FORTY WAYS
TO LOOK AT
JFK

FORTY WAYS
TO LOOK AT
JFK

GRETCHEN RUBIN

To Heather,
I hope you enjoy
the book! *Best wishes,*
Gretchen Rubin

BALLANTINE BOOKS

New York

Published in the United States by Ballantine Books, an imprint of The Random House
Publishing Group, a division of Random House, Inc., New York.

BALLANTINE and colophon are registered trademarks of Random House, Inc.

LIBRARY OF CONGRESS CATALOGING-IN-PUBLICATION DATA

Rubin, Gretchen Craft.
Forty ways to look at John F. Kennedy.
Gretchen Rubin.
p. cm.
Includes bibliographical references and index.
ISBN 0-345-45049-3
1. Kennedy, John F. (John Fitzgerald), 1917–1963. 2. Presidents—United States—
Biography. I. Title.

E842.R83 2005
973.922'092—dc22
[B]
2005041072

Printed in the United States of America

www.ballantinebooks.com

2 4 6 8 9 7 5 3 1

First Edition

Book design by Mary A. Wirth

To Judy and Bob Rubin

He is greatest who is most often in men's good thoughts.

—Samuel Butler

Public sentiment is everything. With public sentiment, nothing can fail; without it, nothing can succeed. Consequently he who molds public sentiment goes deeper than he who enacts statutes or pronounces decisions. He makes statutes and decisions possible or impossible to be executed.

—Abraham Lincoln

Law alone cannot make men see right.

—John F. Kennedy

Contents

FORTY WAYS
TO LOOK AT
JFK

Introduction

The assassination of John F. Kennedy on November 22, 1963, is one of the unforgettable moments of American history. Not only the nation but people around the world shared a sense of profound loss.

The outpouring of grief at Kennedy's death shows the extraordinary regard in which he was held, and in fact, the *most striking* thing about John Kennedy is the astonishing enthusiasm he aroused. It's indisputable that both during and after his life, Kennedy has been the subject of exceptional interest and admiration. Whether or not observers agree that this response is deserved, they must accept that Jack Kennedy was no ordinary politician and that his place in the public imagination is unique. His presidency—one of the shortest in American history—lasted just two years, ten months, and two days, yet Kennedy, decades after his death, remains a dazzling figure in the popular imagination.

I've long been intrigued by Americans' enormous interest in Kennedy—the never-ending flow of biographies, magazine covers, TV specials, documentaries, movies, coffee-table books of photographs, auctions of memorabilia, and cultural references. Of course, not everyone shares this fascination, but enough do that every year brings a fresh outpouring of Kennedy material, and every election cycle, candidates of both parties eagerly claim some version of the Kennedy legacy.

We take the Kennedy phenomenon for granted because it's so familiar, but what accounts for it? What was so beguiling about this well-spoken millionaire, with his Boston accent and modish wife? Why does his memory stir such emotion? What made Kennedy the man into *Kennedy* the icon?

Some years ago, I became determined to solve—for myself—this puzzle. When my husband and I bought our apartment, the elderly previous owners kept only a few possessions, and they left most of their books behind. Along with an admirable Churchill library, they left an astounding number of books about Kennedy as well as several commemorative magazines about JFK, the *New York Journal-American* for January 21, 1961, and Vaughn Meader's famous comedy album *The First Family.* Something about Kennedy had prompted this couple to hoard a Kennedy trove for forty years—and I wanted to analyze the roots of such an impulse.

But why is it important to understand the Kennedy phenomenon?

It's not Kennedy's actions as president but the intensity of the popular interest—both during and after his life—that makes him significant. How did he ignite the public's imagination in such an extraordinary and enduring way, and why is he credited with so much, when, it must be admitted, the plain facts might suggest otherwise? Such tremendous personal power is rare and terrible, and we must try to grasp its source, for as Abigail Adams wrote of George Washington, "If he was really not one of the best-intentioned men in the world, he might be a very dangerous one."

The interest in Kennedy has been attributed to his wit—his glamour—his ideals—his cool—his accomplishments—his excellent press relations—his fortune—his wife and family—his appearance—his terrible death. None of this, however, seems quite satisfactory to explain Kennedy. And it's no answer simply to attribute his appeal to the mystical quality of "charisma" or the "Kennedy style," because these words aren't an explanation, but merely describe the extraordinary effect Kennedy created.

Although Kennedy isn't universally revered, the American public does consistently name him as one of the greatest presidents. A 2004 Gallup poll ranked Kennedy as the second most outstanding president, and a 2003 Gallup poll showed Kennedy and Lincoln tied for first place. Kennedy's stature isn't a recent trend: a 1970 Harris poll showed Kennedy to be by far the most popular president, as did a 1983 Gallup poll, and in *New York Times* / CBS News polls for 1980 and 1996, Americans picked Kennedy as the president they'd choose to run the country today. Kennedy was also enormously popular in office. Of all presidents whose ratings have been measured, Kennedy still holds the record for the highest average job-approval rating, at 70 percent. His first- and second-year averages stood at 76 percent and 70 percent; his drop to an average of 59 percent in the second half of 1963 was likely due to civil rights initiatives.

While the public rates Kennedy high, academics disagree; Kennedy falls in rank significantly when historians are polled. A 1988 *American Heritage* magazine survey of scholars named Kennedy the most overrated figure in U.S. history. A 1997 survey of scholars ranked him in fifteenth place among the presidents. But despite the judgments of historians and pundits, and despite posthumous revelations of unseemly conduct, Kennedy has never lost the deep respect of the public.

My question—what made Kennedy *Kennedy*?—wasn't one that could be answered by gaining access to recently declassified files or by conducting a round of interviews; it would require me to write an account of his life that would make sense of what was *already known*.

Kennedy, of course, hasn't lacked biographers. Thousands of JFK books cram the shelves, not to mention the countless documentaries, movies, and magazine articles about Kennedy and his time. Why another biography now?

I wanted to write a different kind of biography—not in the style of the lengthy, comprehensive biographies or in the style of the brief lives, but something altogether new.

I was struck by Virginia Woolf's diary entry of November 28, 1928, in which she described her ambition for *The Waves:* "I mean to eliminate all waste, deadness, superfluity. . . . Waste, deadness, come from the inclusion of things that don't belong to the moment; this appalling narrative business of the realist: getting on from lunch to dinner: it is false, unreal, merely conventional." That's what I wanted to accomplish: to eliminate as much as possible, to clarify what I thought important. I wanted a way both to sweep in trifles and to slice through the thicket of facts to make sense of what's known. Instead of selecting a single viewpoint—as almost all biographers do—I wanted a structure that would encompass multiple conclusions and would reveal the biographer's machinations to readers.

For my previous book, a biography of Winston Churchill, I hit on the approach of portraying Churchill by looking at him from forty shifting angles. *Forty Ways to Look at Winston Churchill* used this structure to explore the conflicting, overwhelming evidence about Churchill's life and character as well as to demonstrate biography's limits.

I decided to use the same structure to examine the essential aspects of Kennedy's life. Who was his greatest influence? What were his most outstanding qualities, his weaknesses, his most important accomplishments? How did he look? How did he die? Such questions sound naïve when put bluntly, but they are, after all, what we want to learn when we study great lives. In Kennedy's case, many questions address the central puzzle—what made Kennedy *Kennedy*?

The "forty-ways" structure affords several advantages. Because I'm intrigued by how our understanding is shaped by the framework in which facts appear, some chapters exploit unconventional forms. A short time line that contains nothing but a record of Kennedy's illnesses demonstrates the severity of his health problems more cogently than a comprehensive biography. A chapter answering a controversial question—was Kennedy a loving husband? would he have pulled out of Vietnam?—with both a definitive "yes" and an equally definitive "no" shows the difficulty of arriving at confident conclusions. The "Kennedy's Promiscuity" chapter contains a second chapter in a footnote, which discloses the frank details of JFK's sex life in a way that underscores the suppressed quality of these illicit facts. To demonstrate the power of photographs, one chapter contains no text.

The forty-ways design allows me to highlight a striking element of Kennedy's biography: the contrast between what the public knew about Kennedy *during his life* and what emerged *later*. The public sees Kennedy with such intensity—more vividly than almost anyone else—but seeing him isn't knowing him, because Kennedy knew well what to hide and what to display. He overwhelmed the public with material that allowed people to feel they were judging for themselves, but in fact, he controlled the evidence. We know so much more than we did while Kennedy was alive, and we also know more than *he* ever knew. This later-gained knowledge adds a compelling depth and complexity to Kennedy's story.

From this aspect of his life arises one of the critical questions in any Kennedy study: whether the astonishing veneration for him was based on substance or image. It can't be denied that Kennedy—and everyone around him—labored to promote a particular idea of John F. Kennedy. Decades later, his style is just as spectacular as it was in 1960. There was more to Kennedy than that—but how much more? Put another way, was he more like Martin Luther King Jr. or more like Princess Diana in the reverence he inspired?

The forty-ways structure also allows me to adopt, for Kennedy, the venerative forms that people use to celebrate great figures: collections of quotations, of photographs, of homely facts, of personal testimony. Not heroically virtuous himself, Kennedy nevertheless became a secular saint, a political movie star, and an important element of what made Kennedy *Kennedy* was his supporters' efforts to memorialize him. I wanted to use these reverential forms myself, to shed light on them: what they spotlight and what they hide, the needs they answer, the reason these forms persist.

This fragmented approach seemed the most economical and also the most exciting way of pulling out the essential—essential, to be sure, *in my view*—from the vast material about Kennedy. Others have identified central themes for study: the glamour, the brilliant handling of the press, Jackie and Joe. But the forty-ways structure provides a different perspective on these familiar subjects, and in any event, part of the pleasure of studying a well-known life like Kennedy's is reconsidering established facts for fresh insight.

And so this biography of Kennedy is irregular; it dwells on some topics and omits others. Foreground and background, what we saw then and what we see now, the power of pictures, the forms of veneration, the elements of character—all play their part. In the end, I describe my Kennedy—a great man, a glowing example for the whole world, Fortune's favorite. But this biography shows that there are many ways to view Kennedy.

I hope that this biography—irregular as it is—will help others catch the rushing breeze on which Kennedy always seemed to sail, and to bask in the light that shone from him.

1

KENNEDY AS IDEAL LEADER
A Positive Account

Most of those who recount the story of John Kennedy present him in heroic terms—men such as Ben Bradlee, Red Fay, William Manchester, Kenneth O'Donnell, Dave Powers, Pierre Salinger, Arthur Schlesinger Jr., Hugh Sidey, Ted Sorensen, and Theodore White. And of all the mythmakers, none did more than Kennedy and his family to construct the idea of John Kennedy.

Just as in saint-making, when the "Postulator of the Cause" gathers every possible piece of information on the life of a prospective saint to search for signs of extraordinary virtue, these memorializers gather the evidence of Kennedy's character and accomplishments to testify to his merits. They furnish the evidence that proves their conclusion: John F. Kennedy was a great leader who transformed the spirit of America.

During an August 1963 press conference, President John F. Kennedy laughs as he fields questions from reporters.

On November 22, 1963, John Kennedy, the young president who radiated youth, energy, and possibility, was struck down by an assassin—his presidency cut short before he'd served even three years in office.

Kennedy had had a meteoric rise in politics. He was elected to the House of Representatives at age twenty-nine and, six years later, won a Senate seat and, after eight years in the Senate, became president. He never lost an election.

Kennedy was president for only 1,037 days, but during his short tenure, he achieved much. At the Cold War's most dangerous hour, he preserved the peace. He improved relations with the Soviet Union and replaced tension over Berlin with a limited test ban treaty. Despite pressure from advisers, he resisted escalation of dangerous situations during the Bay of Pigs, the Berlin crisis, the Cuban missile crisis, and in Vietnam. At home, he assumed leadership in the struggle for civil rights and galvanized a generation with a renewed zeal for public service.

Kennedy believed it was American ideals, rather than American military might, that would lead the globe, and with his brilliant leadership, he captured the world's imagination.

John Fitzgerald Kennedy was born May 29, 1917, in Brookline, Massachusetts, the second son of nine children born to Joseph Kennedy and Rose Fitzgerald Kennedy. Descended on both sides from Irish Catholic immigrants, Jack had an impressive political ancestry: one grandfather, John Fitzgerald, "Honey Fitz," was the legendary former Boston mayor, and the other, Patrick Kennedy, was a state senator and respected Boston ward leader.

Jack's father, Joseph, was an extraordinarily successful businessman, and by 1957, *Fortune* would rank his family among America's richest, with a fortune estimated at between $200 million and $400 million. But Joe wasn't concerned only with money; in 1929, determined to free his children from the enduring Boston prejudice against Irish Catholics, he moved his family to New York. Joe also became involved in national politics. In 1934, President Franklin Roosevelt appointed him chairman of the new Securities and Exchange Commission and, in 1937, to be the United States' ambassador to Britain.

Although consumed with business and political affairs, Joe was an attentive and loving, if demanding, father who fostered an atmosphere of intense competition, while Rose made sure the Kennedy children had a proper Catholic upbringing, plenty of intellectual stimulation, and training in the social graces. Both parents had the highest expectations for their children—especially for their eldest, Joe Jr.—but despite this pressure, the Kennedy family was very close.

Jack grew up in a happy atmosphere of family affection, political engagement, and affluence, but his childhood was marked by frequent illnesses. Often bedridden, Jack became a voracious reader of biographies, histories, and adventure tales. From age thirteen, he went to boarding school—Canterbury and Choate—and he spent the summer months in Hyannis Port on Cape Cod, Massachusetts, where he and his siblings swam, sailed, golfed, and played touch football.

In 1936, Jack entered Harvard, where he majored in government and was a member of the freshman football and swim teams. Although not particularly studious, Jack was deeply interested in history and politics, and even at Choate, he'd subscribed to the *New York Times*. Jack accomplished something that neither his father nor his older brother, Joe, had been able to do at Harvard: he was accepted by one of the exclusive final clubs, the Spee Club—a considerable accomplishment at a time when prejudice against Catholics was still strong.

After his father became ambassador to the United Kingdom in 1937, Jack went to London to serve as his secretary for six months. Jack was actually present in the House of Commons on September 1, 1939, when Neville Chamberlain declared that Britain was at war with Germany. Although Ambassador Kennedy was initially popular with the British people, he destroyed his reputation by voicing his conviction that Britain would fall to Hitler and that America's only hope lay in staying out of the war. Joe Kennedy resigned his post in November 1940 and thereafter devoted himself to his sons' political careers.

Returning to Harvard, Jack decided to write his senior thesis on Britain's military unpreparedness before World War II. He later expanded his thesis and published it in 1940 as *Why England Slept.* The book won widespread acclaim; a review in the *New York Times* called it "a book of such painstaking scholarship, such mature understanding and fair-mindedness and of such penetrating and timely conclusions, that it is a notable textbook for our times."

In October 1941, Jack entered the navy's Office of Naval Intelligence in Washington, D.C., and after a stint there, was transferred to Charleston, South Carolina. He was eager to get to the combat zones and finally, in March 1943, left San Francisco bound for the South Pacific, where he took command of a patrol torpedo (PT) boat with a crew of twelve.

On the night of August 1, 1943, a Japanese destroyer rammed and split Jack's boat, the *PT-109.* Two men died, and several were badly injured. Jack rallied the survivors to cling to the boat wreckage until morning, and then, determined to lead his men to safety, organized their swim to a tiny island three miles away. For five hours, Jack swam the breaststroke and, ignoring his own injuries, pulled a badly burned man by holding the man's life-jacket strap in his teeth. After more than fifteen hours in the water, the *PT-109* crew reached land. Jack drove himself to exhaustion over the next several days by venturing out to the straits to try to flag down ships and exploring a neighboring island to look for help. On the fourth day, two Solomon Islanders found the survivors and agreed to deliver a message Jack carved on a coconut shell.

NAURO ISL
COMMANDER . . . NATIVE KNOWS
POSIT . . . HE CAN PILOT . . . 11 ALIVE
NEED SMALL BOAT . . . KENNEDY

Rescuers came for the *PT-109* crew two days later.

Jack's heroic actions hit the front page of the *New York Times* and won him the Navy and Marine Corps Medal. Sadly, Jack's

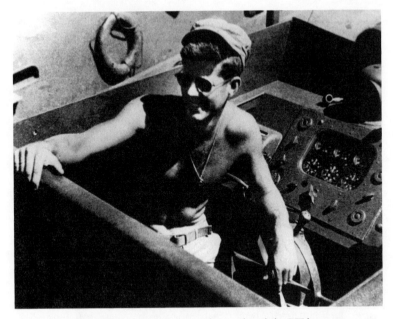

Naval lieutenant Jack Kennedy sits aboard the PT boat
he commands in the southwest Pacific.

brother Joe was not so lucky. In 1944, his plane exploded during a volunteer mission, and his body was never recovered. Another of Jack's siblings, Kathleen (or "Kick"), widow of the heir to the Duke of Devonshire, would be killed in a plane crash in France in 1948.

After the war, Jack began a promising career in journalism but soon turned to politics. As a candidate for Congress from Massachusetts's Eleventh District, he faced a tough race: ten candidates competed in 1946 for the open seat.

A young navy hero, best-selling author, grandson of famous Boston figures P. J. Kennedy and "Honey Fitz," with good looks, an outstanding education, and great wealth, Jack made an intriguing candidate, but he wasn't a natural politician. Even his father admitted later, "I never thought Jack had it in him." With the slogan

"A New Generation Offers a Leader," Jack drove himself hard, and his performance far surpassed expectations. His large family turned out in full force to support him, and his father's resources allowed him to run a professional, well-financed campaign. He won a decisive victory.

Jack served three terms, then, eager for a new challenge, decided to run for the Senate against the popular incumbent Henry Cabot Lodge. Lodge seemed unbeatable, but Kennedy triumphed. His family had again rallied to his support: his mother and sisters held hugely successful "Kennedy teas," and his twenty-seven-year-old brother Bobby ably managed the campaign.

Soon after the election, Jack, dubbed "the Senate's gay young bachelor" by the *Saturday Evening Post,* married Jacqueline Bouvier, a beautiful, accomplished journalist: he was thirty-six; she, twenty-four. Their marriage in Newport on September 12, 1953, was the social event of the season. One of Jack's important actions as a new senator was hiring twenty-four-year-old Ted Sorensen, who started as chief legislative aide and who would become a key adviser and speechwriter.

The early days of Jack and Jackie's marriage were marred by Jack's chronic back trouble. By 1954, the pain was so terrible that Jack decided to undergo an operation, even though he was given only fifty-fifty odds of surviving. He developed a life-threatening infection and had to undergo a second operation just a few months later. Throughout his long recovery, Jackie tirelessly nursed him, doing everything she could to keep his spirits up.

During his convalescence, Jack began work on *Profiles in Courage,* a book of sketches of senators who defied public opinion to vote their consciences. The book became a bestseller and won the 1957 Pulitzer Prize. (Jack donated the prize money to the United Negro College Fund.) The same year, Jack and Jackie's first child, Caroline, was born.

At the 1956 Democratic National Convention, Jack narrated a

film recounting the Democratic Party's history, and his presentation was so well received that he was asked to make the speech nominating Adlai Stevenson. His brilliant performances started talk that he'd make a splendid candidate for vice president.

When, in an unusual move, Stevenson threw the choice of the vice presidential candidate to the convention by popular vote, Jack launched himself into a dramatic contest with Estes Kefauver. Although Jack lost, he proved a surprisingly strong candidate. His near success made him a national figure and convinced him to run for president in 1960.

He spent the next few years crisscrossing the country to build political support. His religion hampered his efforts; no Catholic had ever been elected president, and many voters feared that the Church in Rome would control a Catholic president. Nevertheless, despite his religion, his youth, and the fact that the Democrats hadn't chosen a senator as a presidential nominee for decades, Jack was increasingly seen as a leading candidate. His air of energy, intellect, and grace captivated all who saw him. Kennedy disagreed with those who counseled him to wait. In 1958, he said that if he stayed in the Senate for eight more years, "I'll have to vote politically and I'll end up as both a mediocre senator and a lousy candidate."

In 1960, Jack faced a tough primary battle. Once again, Bobby managed his campaign with tireless and ruthless determination. Jack hoped for a decisive triumph over Hubert Humphrey in the Wisconsin primary, but the vote wasn't conclusive enough to prove that a Catholic could win in a predominantly Protestant state. Jack's subsequent victory in West Virginia proved the strength of his candidacy. Throughout the campaign, he continued to tackle the religion question, telling audiences, "I refuse to believe that I was denied the right to be president on the day I was baptized." In a compelling address to the Greater Houston Ministerial Association, he said, "Side by side with Bowie and Crockett died McCafferty and Bailey and Carey, but no one knows if they were Catholics or not. For there was no religious test at the Alamo."

Jack's travels awakened him to the depth of the nation's problems. Back in Washington during the West Virginia campaign, he told aides, "You can't imagine how those people live down there. I was better off in the war than they are in those coal mines. It's not right. I'm going to do something about it. If we make it."

His hard work paid off at the Democratic National Convention. Jack won the nomination and, to balance the ticket, chose Lyndon Johnson, the powerful Senate majority leader from Texas, as his running mate. Kennedy later explained, "First, I had the feeling that Lyndon takes more of the Catholic flavor off me than anyone else. A Southern Protestant. Second, he obviously helps me in the South. Third, it wouldn't be worthwhile being President if Lyndon were the Majority Leader."

In his ringing acceptance speech, Kennedy announced, "We stand today on the edge of a New Frontier. . . . The New Frontier of which I speak is not a set of promises—it is a set of challenges. It sums up not what I intend to offer the American people, but what I intend to ask of them." He promised the voters "one thousand days of exacting Presidential leadership."

Kennedy then faced his Republican opponent, Richard Nixon. It would be a challenging race. Nixon, who had served two terms as vice president to one of the nation's most popular presidents, was known for his tough stand against communism and had successfully debated Soviet premier Nikita Khrushchev.

Kennedy emphasized three themes: the Soviet Union's outstripping of the United States in military power; the American economy's stagnation; and the failure of the United States to keep pace with demands in public services, education, health, and transportation. Along with his policies, Kennedy offered himself.

Nixon was associated with the Eisenhower administration, which seemed tired, slack, with a chamber-of-commerce mentality. After "eight years of drugged and fitful sleep," as Kennedy described it, the public was ready for something new, and Kennedy offered glamour, intellect, and challenge. Also, the elderly Eisenhower's health had been a source of anxiety; he had suffered a heart attack, a stroke, and an attack of ileitis. The young and energetic Kennedy was a refreshing change.

The contest was bitterly close. In one of the most famous episodes in American political history, Kennedy and Nixon faced each other in an unprecedented series of televised debates. Before the debates, Kennedy had trailed in the polls, and many expected the debates to hurt him, but Kennedy showed himself to be Nixon's equal. As Kennedy himself acknowledged, "It was TV more than anything else that turned the tide."

Kennedy's development as a candidate was remarkable. An old friend recalled of his first campaign, "He was the lousiest speaker! . . . It really amazed me later on, how he learned to speak so well." By the end of the presidential campaign, political journalist Theodore White recalled, his style "began to capture even the newsmen who had heard all he had to say long before, but continued to listen, as one continues to return to a favorite movie."

The race remained tight until the end, when Kennedy won 303 electoral votes to Nixon's 219.

Kennedy spent most of the transition period deciding his appointments. A controversial, but ultimately successful, decision was naming his brother Bobby to be attorney general. Also during this time, John F. Kennedy Jr. was born.

Kennedy took office as the thirty-fifth president on January 20, 1961, and assumed leadership of some 180 million Americans, in the richest, most powerful nation in the world. His youth was striking. He was forty-three years old; his wife, Jacqueline, was only thirty-one; and they had a three-year-old daughter and a two-month-old son.

His inaugural address electrified the nation: "*Ask not what your country can do for you, ask what you can do for your country.*" Although he'd won a narrow victory, the country quickly embraced the new president and his family. The Kennedys, one reporter explained, were "star material." Kennedy's vitality and drive energized the whole country—an accomplishment even more remarkable given that he struggled against pain that would have hobbled most people, especially given the tremendous demands of his office.

As president, Kennedy had an informal, involved style and a huge appetite for information. In place of structured meetings and staff recommendations, Kennedy enjoyed freewheeling discussions in which all points of views were considered. His "New Frontier" encompassed initiatives for an increased minimum wage, federal aid to education, medical care for the elderly, improved housing, aid to depressed areas, civil rights, and tax reform. Kennedy pursued policies to lessen the nuclear threat, to strengthen U.S. defenses, to provide the military with options of "flexible response," and to strengthen democratic governments around the world through trade, education, and financial assistance.

Kennedy encouraged fresh approaches to familiar goals. He took a special interest in the Green Berets, a highly trained force with the mission of fighting wars in a new way, and he launched the Peace Corps, a select group of young people who worked in underdeveloped countries to spread peace and prosperity in a new way.

A series of dramatic international and domestic crises marked Kennedy's tenure in office, and his responses demonstrate his enormous ability to grow to meet the challenges of the presidency.

In April 1961, just a few months after taking office, Kennedy approved an Eisenhower-initiated plan in which fourteen hundred

CIA-trained Cuban exiles made an amphibious landing at the Bay of Pigs in Cuba. From the beginning, Kennedy had doubts about the operation and insisted he wouldn't allow American forces to participate directly. He worried that open U.S. involvement would have grave consequences in Latin America, where he wanted to build good relationships, and, worse, might provoke a Soviet response against Berlin. Although the CIA insisted that the plan could succeed quickly and with no obvious American participation, the invaders were overwhelmed by Castro's forces as soon as they landed. Advisers put Kennedy under tremendous pressure to send in American forces to back up the exiles, but he maintained his refusal to do so. Almost all the men were killed or captured.

Although the Bay of Pigs invasion was a humiliating failure, it taught Kennedy to be skeptical of bold promises and "expert" advice from the CIA, the Pentagon, and the State Department. Kennedy increasingly turned to his brother, and soon Bobby—with his absolute fidelity and profound understanding of JFK's mind and priorities—became the president's most influential adviser for both domestic and foreign affairs.

A few months later, in June 1961, Kennedy met Soviet premier Nikita Khrushchev in Vienna, where they discussed the contentious issue of Berlin. After World War II, Germany had been split into British, French, English, and Soviet zones, with a divided Berlin inside communist East Germany; the Soviets had guaranteed Western access to the city. Khrushchev, however, informed Kennedy that he intended within months to sign a treaty with East Germany that would cut off West Berlin. Kennedy feared that of all possible crises, Berlin was most likely to result in nuclear war. On July 25, 1961, Kennedy gave a televised address to the country to emphasize his resolution to defend Western rights to the city and, among other things, called for a defense-budget increase; a doubled draft call; and a program for civil defense, including construction of public and private bomb shelters.

As a crossing point for East Germans fleeing the Soviet bloc, Berlin posed an urgent problem for Khrushchev, so in August 1961, the East Germans and the Soviets began to erect the Berlin Wall. Once the wall had blocked the stream of refugees, Khrushchev withdrew his deadline for signing the treaty. As abhorrent as Kennedy found the wall, he accepted it because it defused the crisis. "A wall is a hell of a lot better than a war," he observed. Nevertheless, Kennedy deplored its impingement on liberty and pointed to it as a sign of communism's failure. He would give one of his greatest speeches in June 1963, in West Berlin. "All free men, wherever they may live, are citizens of Berlin, and therefore, as a free man, I take pride in the words, *Ich bin ein Berliner.*"

After Berlin, Kennedy's greatest trial with the Soviet Union came in October 1962, when Kennedy—and the world—faced a desperate hour. The two nuclear superpowers faced off, at the brink of war, with the potential to destroy the whole world.

The "thirteen days" of the Cuban missile crisis began on October 16, 1962. National Security Adviser McGeorge Bundy informed Kennedy that a U-2 spy plane had taken photographs showing Soviet missile sites in Cuba, and intelligence revealed that missiles on Soviet ships were headed toward the island. Soon, a group of advisers later dubbed "ExComm" (for Executive Committee of the National Security Council) headed to the White House for secret meetings to discuss possible responses.

ExComm's first instinct was to recommend surprise air strikes against the missiles as quickly as possible, along with a possible invasion. Kennedy was under intense pressure from his military advisers; air force chief of staff General Curtis Lemay emphasized, "I just don't see any other solution except direct military intervention—*right now!*"

Kennedy resisted this advice to follow a more prudent course. In his typical style, he created an atmosphere in which different viewpoints could be aired and assumptions challenged. ExComm member Treasury Secretary Douglas Dillon recalled, "We would argue in front of him. He wouldn't say anything, he would listen and learn. . . . He was very calm, very collected and impressive. . . . He made the right decisions."

After extensive consultation, despite pressure from the Joint Chiefs for a surprise attack on comprehensive targets, to be followed by blockade and invasion, Kennedy decided to take a measured first step. He wanted to give the Soviets the chance to retreat gracefully.

On October 22, 1962, Kennedy appeared on television to alert the country to the discovery and the initial plans for response. To halt the buildup, the United States would enforce a "quarantine" against ships carrying offensive military equipment into Cuba. The United States would continue its surveillance, and armed forces were prepared for action. He would seek the support of the Organization of American States and the United Nations. He warned the country to prepare for "months of sacrifice and self-discipline."

Deeply concerned, as always, about the risks of miscalculation and escalation, Kennedy took no action that risked civilian lives and sought to avoid confrontation—even while work on the missile sites continued and after an American plane was shot down. The world waited in terrified suspense, but despite the extraordinary tension, Kennedy remained cool. Undersecretary of State George Ball remembered him being "by far the most calm and analytical" person in the room.

In the end, Kennedy's strategy was vindicated. On October 24, the deadline for the blockade, Soviet ships headed for Cuba turned back or stopped. Secretary of State Dean Rusk said, "We're eyeball to eyeball and I think the other fella just blinked." Over the next few days, the Americans and the Soviets exchanged messages, and the United States made a proposal: the United States would pledge not to invade Cuba if the Soviet Union would withdraw.

Also, in an agreement kept secret from all but a few advisers, Kennedy pledged to remove U.S. Jupiter missiles on the Soviet border in Turkey. On October 28, the Soviet Union announced its decision to dismantle and withdraw the missiles.

Kennedy's triumph opened the possibility of a more stable relationship with the Soviets. Never again would the two superpowers threaten a direct nuclear confrontation. While some have accused Kennedy of overreacting to a situation that didn't fundamentally alter the strategic balance or threaten U.S. security, Kennedy recognized that in international affairs, appearance and reality often can't be separated. Failing to challenge the Soviet action would have damaged American interests and security. Furthermore, within a year, Kennedy achieved one of his greatest accomplishments: the signing of the Nuclear Test Ban Treaty with the Soviet Union.

In Southeast Asia, Kennedy worried about the growing communist threat to the South Vietnamese government. The 1954 Geneva agreements had split Vietnam, with an anticommunist government in the south and a communist government in the north. In keeping with the widely accepted belief that South Vietnam's fall to communism would threaten its neighbors, the administration supported the tyrannical and corrupt, but staunchly anticommunist, president Ngo Dinh Diem.

The Kennedy administration provided economic and military support to Diem and, in return, tried, without success, to pressure him to make the reforms necessary to build a more effective political base. Kennedy was reluctant to expand American involvement but feared that Vietnam's loss would have severe domestic and international consequences. American support continued, but by the summer of 1963, Diem's regime was on the verge of collapse, and in the fall of 1963, a group of generals overthrew and killed Diem. A few weeks later, Kennedy himself would be assassinated.

At home, the momentum of the civil rights movement continued to build. In part inspired by Kennedy's insistence that "we can do better," people throughout the country were peacefully protesting racial injustice. Kennedy understood the importance of their fight. When someone asked him, "What do you think of those who are sitting in?" he responded, "By sitting in, they're standing up."

Just a month before Kennedy's inauguration, the Supreme Court had ruled that segregation was illegal in facilities serving interstate travelers. In the summer of 1961, the "Freedom Riders," integrated busloads of civil rights activists, traveled across the South to challenge remaining restrictions. Kennedy believed the Freedom Rides to be self-defeatingly provocative, and he urged activists to work through legal reform and the courts. Nevertheless, he intervened to protect the riders from violence and to press for progress.

A major crisis arose in the fall of 1962, when a black man, James Meredith, tried to register at the all-white University of Mississippi. Kennedy wanted to avoid confrontation or the use of federal troops, but Governor Ross Barnett did everything he could to resist the court order commanding Meredith's enrollment. Kennedy first sent marshals and then, when a violent riot broke out, federal troops. By the time troops arrived, two hundred people had been injured and two were killed. Thanks to Kennedy's intervention, however, Meredith was successfully enrolled.

Before many months had passed, in the spring of 1963, Martin Luther King Jr. launched a campaign of dramatic civil disobedience in Birmingham. As part of this push, King enlisted more than a thousand children—some as young as six. Police Chief Eugene "Bull" Connor used brutal tactics against the demonstrators, and the country was shocked by pictures of policemen turning high-pressure fire hoses and attack dogs on nonviolent protesters. These violent images swayed public sentiment in greater favor of racial equality, and Kennedy would later describe his civil rights bill as "Bull Connor's Bill."

Not long after, in June 1963, a pair of black students prepared to enroll at the University of Alabama. Publicity-hungry governor George Wallace stood in the doorway to block the court-ordered desegregation, but Kennedy federalized the state's National Guard and forced Wallace to yield. After watching a replay of Wallace's defiance, Kennedy announced, "I want to go on television tonight," and he, Bobby, and Ted Sorensen rushed to prepare his remarks in the few hours before he went on the air. That speech was one of Kennedy's greatest. He spoke for eighteen minutes— much of it improvised from an unfinished text. In this speech, Kennedy fully committed the prestige of his presidency to the battle for civil rights. "It is better to settle these matters in the courts than on the streets, and new laws are needed at every level, but law alone cannot make men see right. . . . We are confronted primarily with a moral issue. It is as old as the scriptures and is as clear as the American Constitution." Soon after, Kennedy submitted sweeping civil rights legislation to Congress.

Apart from civil rights, one of Kennedy's most important domestic legacies was his championship of a new economic approach. In 1962, he advocated a tax cut and a planned budget deficit. He'd initially been wary of such action, and when Walter Heller, head of the Council of Economic Advisers, argued for a tax cut as an antirecession measure, Kennedy said, "Do you think for a minute that I, coming in on a platform of sacrifice, can, as the very first thing, hand the voters a tax cut?" But Kennedy came to recognize that a tax cut could be a key tool to stimulate growth and job creation.

Together, Jack and Jackie Kennedy transformed the staid atmosphere of Washington, D.C. Under Jackie's direction, the White House became a glamorous center for American arts, history, and culture. Although Jackie considered her chief responsibility to be her family, she devoted herself to making the White House a historical showcase as well as a celebrated residence. Her elegance and sophistication helped make the Kennedys' brief years in the White House into "Camelot."

On November 21, 1963, John Kennedy flew to Texas to make several appearances, and for the first time since 1960, Jackie accompanied him on a political trip. The recent death of their son Patrick, who had been born in August but lived just two days, had brought the couple even closer.

Kennedy was warned that Dallas was a hotbed of antiadministration sentiment. Many advised Kennedy not to go to Texas, and a few days before he left, Kennedy told a friend that he wished the trip were over.

The morning of Friday, November 22, 1963, the Kennedys landed at Dallas's Love Field. At other Texas stops, Jackie had been given the famous yellow roses of Texas, but in Dallas, she carried red roses. The Kennedys headed into town in the backseat of an open convertible, with Texas governor John Connally and his wife riding in front.

At 12:30 p.m., as Kennedy's motorcade drove slowly past cheering crowds and through Dealey Plaza, twenty-four-year-old Lee Harvey Oswald fired three shots from the sixth floor of the Texas School Book Depository, where he worked. The first bullet failed to hit its target; the second bullet passed through the back of Kennedy's neck and exited his throat but didn't mortally injure him; the third bullet smashed into the back of his head. Kennedy was rushed to Parkland Hospital and pronounced dead at 1:00 p.m.

Word of Kennedy's death swept the country. Within thirty minutes of the shooting, 68 percent of American adults knew of it, and by evening, 99.8 percent. Bobby was dressing to rush to Dallas when he heard his brother had died. "He had the most wonderful life," Bobby said.

Kennedy's body was flown back to Washington, D.C., and taken to Bethesda Medical Center for an autopsy and preparation for burial. Back in Dallas, within ninety minutes of the assassination, the police arrested Lee Harvey Oswald and charged him with the murder of Kennedy as well as Dallas police officer J. D. Tippit. Two days later, on November 24, while Oswald stood in a crowd of seventy policemen in the basement of police headquarters as he was being transferred to another facility, local nightclub owner Jack Ruby shot and killed him—the first murder to occur "live" on television. In Washington, Johnson aide George Reedy had the TV on in his office and thought the network had replaced Kennedy coverage with a gangster movie.

The entire country drew together to witness the solemn events surrounding Kennedy's funeral, which, in accordance with Jackie's directions, was modeled after Abraham Lincoln's. On Saturday morning, the coffin traveled from the hospital to the White House. On Sunday, Kennedy's body lay in state in the Capitol Rotunda, where hundreds of thousands of mourners passed by. The next morning, Kennedy's body was returned to the White House, and from there, Kennedy's family, friends, and world leaders walked in a solemn procession behind the coffin the several blocks to St. Matthew's Cathedral. Kennedy's body was then taken to Arlington National Cemetery. Nearly all previous presidents had been buried near their homes, but Jackie wanted to place her husband's grave in a site of national, rather than local, significance. She lit an eternal flame at his gravesite, and fifty jet planes flew overhead, one to represent each state of the Union, followed by *Air Force One,* the president's personal plane.

Kennedy's death caused an extraordinary outpouring of sorrow. In the United States, the three television networks suspended regular programming to cover the events surrounding the funeral, and at times, nine out of ten Americans were watching as well as millions of people all over the world. The exhaustive coverage of the funeral made Kennedy's death immediate and unforgettable, and the solemn rituals of grief and loss moved the public deeply.

Although he held office for such a short time, Kennedy is remembered as one of the country's most beloved leaders. Decades have passed since Kennedy's one thousand days as president, but his eloquence, his idealism, and his grace are all remembered as Camelot.

2

KENNEDY AS SHOWY OPPORTUNIST
A Critical Account

Laboring beside the Kennedy mythmakers are the demytholo-
gizers who challenge the heroic view. Just as the Postulator of the
Cause gathers all possible evidence about a subject, in the hopes of
proving exceptional virtue, the Promoter of the Faith—the
"Devil's Advocate"—scrutinizes this evidence for signs of faults
and exaggeration.

Many embrace this function, because the kind of figure who
inspires veneration also rouses the urge to tear down and to ex-
pose. Seymour Hersh, Victor Lasky, Thomas Reeves, Garry
Wills, and others focus on Kennedy's family advantages, his ma-
nipulation of the press, his lies, and his hypocrisy.

Their evidence can't be ignored in making a judgment of
Kennedy.

*March 1963.
Photographers
crowd to snap Jack
Kennedy's picture
as he leaves the
White House.*

During his short presidency, Kennedy's greatest accomplishment was his successful management of his image. His wit, good looks, money, and photogenic family distracted the public from his performance in office.

In foreign policy, Kennedy's mindless activism, love of crisis, and need to prove his toughness not only produced the failed Bay of Pigs invasion but also contributed to the perilous episodes in Berlin and Cuba that Kennedy would count among his victories, and to the deepened American commitment in Vietnam. Domestically, Kennedy achieved little. In the area of civil rights, he acted only when events left him no choice. Celebrated New Frontier initiatives—the Peace Corps, the race to the moon, White House cultural performances—held little interest for Kennedy apart from their public relations potential. He never built an effective relationship with Congress and achieved few legislative successes. In his private life, Kennedy's sordid conduct belied his carefully constructed reputation as a loving family man and dignified statesman.

Kennedy's much-celebrated "Camelot" yields an endless supply of glamorous photographs and volumes of effusive prose, but little of enduring significance.

John F. Kennedy was born on May 29, 1917, in Brookline, Massachusetts, the great-grandson of poor Irish immigrants and son of Rose and Joseph Kennedy. Joe Kennedy was an ambitious businessman who worked ruthlessly to secure social prestige and a fortune through his activities as a bank president, shipyard manager, Hollywood movie producer, liquor importer, and consultant. Once his financial position was secure, Joe turned his attention to conquering Washington. He became a major Democratic contributor and a prominent supporter of President Franklin Roosevelt. Throughout, Joe was a master at winning positive press attention for the Kennedy family.

Although Joe was in many ways dedicated to his children, he spent a huge amount of time away from them and openly carried on affairs. Such behavior drove Rose to take refuge in her Catholic faith, solitude, and profligate spending on couture clothing. She took frequent long trips without her children and once left behind five children between the ages of two and eight to take a six-week vacation.

From an early age, and for his entire life, Jack Kennedy was plagued by poor health, and his childhood was marked by frequent periods of illness. Despite being sickly, he was in constant competition with his older brother, Joe Jr., who, as eldest son, was favored by his traditional family as well as being more athletic, studious, and outgoing than Jack.

In high school, Jack was a mediocre student and, at Harvard, was mostly interested in his social life and athletics, as demonstrated by his failure to earn even a single A. He ran for a seat on the student council but lost.

While Jack was in college, in 1937, his family moved to London when his father became the United States ambassador to the Court of St. James's. Jack capitalized on his father's position by writing his senior thesis on the origins of Britain's appeasement policy, and in the grim months as Britain braced for war, young Jack nagged the U.S. embassy staff in London to act as his personal research assistants by sending him pamphlets, books, and other obscure materials. After Jack finished his thesis, Joe enlisted the help of journalist Arthur Krock and several others to get it published as a book, *Why England Slept*. Joe Kennedy resigned from his post in 1940. Although he initially had been popular as ambassador, as war approached, the British turned against him because of his openly defeatist views.

Jack's health continued to be very poor. In 1941, he volunteered for the Army Officer Candidate School but failed the physical; he then failed the navy physical, too. Only with the help of his father's connections did he manage to "pass" the medical exam.

In October 1941, Jack went to work in the Office of Naval Intelligence in Washington, D.C. He promptly began an affair with a former Danish beauty queen, Inga Arvad, who was both married and a suspected Nazi spy. She'd spent time with Hitler at the 1936 Berlin Olympic Games and wrote that he was "very kind. . . . He is not evil as he is depicted by the enemies of Germany." Because of her Nazi associations, made more suspicious by her affair with an intelligence officer, the FBI put her under surveillance and recorded her sexual encounters with Jack. When rumors of the affair began to circulate, the ONI—and perhaps Joe as well—became concerned that an officer was consorting with a suspected spy. After only three months in Washington, in January 1942, Kennedy was reassigned to a desk job in South Carolina.

Jack, however, was eager for sea duty and, in July 1942, was sent to midshipman's school in Chicago. He used the combined influence of his father and grandfather to win a coveted assignment to command a patrol torpedo (PT) boat and to be assigned to the Solomon Islands.

After Jack had taken up his duties on the *PT-109* in the South Pacific, at about 2:30 a.m. on August 2, 1943, a Japanese destroyer rammed and split his small boat. During all of World War II, this was the *only* time a Japanese destroyer hit a PT boat, and why the crew failed to notice a destroyer bearing down on them—when other PTs had picked it up a mile or more distant—was never fully explained. Kennedy later emphasized that he was on the attack when hit, but crew members made it clear that no attack was actually attempted. The crash killed two men; the others were thrown into the water. While many accounts suggest that the crew was given up for dead, in fact, fighter planes searched for the ship and Solomon Islanders combed the islands for survivors.

The *PT-109* crew decided to swim for a nearby island. Over the next few days, Jack repeatedly struck off to seek help—efforts that showed bravery but were also impulsive, futile wastes of energy. As it happened, before long, some Solomon Islanders discovered the men and took back messages requesting help. The U.S. authorities were alerted, as well as two wire-service war correspondents, who reported the rescue of Ambassador Kennedy's son and his crew. Their dramatic stories painted Jack as a hero—a crucial boost to his future political career. A glowing account made the *New York Times*'s front page, and in 1944, John Hersey wrote a *New Yorker* piece, "Survival," that recounted Jack's adventures. Overlooked, however, was the crucial point: how had the small, highly maneuverable *PT-109* been rammed by a Japanese destroyer? Jack's brother Joe didn't hesitate to ask pointed questions: "Where the hell were you when the destroyer hove into sight, and exactly what were your moves, and where the hell was your radar." Jack later admitted he hadn't been sure whether the navy would award him a medal or throw him out.

Several months later, Jack returned home due to chronic back problems. His campaigns would emphasize his heroic experiences in the South Pacific, but in fact, he spent nine months on active duty there.

In contrast to Jack, who became an accidental hero after his boat was hit, in August 1944, Joe Jr. volunteered to fly a bomber loaded with explosives to a German V-1 launch site; he died when his plane exploded. Joe Jr.'s death devastated the Kennedy family, especially Joe. Joe had once dreamed of being president himself and had even begun the machinations to make himself a serious candidate, but his outspokenly pessimistic views during the war had destroyed his chances: "I'm willing to spend all I've got left to keep us out of the war. . . . Democracy is finished in England. It may be here." His own hopes dashed, Joe then expected his oldest son to be president; after Joe Jr. died, he turned his attention to building the career of his second son.

To keep Jack in the forefront of the public mind, in 1945, Joe asked his friend William Randolph Hearst to give Jack a temporary assignment writing for a Hearst newspaper. Although Jack would later be described as a "former journalist," his experience was limited to a few months' work. Each dispatch was a piece of self-promotion, identifying him as a PT boat hero, author of *Why England Slept,* and son of the former ambassador. Jack produced a total of about five thousand words before quitting to run for Congress from Massachusetts.

Jack was an unlikely candidate to represent the largely working-class, immigrant Eleventh District. He was young and looked younger, was in terrible health, and hadn't lived in Boston since he was nine years old. He spent summers at Hyannis Port, winters in Palm Beach, and was a product of Choate, Harvard, and the Stork Club, with no real work experience outside the navy. He was fortunate to have a rich father—Joe spent a staggering sum on the campaign—but unfortunately, that same father was despised by many. Jack's main selling point was his wartime experience, and his time in the South Pacific also became a convenient cover for his longtime medical problems. Jack's own strenuous work in the campaign, and the advantages granted him by his father's fortune, paid off: he won the race handily.

1946. A young, gaunt, and tan Jack Kennedy grips the podium during his first campaign.

As a congressman, Jack had one of the worst absentee ratings in the House and sponsored no noteworthy legislation. This may have been due, in part, to ill health. In 1947, Jack was diagnosed with life-threatening Addison's disease, in which the adrenal gland malfunctions—a condition from which, in the future, he would repeatedly claim he didn't suffer. Despite his lackluster record, in 1952, Jack ran for the Senate against incumbent Henry Cabot Lodge. Again, Kennedy's determination, organization, and money prevailed, and against high odds, Jack won.

Although Jack's Senate career was no more distinguished than his House career, he always managed to get good press. Fellow Massachusetts congressman Tip O'Neill observed, "In all my years in public life, I've never seen a congressman get so much press while doing so little work."

Jack was a confirmed and active bachelor, but in 1953, needing a wife to advance politically, he married the twenty-four-year-old Jacqueline Bouvier. Against the wishes of Jackie's mother, who wanted a small, tasteful ceremony, the Kennedys insisted on a huge wedding with maximum publicity.

During his Senate years, Jack's back pain became debilitating. Desperate for relief, he endured two back operations in 1954 and 1955. He was recuperating when, in December 1954, the Senate voted to censure communist witch-hunter Senator Joseph McCarthy. Jack was the only Democrat who failed either to vote against McCarthy or to place himself on the record by "pairing" his vote to the vote of an absent senator who opposed censure—a lapse that would dog him for the rest of his life. Although he and his defenders blamed this failure on his convalescence, he easily could have paired his vote. Why the refusal to stand up to McCarthy? Joe Kennedy had contributed to McCarthy, Bobby had worked on his investigating committee, Eunice and Pat had dated him, and most important, most of Jack's constituents considered McCarthy a hero.

In an often-noted irony, it was at this time that Jack started work on *Profiles in Courage,* a book about senators who risked their careers to take principled stands. His book proved controversial: after it won a 1957 Pulitzer Prize, Drew Pearson claimed that Jack hadn't written it himself. Realizing the threat to JFK's reputation, the Kennedys forced the network that had broadcast Pearson's remark to apologize.

At the 1956 Democratic Convention, Jack gave a terrific performance as the narrator of a film about the history of the Democratic Party; the *New York Times* reported that he "came before the convention tonight as a movie star," and as a result, Jack came close to becoming Adlai Stevenson's vice presidential running mate. This brush with high office immediately spurred him to concentrate on running for president.

His advantages were his famous name, the prestige of his books, his reputation as a war hero, his friendly press relations, and his appealing image. His disadvantages were his youth (if he won, he would be the youngest president ever elected) and his religion (no Catholic had ever been elected president). He had no real experience in the private sector. He wasn't a prominent party figure and lacked the backing of most national Democratic leaders. He'd never been a governor, cabinet officer, or general. He wasn't associated with any great national issue or major legislation.

Kennedy money, however, paid for advantages like a private campaign plane, unprecedented use of public opinion polls, and ample staff. Jack's campaign was also made glamorous by the presence of celebrity supporters such as singer Frank Sinatra and British actor Peter Lawford, who had married Jack's sister Pat. With this support, Jack built an image of himself as an intellectual, tough politician with fresh ideas.

Although Jack sought to portray the public as eager for change in 1960, Eisenhower would have been overwhelmingly reelected had he been eligible for a third term. He'd led the country in a period of growing affluence and peace, and the public embraced his program of moderate conservatism and firm anticommunism. Jack knew that to win, he must convince the public that peace and prosperity were illusory. He charged Eisenhower with permitting the Soviet Union to pull ahead of the United States in nuclear capacity in a "missile gap" and stressed the threat of Cuba's communist regime.

Jack had one particular strength that proved critical: he was outstandingly telegenic. The televised presidential debates with opponent Richard Nixon showed Jack to be the more self-possessed and attractive candidate. He appreciated the importance of the debates to his success and did all he could to prepare: he reviewed three-by-five cards crammed with facts, rehearsed his answers— and less conventionally, sat outside to deepen his tan, received an injection from "Dr. Feelgood," and according to aide Langdon Marvin, a few hours before airtime, spent fifteen minutes with a prepaid prostitute in a hotel.

Jack had an additional advantage over Nixon: he had a deep rapport with the journalists who covered him. In fact, journalist Theodore White admitted that reporters' personal enthusiasm for Jack caused them to misread political reality. They saw the evidence of the "jumpers," the frenzied crowds, the excitement generated by Jack's personality and careful staff work; they forgot about the unenthusiastic voters who stayed home.

In the end, despite Kennedy's image as a charismatic, popular candidate, he won by only 118,574 votes, out of a total vote of 68,837,000. He'd been confident of a victory, and it should have been fairly easy. The 1952 and 1956 elections had been personal victories for Eisenhower, not party victories; Nixon was not well liked, and Eisenhower had undermined his candidacy—for example, asked what major ideas Nixon had contributed, Eisenhower replied, "If you give me a week, I might think of one." Particularly considering suspicions of voter fraud, this margin reveals the weakness of Kennedy's public support. But he had won.

Kennedy's impact as president was largely a matter of image and packaging. The fifties had been a safe, prosperous period when people sought to establish themselves in the inconspicuous mass of the middle class. Now people were ready for something new, and the glamorous, dashing Kennedy satisfied this hunger, and his wife, with her elaborate coiffures, feathery whispers, and taste for antiques, even more so.

Kennedy's initial appointments stunned committed Democrats, who were dismayed by his decision to retain CIA head Allen Dulles and FBI head J. Edgar Hoover and to place Republicans in the top jobs at Defense, Treasury, and the National Security Council. During the campaign, a TV interviewer had asked Bobby, "If your brother is elected, how much truth is there, if any, to the persistent rumor that you will be appointed U.S. Attorney General?" "There is absolutely no truth to that," Bobby answered. "That would be nepotism of the worst sort." Nevertheless, Jack's most controversial decision—at his father's insistence—was appointing his thirty-four-year-old brother to be attorney general. In that office, Bobby directed thirty thousand employees and a $30 million budget, but he was little equipped for this responsibility. He'd earned mostly Cs and Ds in college, had barely been admitted to the University of Virginia Law School, had worked briefly in the Justice Department, and had served as investigator for two Senate committees—on the first, for Joseph McCarthy. Also, Bobby had an angry, bullying temperament that made him ill suited for the nation's most important legal office.

But as Joe Kennedy had foreseen, as attorney general, Bobby would play a critical role as Jack's protector. There, he supervised Hoover, whose files contained explosive material about Jack's sex life. Bobby also used his position in other ways to protect his brother, as when Justice Department employees investigated Victor Lasky, author of the highly critical *J.F.K.: The Man and the Myth.* In addition to his role as attorney general, Bobby—with even less experience than he possessed in law—also became one of his brother's most influential foreign policy advisers.

Kennedy had high expectations for himself as president, but once elected, he learned that governing wasn't as easy as it had looked from the sidelines. During the campaign, Kennedy had argued that the presidency needed to be rebuilt by "a man who will formulate and fight for legislative policies, not by a casual bystander." Kennedy, however, never mastered the legislative process, and his victories were few. Although Kennedy presented himself as a dramatic alternative to Eisenhower, in matters of policy, he differed little from his predecessor. Even the worshipful writer William Manchester admitted that he heard cocktail party jokes about the "third Eisenhower Administration," and columnist Walter Lippmann criticized the New Frontier as "the Eisenhower Administration thirty years younger."

Notable exceptions to this continuity were Kennedy's disasters in Cuba and Vietnam. In his first days as president, Kennedy, the former PT boat skipper, saw fit to sweep aside, as mere layers of fat, much of the apparatus that Eisenhower, the former supreme commander of the Allied Forces, had deigned to use to oversee national security matters. As a result, Kennedy created a White House that lacked structure and procedures to establish information flow and accountability.

Kennedy had inherited from Eisenhower the broad outlines of a plan to use a group of Cuban exiles against Castro. Kennedy had ample opportunity to cancel the operation, but given his persistent criticism of the Republicans for allowing communism to take hold ninety miles from American shores, could he pass up the opportunity to act? Bobby explained that if Jack "hadn't gone through with it, everybody would have said it showed that he had no courage."

So, within a few months of taking office, on April 17, 1961, Kennedy sent fourteen hundred U.S.-trained Cuban exiles to invade Cuba, which boasted a well-equipped army of more than two hundred thousand. Predictably, almost all the men were killed or captured. Kennedy bore great responsibility for the debacle. He had removed the White House structures that would have revealed the plan's flaws; until the last minute, he meddled with critical details, with no understanding of the consequences; he insisted the U.S. role be kept secret, when that stricture both doomed the invasion to failure and was obviously impossible—newspapers, after all, had widely reported the invasion plans.

Soon after, in June 1961, Kennedy had an unsuccessful meeting with Soviet premier Nikita Khrushchev in Vienna. Khrushchev's belligerence visibly shook Kennedy, and afterward, Khrushchev described Kennedy as young and weak. During the summit, Khrushchev announced his intention to sign a separate peace treaty with East Germany that would make all of Berlin into East German territory, thereby cutting off allied access to West Berlin.

On July 25, 1961, after his return, Kennedy gave an alarming report on Berlin to the American people. Kennedy evoked all the horrors of nuclear war as he emphasized the advisability of building and stocking bomb shelters—and thus set off a public panic. Within weeks, the Soviets threw up the Berlin Wall to bar the exit of refugees fleeing to the West through the city. Far from being dismayed, Kennedy seemed relieved the Soviets had found a way to cool the explosive situation.

Kennedy's most severe test came in October 1962, during the Cuban missile crisis. This episode was indeed the most dangerous hour of the Cold War, but Kennedy himself bore much responsibility for Khrushchev's decision to try to place missiles in Cuba.

After the failure at the Bay of Pigs, Kennedy had charged Bobby with the clandestine "Operation Mongoose" to topple Castro, and in January 1962, Bobby told the CIA that getting rid of Castro was "the top priority of the United States government. All else is secondary. No time, money, effort, or manpower is to be spared." Under Bobby's goading, those involved in Operation Mongoose attempted to spy, to cripple the Cuban economy through sabotage, and to plot Castro's assassination. Nevertheless, they accomplished little—except to convince Castro and Khrushchev that the United States was planning to invade Cuba sometime in 1962.

Eisenhower had used his vast prestige to reassure Americans that despite Soviet boasts of nuclear superiority, they had no reason to fear for their security. Kennedy had campaigned on the supposed "missile gap" but, as president, revealed the actual superiority of the American position. The undermining of Khrushchev's claims had put pressure on the Soviet leader to increase defense spending and to score a bold success to enhance his position. Khrushchev decided to put missiles in Cuba, so that in a quick stroke, he would build Soviet prestige, offset Soviet weakness, deter any U.S. first strike, and protect Cuba.

On October 16, 1962, Kennedy learned of the discovery of missile bases in Cuba. A group of top advisers gathered in secret to debate the proper course of action. On October 22, Kennedy gave a TV address to alert the public to the missiles' discovery. Choosing an approach that was highly dramatic and confrontational, Kennedy announced a "quarantine" to block additional weapons from reaching Cuba and demanded the installations' removal. After several days of suspense, and once the United States pledged not to invade Cuba, Khrushchev announced that the weapons would be withdrawn. Kennedy won ecstatic praise for his resolute stance; however, what was *not* disclosed was his pledge to remove Jupiter missiles from the Soviet border in Turkey. This agreement was so secret that even most of Kennedy's top advisers didn't know about it, not to mention Congress, the American public, or NATO allies. Later, when the administration ordered the withdrawal of the Jupiter missiles, and some congressmen asked pointed questions about a possible connection, Defense Secretary McNamara insisted, "The Soviet government did raise the issue, [but the] President absolutely refused even to discuss it."

In Southeast Asia, Kennedy supported the oppressive government of South Vietnamese president Ngo Dinh Diem. The administration approved the CIA's most aggressive operations, greatly expanded the American military presence, and violated the Geneva Convention. The number of American military advisers rose from 948 in November 1961 to more than 16,000 by November 1963. Kennedy tried to stay the course without challenging the assumptions at the basis of the conflict, and so, for example, although he initially opposed measures such as the use of napalm, defoliants, and free-fire zones, he eventually approved them. By the summer of 1963, Diem's regime was weakening. In a series of misunderstandings and mistakes, Washington tacitly authorized a coup against Diem despite uncertainty about how such a change would further U.S. objectives. During the coup, on November 1, 1963, Diem was assassinated. Many observers commented on Kennedy's distress at the news of Diem's death, but as General Maxwell Taylor asked, "What did he expect?"

On the domestic front, despite an eighty-nine-seat House margin and a twenty-eight-seat Senate margin, Kennedy never managed to persuade Congress to move on his principal legislative initiatives. On civil rights, the movement's energy, as well as the need to protect a political base, forced him to play a more active role than he wished. Only in the last months of his presidency did Kennedy make a major speech on civil rights or propose sweeping civil rights legislation. The Peace Corps was the New Frontier's signature initiative, but as Sargent Shriver, the Kennedy brother-in-law installed as its first director, admitted, "Jack never uttered more than thirty words to me about the Peace Corps."

Private life at the White House didn't set an example of high-minded sacrifice or activity. Kennedy's interest in books and intellectual company, fondly emphasized by the Ivy League professors he hired, was largely a matter of spin. Writers, academics, and artists were so thrilled to join Kennedy's golden circle that they suspended their usual skepticism. As Saul Bellow put it, "Mr. Kennedy was getting ready to exploit the eggheads. He could get them cheap, and they were falling all over themselves." Kennedy projected a vigorous image to hide the fact that he was sickly, heavily medicated, and often crippled by back pain. Jackie, for her part, refused to carry out most of the traditional duties of the first lady and instead used her platform to arrange for her home to be lavishly redecorated at others' expense. She spent much of her time vacationing outside Washington, and Kennedy took advantage of her absences to hurry in women for sex. His promiscuity was an open secret among many.

Kennedy's sexual adventurism entangled him in possible scandal. Kennedy shared a lover, Judith Campbell, with organized crime figures Sam Giancana and John Roselli. Not only that but—incredibly—the same Giancana and Roselli had been recruited by the CIA in 1960 in a plot to assassinate Castro. Also, Kennedy had a relationship with a prostitute, Ellen Rometsch, whom the FBI suspected of spying. Rometsch was associated with Bobby Baker, who had come under scrutiny for influence peddling, and the Baker investigation threatened to uncover Rometsch's connection to Kennedy.

But soon all this would come to an end.

In November 1963, Kennedy made a political trip to Texas. On November 22, Jack and Jackie Kennedy landed in Dallas and, despite warnings of possible violence, drove into town in an open car along a well-publicized motorcade route. At 12:30 p.m., Lee Harvey Oswald, a Texas School Book Depository employee, fired three bullets from the sixth floor of that building. Oswald's third shot hit Kennedy's head and killed him.

President John F. Kennedy was dead at age forty-six.

Directing the ceremonies surrounding her husband's funeral, determined to build his legend as a great president and hero, Jackie adopted many of the elements of Abraham Lincoln's funeral. She insisted upon dramatic flourishes such as a walking procession of family and dignitaries, a riderless horse with boots reversed in the stirrups, and an eternal flame, which even a family member questioned as "ostentatious."

Even now, decades after his death, the JFK image is kept vivid in the public mind with sentimental books of Kennedy photographs, retrospectives on Jackie's dress and entertainment style, and new revelations about Kennedy's sordid sex life. Nevertheless, despite the extraordinary public interest in John Kennedy, it's apparent that although he raised expectations high, his real accomplishments were few. His principal contribution was his introduction of the concept of president-as-entertainer.

3

KENNEDY'S EXCELLENCE

His Most Outstanding Quality

Assessments of Kennedy must tackle the essential question: what made Kennedy Kennedy? One factor, certainly, was the standard of excellence he represented.

Often, people are attracted to a leader because they recognize themselves in their leader's virtues, habits, and limitations. In the more rare and strenuous case, however, their identification is aspirational: they see in a leader not what they are but what they could be. In general, people don't want to exert themselves, and it's an exceptional leader who can inspire them with the desire to do better.

Somehow, Kennedy corresponded perfectly with what Americans wanted to see in their president. Kennedy seemed the embodiment of matchless excellence, and from him, the country caught a spirit of challenge and renewal.

Kennedy's most distinctive quality was his striving toward excellence. He personified the best America had to offer, and he inspired others to live up to the level of his vision. He believed the United States should have higher aims and, in the presidential campaign, often insisted, "I am not satisfied when . . ." or "I think we can do better." In the first televised debate, he emphasized, "This is a great country, but I think it could be a greater country, and this is a powerful country, but I think it could be a more powerful country." Said by Kennedy, such statements didn't sound like pessimism but, instead, a stirring call to action.

Whatever Kennedy sought to do, he seemed to do easily and well. When he went to war, he came back a hero. When he ran for office, he won. When he wrote a book, it became a bestseller and won a Pulitzer Prize. He knew the king of England and Grace Kelly. He was a millionaire. His elegant, intelligent, Emmy Award–winning wife dedicated herself to supporting him and his career, and she *and* his mother *and* his sister-in-law had appeared on the "best dressed" lists. He had two delightful young children, a girl and a boy. His sex appeal was legendary. His controversial father was a tremendous source of support but knew to stay well out of sight. His brothers, unlike many presidential brothers, were a credit. He was relentlessly curious and able to absorb huge amounts of information without effort. He was handsome, tan, and well dressed, without seeming vain, foppish, or unmanly. Despite the constant pain he endured, he was lean, graceful, energetic. He actually had to hide his excellent golf scores, because he didn't want to appear a golf-obsessed duffer like Eisenhower. He seemed to win every contest, however trivial: as a freshman congressman, he was named by the Associated Press as one of the country's fifteen most eligible bachelors; in 1952, the *Capitol News* named him the "handsomest member of Congress." These achievements were graced with a *sprezzatura* that made them all the more dazzling.

He seemed utterly himself, with nothing to disguise or embellish. He never tried to hide the Harvard accent, the Sunday mornings at Mass, and the summer houses that were part of his life. John

John F. Kennedy waves to the crowd.

Kenneth Galbraith noted he'd never met a man who took such pleasure in being himself and had as little insecurity as Kennedy. Kennedy remained true to his nature; when asked why he always wore the same gray suits, he answered, "That's me. I keep it that way." Looking over a speech his advisers considered "excellent," Kennedy said, "I just can't give that speech. . . . We're stuck with my personality. And we have to give the speeches that conform to my personality."

Kennedy didn't tailor himself to the public taste—for example, just as he didn't hide his rocking chair, despite its associations with age and inactivity, he never hid his regard for poetry. Not many

politicians could have ended a speech with a quote from Tennyson's "Ulysses" or paraphrased a Robert Frost poem in a campaign speech without sounding affected, but done by Kennedy, it
was winning: "Iowa City is lovely, dark and deep / But I have . . .
miles to go before I sleep." Kennedy often included unself-
conscious references to poetry in his remarks. In an address made
in January 1960, he joked that Eisenhower's State of the Union
message "reminded me of the exhortation from *King Lear* that
goes: 'I will do such things—what they are I know not . . . but they
shall be the wonders of the earth.' " In a speech in October 1960,
he said, "I do not want it said of our generation what T. S. Eliot
wrote in his poem, 'The Rock'—'and the wind shall say: "these
were decent people, their only monument the asphalt road and a
thousand lost golf balls." ' We can do better than that." In the last
press conference he gave, Kennedy offhandedly threw in a line of
poetry: "In the fields of education, mental health, taxes, civil
rights . . . however dark it looks now, I think that 'westward, look,
the land is bright,' and I think that by next summer it may be."

Confident of himself, he put others at ease. A friend recalled,
"He was the same in person as he was on the television screen. . . .
He wasn't two different people." Kennedy's self-assurance con-
trasted brightly with Nixon's fake piety and dreary insistence that
he was a "regular fellow." Kennedy reflected, "Nixon has always
the problem as to who he is. I know who I am." The television debates highlighted their differences. Kennedy was cool and relaxed;
Nixon was haggard, nervous, shifty-eyed. When asked if he felt he
should apologize for President Truman's comment suggesting
where voters for Nixon "could go," Kennedy answered, "I really
don't think there's anything that I can say to President Truman
that's going to cause him, at the age of 76, to change his particular
speaking manner. Perhaps Mrs. Truman can, but I don't think I
can." That was Kennedy—self-deprecating, good-humored.
Nixon's priggish answer: "Whoever is President is going to be a

man that all the children of America will either look up to, or will look down to. . . . I'm very proud that President Eisenhower restored dignity and decency and, frankly, good language to the conduct of the presidency." Kennedy's self-assurance extended to Jackie. Many advisers thought her too sophisticated and wanted her to dress and act differently, but despite her influence on his own political fortune, Kennedy didn't press her to change. "A man marries a woman, not a first lady," he said. "If he becomes president, she must fit her own personality into her own concept of a first lady's role. People do best what comes naturally."

Being self-assured didn't mean Kennedy didn't work hard on self-presentation. He thought carefully about his effect on other people. He disliked his high, nasal voice, and so, on the advice of a vocal coach, for a time, he spent thirty minutes each morning barking like a dog to deepen his voice. Tradition dictated that the president toss out the first ball for the Washington Senators' season opener, so Kennedy practiced his pitching. He wasn't a natural backslapper or public speaker, but through experience and diligence, he transformed himself into a tremendously charismatic politician. "I never saw anybody grow the way Jack did," Congressman Tip O'Neill said: "He turned into a great personality and a beautiful talker. But until he was in the Senate you just couldn't imagine that he was really going anywhere."

Kennedy's advisers revered him as their master. "Kennedy amazed his own men," Hugh Sidey wrote, "with his detailed knowledge of the party machinery . . . the names of key workers, of the political feelings in various regions." One aide admitted, "When asked who is the most knowledgeable of the President's advisers he always felt obliged to remind his questioners that none was half so well-informed as the President himself." Kennedy's ambassador to the Soviet Union recalled how Kennedy "drained me dry of all I knew. And on the rare occasions when there was a difference of opinion between us, he was right and I was wrong."

Kennedy absorbed innumerable memos, newspapers, magazines, and letters, and he was interested in everything from the daily morning intelligence report to Hollywood rumors. After one free-wheeling, highly substantive discussion with top officials and diplomats, Charles Bohlen was struck by Kennedy's impatience to learn. "I never heard of a President who wanted to know so much." British prime minister Harold Macmillan recalled JFK as "one of the best-informed statesmen whom it has ever been my lot to meet . . . altogether without pedantry or any trace of intellectual arrogance."

Kennedy displayed his erudition with grace and quoted without affectation from Lincoln and Jefferson, from Emerson and Thoreau, from Goethe and Frost. Schlesinger ventured he was probably the one politician who had quoted Madame de Staël on *Meet the Press.* Theodore White described Kennedy's campaign as "a transcontinental lecture in American history; the stories not only entertained but gave a lift to his audiences, making them see their connection with America's past." As his ready and witty allusions showed, Kennedy's particular interests were history and biography. He once reminded listeners that for "one brief moment of glory," he'd been a candidate for vice president. "Socrates once said that it was the duty of a man of real principle to avoid high national office, and evidently the delegates at Chicago recognized my principles even before I did." When the microphone at the St. Paul airport didn't work, he joked, "I understand that Daniel Webster used to address 100,000 people . . . without a mike. We are a little softer than they used to be, however."

One of Kennedy's strengths as a leader was his shrewd understanding of human nature. His brother-in-law Sargent Shriver recalled, "Kennedy was one of the most astute, sensitive political personalities I have ever met. He knew people extraordinarily well; it was almost like a sixth sense. He knew people's strengths and weaknesses." For example, Kennedy said in 1959, "Nixon is a nice fellow in private, and a very able man. I worked with him on the Hill for a long time, but it seems he has a split personality and he is very bad in public, and nobody likes him." When Theodore White told Kennedy that New York governor Nelson Rockefeller, who was a likely 1964 presidential challenger, held him in warm regard, Kennedy replied, "I like him too. But that's not important. He'll get to hate me. That's inevitable."

And along with his other gifts, Kennedy was enormously *likable,* with a wonderful sense of fun, easy conversation, and graceful manners. Columnist Rowland Evans said, "Jack was simply the most appealing human being I ever met." Longtime friend Lem Billings thought Kennedy had the best sense of humor of anyone he knew. Columnist Joseph Alsop observed that while Franklin Roosevelt was loved by the public, he wasn't loved by those around him; Kennedy was "loved by an astonishing number of the people who served him—not just the very able men like Ted Sorensen and Kenny O'Donnell, who gave their whole lives to him, but many others like Bob McNamara and McGeorge Bundy, and still others further out on the fringe like myself." Charley Bartlett recalled, "There was gaiety—the amazing thing is that it wasn't a bubbling gaiety, but it was there. There was a very deep gaiety to John Kennedy." This high-spiritedness is all the more extraordinary considering that Kennedy was almost constantly in pain.

Kennedy's teasing humor drew people to him. When special counsel and chief speechwriter Ted Sorensen gave a speech that was heavily criticized, Kennedy said, "That's what happens when you permit a speech-writer to write his own speech!" When Sorensen apologized for embarrassing Kennedy, Kennedy laughed. "I don't mind. They can criticize *you* all they like!" When Schlesinger asked permission to write a film column, Kennedy responded, "It is fine . . . as long as you treat Peter Lawford with respect." He had a light touch. Bobby Baker, who named his children

Lynda and Lyndon after LBJ, said, "I loved him—more than I did Johnson. . . . He was not mean; he was thoughtful. He had a zest for living."

Not only did Kennedy set a personal example of excellence, he also chose to associate his administration with people of outstanding accomplishment. Kennedy hosted Congressional Medal of Honor winners and Nobel laureates—who comprised, he observed, "the most extraordinary collection of talent, of human knowledge, that has ever been gathered together at the White House, with the possible exception of when Thomas Jefferson dined alone." Unlike many political and business leaders who consider the arts mere frippery, Kennedy believed artistic achievement essential to the greatness of the United States, and he made the White House the setting for great performances, such as a concert by cellist Pablo Casals and Jerome Robbins's *Ballets USA*. Kennedy's support for such events is the more admirable given that he himself didn't much appreciate them. For example, Kennedy—who loved Frank Sinatra, Broadway show tunes, and Irish ballads—didn't enjoy classical music, and at White House concerts, he twice hurried to the stage to thank the musicians before they'd finished. As president, however, he wanted to lend his prestige to performances of distinction. Jackie agreed: "People seem so interested in whatever the first family likes. This is where I think one can lead."

There's no question that Kennedy relished displaying his relationships with Nobel Prize winners, artists, and scholars. But this is, in itself, remarkable for a politician. The public is often suspicious of highbrows and eggheads, but Kennedy deliberately cultivated the reputation of being an intellectual and a voracious reader. He wanted the country to admire intellectual accomplishments, and with his supreme self-knowledge, he recognized that he could make such achievements attractive by associating with them.

Perhaps the country more willingly accepted Kennedy's support of Shakespeare and ballet because the Kennedys—with their sailing, swimming, touch football, tennis, riding, and waterskiing—were hardly effete. Kennedy wanted nothing flabby or second-rate about himself, his circle, or his country. At one point, Kennedy asked his staff each to lose five pounds. He famously challenged Americans to march fifty miles. Kennedy himself had a regular exercise regime and made daily use of the White House swimming pool.

Kennedy strove for excellence in everything he did, and this ideal was a guiding force, a moral pressure on him. For example, though some advisers urged him to take more vigorous action for civil rights, Kennedy hesitated to get too far ahead of the country; at the same time, his civil rights aide Harris Wofford observed,

March 1963. President Kennedy is a blur of motion as he leaves the State Department auditorium after a press conference.

"Our best ally (and defense) was his own self-image; he saw himself as a strong President, open to criticism and prepared to give courageous moral leadership."

Mesmerized by his splendid standard, the American public saw Kennedy's excellence as both an example and a challenge.

4

TIME LINE OF KENNEDY'S PRESIDENCY

What He Accomplished

Presidents are judged by their ability to win approval of signature legislation, to preserve national security, to score diplomatic victories, to settle domestic and international crises, to strengthen the economy, and to maintain the public's trust.

This time line of the key events in Kennedy's truncated presidency summarizes such milestones—but without the explanations and effusions that usually pad accounts of Kennedy's administration.

1961

JANUARY	Sworn in as thirty-fifth president of the United States
MARCH	Proposes the Alliance for Progress; creates the Peace Corps
APRIL	Launches the Bay of Pigs invasion
MAY	Signs area redevelopment bill to aid communities with chronic unemployment; pledges that U.S. space team will reach the moon by 1970
JUNE	Meets with de Gaulle in Paris and Khrushchev in Vienna; signs bill extending Social Security benefits; signs bill providing funds to build low-income housing in urban areas
JULY	Signs bill increasing federal efforts to halt water pollution; grapples with severe tensions in Berlin
SEPTEMBER	Signs bill raising the minimum wage; signs bill establishing a program to help combat juvenile delinquency

1962

MARCH	Announces that Soviet resumption of atmospheric nuclear testing necessitates U.S. testing
APRIL	Obtains rescission of steel price increase
JUNE	Announces Geneva Conference agreement on neutral Laos

JULY	Signs revision of public welfare legislation
SEPTEMBER	Sends federal marshals and troops to enforce a court order requiring the University of Mississippi's desegregation
OCTOBER	Signs trade expansion bill; after discovery of Soviet missiles in Cuba, imposes a naval "quarantine" on all weapons shipments to Cuba and successfully demands that Soviets withdraw nuclear missiles from Cuba
NOVEMBER	Issues an executive order banning racial discrimination in federal housing

1963

JUNE	Sends federalized Alabama National Guard to enforce a court order requiring the University of Alabama's desegregation; gives three key speeches on democracy, freedom, and civil rights
OCTOBER	Signs the Nuclear Test Ban Treaty

5

KENNEDY AND MONEY
A Circumstance That Shaped Him

Money dictates the conditions of a person's life and, whether plentiful or scarce, exerts an enormous influence. Kennedy grew up in a household of great wealth, and thanks to his father, was a millionaire as an adult. This background gave Kennedy his air of command, the ability to concentrate his energies on great issues, a lordly disdain for cost, and a sense of impunity.

Perhaps surprisingly, the public didn't resent Kennedy's circumstances. It's natural to expect a magnificent setting for those who seem truly great, and so it seemed quite right that Kennedy should enjoy a life of wealth, privilege, and power.

One of Jack Kennedy's most winning qualities was his calm air of self-assurance. He seemed focused, relaxed, lighthearted. He never grubbed over minor details or looked for a way to turn a personal profit or settled for anything shoddy or second-rate. And why should he? He was rich.

Unlike political contemporaries such as Hubert Humphrey,

Richard Nixon, or Lyndon Johnson, Kennedy never worried about supporting his family. A wall of money, thrown up around him by his enormously wealthy father, insulated him from financial worries and temptations.

Although Joe Kennedy drove himself to amass a fortune, he taught his children to have an aristocratic disdain for earning. "I have never discussed money with my wife and family," he emphasized, "and I never will." Jack Kennedy had no interest in the family business or money matters and, even as an adult, trusted his financial affairs to his father's office.

But Kennedy's air of calm and self-assurance wasn't solely due to the fact that he didn't worry about paying bills. It also rose from his life of servants and staff, in which he delegated the daily details that madden and distract most people. He didn't run his own bath or choose his own clothes or stop to pick up something at the grocery store. Anxious on the day of the West Virginia primary, Kennedy didn't want to face public scrutiny if he was defeated. So that morning, he headed to Washington on his private plane—complete with desk, bedroom, and galley, and crew of three—and when he found out at 11:30 p.m. that he'd won, he flew back to West Virginia that night.

Money released Kennedy from ordinary restrictions. Racing to complete his Harvard thesis, he hired a personal secretary and five stenographers. In his first House race, when he missed the deadline to file the papers necessary to qualify as a candidate, Kennedy clout persuaded a clerk to open the office so he could complete the forms. In his presidential race, the Kennedy fortune paid for TV airtime and newspaper ads, the salaries of research and support staff, the elegant Kennedy teas, and the renting of meeting halls. The lack of money worries allowed Kennedy to concentrate his mind and energies on winning.

Being raised rich helped give Kennedy a pleasing air of authority. He expected others to do things for him. As a boy, he was served by maids and cooks and secretaries; at Harvard, he had a part-time valet who came to his room daily to tidy up. Even when Kennedy lived in a dingy Boston apartment during his congressional campaigns, he didn't fix his own breakfast. The janitor would make eggs and bacon in his own apartment and bring it up to Jack on a tray. When Jack and his sister shared a house in Washington, D.C., they were attended by a longtime Kennedy family cook and a valet, George Thomas. (Twenty years later, in the White House, Thomas wouldn't have much to do: Kennedy joked, "George opens the door for the butler to bring in the breakfast tray.")

Kennedy ignored money as only a rich person could do. He never carried cash and, despite his wealth, was notorious for cadging money from aides for milkshakes, newspapers, taxi fares, or the church collection plate; some sent expense vouchers to the Kennedy office to be paid back. Like many rich people, he exercised a sporadic, haphazard frugality. In the White House, he complained about the expense of food and entertaining. While Jackie racked up a forty-thousand-dollar department store bill, Jack imposed modest economies, such as moving the Kennedy grocery account from an upscale Georgetown market to a wholesaler.

Despite occasional halfhearted attempts to pinch pennies, Kennedy lived the life of a very wealthy man. He himself wasn't much concerned with possessions; he didn't need to be, because his wife worked ceaselessly to create an elegant atmosphere around him. Beautiful clothes, lovely rooms, sophisticated parties—all this required money and the knowledge, exercised by Jackie, of how to spend to achieve the proper effect. She had a passion for decorating. In one Kennedy household, she changed the kitchen wallpaper three times in three months; in another, she redecorated the living room at least three times in their first four months in the house; and her chief ambition as first lady was to refurbish the White House with beautiful antiques and fabrics. For his part, Kennedy indulged in many luxuries that only a very rich man could afford. He wore three separate suits of clothes each day and sometimes wore as many as six shirts, with no thought for the expense and effort required.

Growing up rich shaped another aspect of Kennedy's success. People marveled at Kennedy's natural, unguarded air in the White House. Surrounded by household staff from boyhood, Kennedy—and his wife, too—had been trained by years without privacy; in houses staffed with servants, someone is always listening, watching who comes and goes, observing the sleeping arrangements. Servants require those they serve to pose, to assume a role, to maintain a public face. By the time Caroline was born, the small Kennedy family employed a staff of nanny, valet, cook, and housemaid. This exposed way of life prepared the Kennedys for constant public scrutiny and vigilant press attention.

The public didn't resent Kennedy's position as a man of inherited money. As Congressman Roman Puchinski observed, "His wealth never bothered anybody." People seemed to accept, as right and natural, Kennedy's opulent manner of life.

In fact, while another politician might have tried to conceal the facts of such a privileged existence, Kennedy—with his unfailing insight into the public mind—understood that the public craves glimpses into the lives of the very rich. Of course, he was careful not to show off his wealth in an obnoxious way. When Jackie gave him a white Jaguar for Christmas in 1957, he returned it as "too flashy." He didn't allow photographers to come to opulent Palm Beach or to photograph his quarters on *Air Force One,* and he sometimes discouraged Jackie from flaunting her upper-class activities, such as foxhunting. When word got out that Jackie had constructed a small golf course at the Kennedys' rented country house, Glen Ora, as a birthday gift—as she had—the White House denied the story as "ridiculous and untrue." Generally, however, Kennedy didn't try to hide his rich man's life. People were fascinated by the frequent moves among the White House and the two-story penthouse suite at the Carlyle Hotel in New York City, the hunt-country house in Virginia, the villa in Florida, Jackie's mother's estate of Hammersmith Farm, and the Kennedy family compound in Hyannis Port, with its private movie theater, tennis courts, and four sailboats. They loved to read about Kennedy's forty-sixth birthday party, held on a yacht. They pored over pictures of Jackie's clothes, hair, and jewelry.

It's true, too, that the public approved of the way Kennedy lived; it seemed the right way to be rich. He had money, horses, parties, houses, travel, with vigorous pastimes such as football and sailing—but also children, study, church, and heavy public responsibilities. It seemed quite proper that the man who was president—and who was therefore tied, in the public mind, to a noble calling and great events—should live in splendid circumstances, with wealth and dignity.

6

Kennedy Fact Sheet
Details from His Life

For admirers studying an adored figure, no fact is too trivial. Shoe size, favorite poem, favorite food—every fact seems to shed some light on the character or life of the revered one. But do these enthusiasts really want to know everything?

Kennedy Facts

HAIR COLOR: reddish brown.
EYE COLOR: greenish gray.
HEIGHT: six feet.
IQ: 119.
ASTROLOGICAL SIGN: Gemini.
CHINESE ZODIAC YEAR: Year of the Snake.
WEIGHT WHEN ELECTED: 167 pounds.
BODY MASS INDEX: 22.6.

Cholesterol level: 410.

Blood type: O positive.

Hat size: 7⅝ (extremely large).

Jacket size: 40 inches.

Waistline: 32 inches.

Shoe size: 10C.

House at Harvard: Winthrop.

Age at which he lost his virginity:

seventeen, when he and Lem Billings went to the same New York City prostitute, who charged three dollars.

Medals he won for wartime service:

Purple Heart and Navy and Marine Corps Medal.

First year he voted in a local primary election:

in 1946, aged twenty-nine, when his own name was on the ballot.

Gift to ushers at his wedding:

a Brooks Brothers umbrella engraved with the recipient's initials and the wedding date.

Nervous habits:

tapping his teeth, playing with the button on his suit coat, putting his hands in his pockets, swinging his foot.

Usual breakfast:

freshly squeezed orange juice, coffee, toast, two four-and-a-half-minute boiled eggs, and four pieces of bacon (except on Friday).

How many children he wanted:

five, at least, but not too close together.

Year he was *Time* magazine's "Man of the Year":   1961.

Temperature of the White House pool:

ninety degrees, to ease the pain in his back.

Actor whom he chose to play him in the 1963 movie based on his *PT-109* adventure: Warren Beatty. (Beatty declined, and Cliff Robertson played JFK.)

ROUTINE GIFTS HE GAVE: to acquaintances, a copy of
Bartlett's Quotations; to friends, an inscribed silver
bowl.

HIS FIRST EXECUTIVE ORDER:
Executive Order Number 1, January 21, 1961, to increase the
variety and double the quantity of surplus foods for 4 million
poor Americans.

HIS GOLF SCORE: high 70s and low 80s.

COUNTY IN IRELAND FROM WHICH THE KENNEDY FAMILY CAME:
County Wexford.

HIS IDEAS FOR A POSTPRESIDENTIAL CAREER:
to be president of Harvard, ambassador to Ireland, a senator
or to found or buy a newspaper. He suggested that the
Senate consider passing a bill that would make every former
president an honorary member.

MAGAZINES HE READ REGULARLY IN THE WHITE HOUSE:
*Time, Life, Newsweek, U.S. News & World Report, Business
Week, Nation's Business, Saturday Review, The New Yorker,
Harper's, Atlantic Monthly, The Spectator, The New Republic,
History Today, Foreign Affairs, Manchester Guardian Weekly,
London Economist.*

HAPPIEST DAY OF HIS LIFE:
July 10, 1963, the day he signed the instruments of
ratification for the Nuclear Test Ban Treaty.

MOST UNHAPPY PERIODS OF HIS LIFE:
during the time of his back operations in 1954 and 1955 and
after the failure of the Bay of Pigs invasion.

WHAT HE BELIEVED TO BE THE GREATEST SINGLE PROBLEM IN THE
1960s: nuclear proliferation.

THE OPPONENT HE HOPED TO FACE IN THE 1964 ELECTION:
Barry Goldwater.

THE OPPONENT HE FEARED TO FACE IN THE 1964 ELECTION:
Nelson Rockefeller.

THE HONOR THAT MADE HIM HAPPIEST:
winning the Pulitzer Prize for Biography.
WHAT HE CONSIDERED THE MOST ADMIRABLE OF HUMAN
VIRTUES: courage.
THE QUALITY HE THOUGHT MOST IMPORTANT: vitality.
WHAT HE SAID WAS HIS BEST QUALITY: curiosity.
WHAT HE SAID WAS HIS WORST QUALITY:
irritability—impatience with the boring or mediocre.
HIS GREATEST FEAR:
that he might be the president to start a nuclear war.
THINGS AT WHICH HE DIDN'T EXCEL:
playing poker and learning foreign languages.
ESSENCE OF THE KENNEDY LEGACY, ACCORDING TO BOBBY
KENNEDY: "a willingness to try and to dare and to change,
to hope for the uncertain and risk the unknown."
WHAT HE WANTED TO BE SAID OF HIS PRESIDENCY:
"He kept the peace."
NUMBER OF TIMES HE RECEIVED LAST RITES: four.
HIS JOB-APPROVAL RATING IN NOVEMBER 1963,
ACCORDING TO THE GALLUP POLL: 58 percent.
PROPORTION OF PRESIDENTS WHO'D DIED IN OFFICE, BY
KENNEDY'S TIME: about one out of four.

KENNEDY'S FAVORITES

SOME FAVORITE BOOKS AS A CHILD:
the Billy Whiskers series (brightly illustrated books about the
adventures of a billy goat), Sir Walter Scott's *Waverly* novels,
biographies, *King Arthur and the Round Table.*
SOME FAVORITE BOOKS AS AN ADULT:
John Buchan's *Pilgrim's Way,* David Cecil's *The Young
Melbourne,* T. E. Lawrence's *Seven Pillars of Wisdom,* Samuel

Flagg Bemis's *John Quincy Adams,* Allan Nevins's *The Emergence of Lincoln.* He also read every book by Winston Churchill, of which his favorite was *Marlborough,* and numerous books on American presidents.

BOOKS HE'D TAKE TO A DESERT ISLAND:

the Bible, John Buchan's *Pilgrim's Way, The Oxford Book of American Verse,* and *The Oxford Anthology of American Literature.*

BOOK HE ENCOURAGED THOSE AROUND HIM TO READ:

Barbara Tuchman's *The Guns of August,* because it illustrated one of his greatest fears, the danger of war by miscalculation; Mao and Che Guevara, on guerrilla training.

SOME FAVORITE SONGS:

"Hooray for Hollywood"; "Bill Bailey, Won't You Please Come Home?"; "Blue Skies"; "Heart of My Heart"; "Younger Than Springtime."

FAVORITE DRINKS:

daiquiri, scotch and water, brandy stinger.

FAVORITE FOODS:

ice cream and soup, especially tomato and clam chowder.

A FAVORITE QUOTE FROM EDMUND BURKE:

"The only thing necessary for the triumph of evil is for good men to do nothing."

SOME FAVORITE POEMS: Tennyson's "Ulysses," Alan Seeger's "A Rendezvous with Death."

A FAVORITE PASSAGE FROM SHAKESPEARE:

Saint Crispin's Day speech from *Henry V:*

> We few, we happy few, we band of brothers;
> For he to-day that sheds his blood with me
> Shall be my brother; be he ne'er so vile,
> This day shall gentle his condition;

And gentlemen in England now a-bed
Shall think themselves accurs'd they were not here,
And hold their manhoods cheap whiles any speaks
That fought with us upon Saint Crispin's day.

A FAVORITE QUOTE FROM ABRAHAM LINCOLN, AS PARAPHRASED
   BY JFK: "I know there is a God, and I know He hates
   injustice. I see the storm coming and I know His hand is in
   it. But if He has a place and a part for me, I believe that I am
   ready."

FAVORITE SPORT: college and professional football.

STATESMAN HE MOST ADMIRED: Winston Churchill.

A FAVORITE QUOTE FROM CHURCHILL: "We arm to parley."

WHERE HE MET CHURCHILL: with Jackie on Aristotle Onassis's
   yacht in 1955.

FAVORITE STORY ABOUT VICE PRESIDENT JOHNSON: after the
   success of the mission to put John Glenn into orbit, Johnson
   commented, "If only he were a Negro."

FAVORITE NEW YORK RESTAURANT: Le Pavillon.

A FAVORITE MOVIE: *Red River.*

A FAVORITE APHORISM: "In politics, there are no friends, only
   allies."

FAVORITE MUSICALS: *My Fair Lady* and *Camelot.* (On the
   Kennedys' last night in the White House before leaving for
   Texas, the Marine Band had played songs from *Camelot.*)

FAVORITE PHOTOGRAPH OF HIMSELF:
   Mark Shaw's unconventional 1960 picture of JFK walking in
   the dunes at Hyannis Port.

John Kennedy walking in the dunes.

7

KENNEDY AND HIS FATHER
His Most Significant Influence

What made Kennedy Kennedy? Many people influenced him. His wife, Jackie, taught him appreciation for arts and culture. His aide Ted Sorensen helped shape the graceful prose that became his hallmark. His brother Bobby was his most trusted adviser.

But an earlier and greater influence than these was his father, Joseph Kennedy. It was Joe Kennedy who encouraged Jack at every step, who promoted his reputation at every turn, who pushed him to run for office, who pulled the strings to win him every advantage. Kennedy never denied his father's influence. "He's the one who made all this possible," JFK told a friend not long before the assassination.

The dominant force in the life of John F. Kennedy was, from his earliest days, his father, Joseph Kennedy.

Joe Kennedy was an unremittingly demanding father. Although engrossed in building a fortune and polishing his reputation, he took his paternal role very seriously. He was absent for long stretches when his children were young—he wasn't present for several of their births and didn't see Pat until she was almost a month old—but paid close attention to their upbringing as they grew older.

He gave his children a rage for distinction and whipped them into a frenzy of competition among themselves and with others. He expected his sons to enter public life and his daughters to marry distinguished men who would contribute to the Kennedy dynasty. More than anything, Joe insisted on success: "We don't want any losers around here. In this family we want winners." His expectations were highest for his oldest son, Joseph P. Kennedy Jr.

Joe was determined to use his money and connections to thrust his children into the highest society. He worked tirelessly to build the Kennedy reputation, and by the 1930s, the Kennedys had one of the most celebrated names in America. For example, the 1930s Broadway musical *Leave It to Me* and the 1940s West End comedy *The Chiltern Hundreds* made recognizable reference to the Kennedy family.

But if Joe was dictatorial and demanding, he was also loving, encouraging, and deeply engaged in his children's activities. "All my ducks are swans," he said. All his ducks, that is, except one. Rosemary, his eldest daughter, was mildly retarded. The family went to great lengths to hide her condition—in London in 1938, she was even presented at court with her sister Kick—but when Rosemary reached her twenties, she became frustrated, restless, and increasingly difficult to supervise. Without Rose's knowledge, Joe subjected Rosemary to a prefrontal lobotomy in the hope she'd become less agitated. The disastrous surgery left Rosemary profoundly retarded and slightly paralyzed, and she was institutionalized for the rest of her life.

Joe was eager to hide the less-than-perfect Rosemary; however, he did everything he could to support the other children. He gave careful consideration to their education, wrote them thoughtful letters, placed them in broadening situations, spotlighted their achievements, and used his contacts to win them advantages. He also hired private detectives and informants to investigate them and their friends.

Joe succeeded brilliantly in shaping his children; they were fiercely competitive, concerned with public issues, and loyal to the family. As adults, they achieved several kinds of success he admired. His three sons became prominent politicians. Daughter Kick married into the highest levels of the British aristocracy, in line to be the Duchess of Devonshire. Pat married a Hollywood movie star. Eunice and Jean married men who worked in the Kennedy family business and in the administration. The whole family pitched in to help the Kennedy brothers win public office. Later, when asked how he and Rose shaped their children, Joe replied, "I could give you some pat answers, but . . . I can't think of a single thing we tried that some of my friends haven't tried with very different results." He added, "Competition—that's what makes them go."

Joe was indeed competitive on behalf of his children, and a glance at his intervention on Jack's behalf demonstrates his determination to help Jack succeed.

While Jack was writing his Harvard senior thesis, Joe was still in London as ambassador to the Court of St. James's. Joe wrote his son letters furnishing ideas and text—from which Jack lifted some passages almost verbatim—and when Jack finished, Joe was determined to see the thesis published. Influential *New York Times* journalist Arthur Krock, who acted as the Kennedy family's personal publicity man, retitled Jack's work as *Why England Slept,* edited it, and helped find a publisher. Joe then convinced *Time-Life* publisher Henry Luce to write the foreword. After its publication, Joe bought large quantities of the book to create the illusion of popular demand. Joe believed these efforts would pay off for Jack, because, as he wrote his son in 1940, "a book that really makes the grade with high-class people stands you in good stead for years to come."

In 1941, due to his colon, stomach, and back problems, Jack failed the physical examination for both the army's and the navy's officer candidate schools. Although Jack later claimed he did a summer's worth of back-strengthening exercises to pass the test, in reality, Joe used his influence to find doctors who overlooked Jack's true medical condition. Once in the navy, Jack wanted command of a patrol torpedo boat, a glamorous role that afforded autonomy and opportunities for heroic action. The competition was fierce, but again, Joe pulled strings for his son. By the spring of 1943, Jack was on his way to the South Pacific to a PT boat command.

In August 1943, a Japanese destroyer smashed Jack's boat, and Jack led his crew for several days until their rescue. Upon their return, Jack's standing as the son of the former British ambassador ensured that he was hailed as a hero. Joe made sure the incident received as much acclaim as possible.

Joe had planned to see his eldest son become president, and he was devastated when, in August 1944, Joe Jr. was killed on a daring volunteer mission. Joe wrote a friend, "All my plans for my own future were all tied up with young Joe and that has gone smash." With Joe Jr. gone, Joe became determined to put Jack in the White House. Jack explained, "My father wanted his eldest son in politics. 'Wanted' isn't the right word. He *demanded* it." (Later, Jack would deny that his father had pressured him to run.)

Joe's influence and fortune had an incalculable impact at every step of Jack's political career. Joe financed the campaigns and was consulted on every important matter, though he was chiefly concerned with tactics, not substance. One of his most important contributions was his decision—despite his domineering personality and love for the spotlight—to remain out of view. He well understood that given his notorious history and controversial views, his obvious involvement would only hurt Jack's chances.

Joe's first step was to identify a seat for Jack. After discovering that Congressman James Michael Curley had serious financial problems, Joe sent him twelve thousand dollars and promised financial support if Curley would leave his Eleventh District seat to run for mayor of Boston. Curley did.

Ten men ran for the open seat. The Kennedys offered the front-runner, Mike Neville, a job for life if he would drop out. When he refused, Joe prevailed on William Randolph Hearst to ensure that for two months before election day, Hearst-owned newspapers wouldn't run a Neville advertisement, photograph, or his name. Another candidate was Joseph Russo; Joe paid a young janitor, also named Joseph Russo, to put his name on the ballot to dilute the Russo vote.

With his Hollywood experience, Joe understood the importance of managing Jack's image. He was among the first to appreciate the role of "public relations" in politics, and he hired a PR firm to represent Jack. It was Joe who pushed the notion that Jack should run as a young veteran, after a private poll showed that the public was more interested in Jack as a war hero than as a politician. Joe lobbied his friend James Forrestal, secretary of the navy, to name a Boston-built destroyer the USS *Joseph P. Kennedy, Jr.,* to remind the public of the Kennedy boys' heroic war records. When John Hersey wrote the *New Yorker* story "Survival" about Jack's *PT-109* exploits, Joe arranged for it to be republished in *Reader's Digest* and paid an astronomical amount for one hundred thousand reprints to be mailed to voters. Joe used his fortune to build Jack's reputation in the community, where he hadn't lived for years. In 1946, the Kennedys—represented by Jack—gave six hundred thousand dollars for a children's hospital in Jack's district. This check, and many others that followed, meant goodwill for the Kennedys and newspaper coverage for Jack. And Joe's money gave Jack the important advantage, not enjoyed by his opponents, of not having to hold down a job outside the campaign.

After Jack won—handily—Joe's support continued. He used a press agent to get Jack named one of the U.S. Junior Chamber of

Commerce's Ten Outstanding Men of 1946. (In 1954, Bobby would have his turn.) Joe's money paid for Jack to hire more staff members than official congressional payrolls would cover.

When Jack decided to run for the Senate against popular incumbent Henry Cabot Lodge, Joe again spent a huge amount to cover campaign expenses, to donate to other candidates, to hire planes and cars, even to order engraved invitations for the ladies' teas, which proved so effective. He bought the *Boston Post* endorsement—worth an estimated forty thousand votes—by promising a $500,000 loan to the publisher. Jack admitted to reporter Fletcher Knebel, "We had to buy that fucking paper or I'd have been licked." When Jack ran for reelection in 1958, Joe spent an estimated $1.5 million to secure Jack an impressive margin, to boost his chances for the presidency.

Joe was so confident of ultimate Kennedy triumph that in 1957, well before Jack's Senate victory, a journalist reported that Joe looked forward to a time when "Jack will be in the White House, Bobby will serve in the Cabinet as Attorney General, and Teddy will be the Senator from Massachusetts." Over the next five years, Joe's efforts and money would help ensure his predictions came true.

After Jack began his presidential campaign, Joe worked doggedly to help, and Rose Kennedy wrote in her diary that she didn't think Joe would "ever get credit for the constant, unremitting labor he has devoted to making his son President." Jack enjoyed every advantage that money could buy, and as before, Joe's contribution was far greater than merely acting as a moneybags. Thanks to Joe's efforts to promote the Kennedy family, by 1960, Jack had been well known to the American public for years. He'd been featured in newsreel footage since boyhood; in 1940, the AP circulated a photograph of Jack spotting his draft number, one of the first chosen in the lottery; his wedding was on the front page of the *New York Times.* This groundwork of familiarity helped Kennedy enormously. As

Theodore White observed about Humphrey's difficulties in the primaries, "Humphrey had, above all, to become known." Joe also began lining up support from political bosses starting in 1957 and had the idea to recruit Franklin D. Roosevelt Jr. to stump for Jack in West Virginia, where FDR was revered—a move that many observers believed played a decisive role. (Despite long-standing rumors, no solid evidence links Joe to organized crime, and although some claim Jack won Illinois because of Joe's Mob connections— or because Chicago mayor Richard Daley's organization stole the election—Jack would have had enough electoral votes, 276 to 246, to win even without Illinois.)

Joe's influence remained strong after Jack's victory, although, as always, his role was concealed. Kennedy called his father frequently, sometimes as many as six times a day. Joe continued to push Jack's interests however he could: when Kennedy friend and author Robert Donovan wanted a movie deal for his highly flattering book *PT 109: John F. Kennedy in World War II*, Joe used his Hollywood connections to sell the book over the phone to Warner Bros. Joe was also extremely close to Jackie, who considered Joe her champion in the competitive Kennedy household. With his instinct for understanding how to appeal to the public, Joe grasped Jackie's importance to the Kennedy presidency. Although Jack struggled without success to rein in Jackie's spending, Joe told her clothes designer, Oleg Cassini, "Don't bother them at all about the money, just send me an accounting at the end of the year. I'll take care of it."

On December 19, 1961, however, Joe suffered a severe and debilitating stroke that garbled his speech and left him almost immobile. He could no longer act as his son's counselor. Bobby recalled later that Jack often said how he wished he could talk to their father as he had before.

If Joe had an enormous influence on Jack's public career, he had a similar influence on his son's private conduct. Joe was a notorious philanderer who flaunted his indiscretions in front of his family; he insisted, for example, that his mistress Gloria Swanson visit Hyannis Port and accompany the family on a voyage to Europe. Joe encouraged his sons to follow his lead. "Dad," Jack once confided, "told all the boys to get laid as often as possible," and Joe taught his sons to compete with one another in the sexual realm. One friend recalled, "Jack would take a girl away from his brothers, or a friend, at any time." For his part, Joe tried to seduce his sons' girlfriends and his daughters' friends. Inga Arvad recalled that "if Jack left the room, [Joe would] try to hop in the sack with her. . . . She thought it was a totally amoral situation, that there was something incestuous about the whole family." Jack warned female visitors to the Joe Kennedy house to lock their bedroom doors: "The Ambassador has a tendency to prowl late at night." Although Jack couldn't be so open about his affairs, he certainly matched his father's lechery.

Remarkably, given Joe's relentless demands, neither Jack nor any of the Kennedy children seemed to resent or rebel against their father. Joe managed to invest them with his goals, and they were loving and grateful. Eunice toasted her bridegroom, Sargent Shriver: "I searched all my life for someone like my father, and Sarge came closest." One of Jack's lovers recalled that he told her that if his daughter, Caroline, ever got into trouble, he hoped she'd come to him with her problem instead of trying to hide it. "His father had always wanted him to have that feeling about him, and that was a really important thing." During the inaugural parade, as the new president approached the stand, Joe—always before the family's ruling figure—stood up and removed his hat in a gesture of respect. And when Jack passed, he tipped his own hat to his father, the only person he honored that way that day. "What nobody should ever forget," old friend and senator George Smathers said, "was that Jack had a tremendous respect for his father . . . He had the greatest admiration for him of anyone, and I mean *anyone!*"

8

KENNEDY AND HIS WIFE
His Most Important Partner

Most great figures are remembered singly. Not Kennedy. It's impossible to describe his presidency without detailing the contribution made by his wife, Jackie. Although Jackie Kennedy was first lady for only thirty-four months, she transformed that role as profoundly as John Kennedy transformed the presidency.

Kennedy friend Chuck Spalding reflected that Jackie "filled out the picture for Jack. If you look at pictures of the two of them and take her out . . . you'll see what I mean. Sometimes I wonder if he ever knew."

Jacqueline Bouvier was born July 28, 1929, in Southampton, New York. She grew up in households with large staffs of servants, frequent trips abroad, education at the best schools, and a knowledge of languages, art, antiques, and fashion.

In 1951, while working as the "inquiring photographer" for Washington, D.C.'s *Times-Herald,* she met Jack Kennedy at a dinner party. After a two-year courtship, the two were married on September 12, 1953.

Jackie's interests didn't extend to politics—she didn't vote until she married—and she hated campaigning. But interested or not, when her husband was elected president, Jackie, then thirty-one, became first lady, and her success in that role would far exceed everyone's expectations.

Initially, many JFK aides wanted Jackie to be a different kind of first lady: she should be more frugal, or more politically outgoing, or more homey. Jackie paid no attention. From the beginning, she handled the position in her own way. She told one friend, "People have told me ninety-nine things that I had to do as First Lady, and I haven't done one of them."

She ignored many of the customary duties of the president's wife, and during her first year, Mrs. Johnson substituted for her for more than fifty social obligations. At the same time, however, Jackie embraced her traditional role within her family. When asked what she wanted to do as first lady, Jackie said, "I'm a mother. I'm a wife. I'm not a public official." She considered herself a helpmate to her husband, not his colleague in politics: "What I really want is to be behind him and to be a good wife and mother. I have no desire to be a public personality on my own." Bobby said, "She's good for Jack because he knows that she's not the kind of wife when he comes home at night who's going to say, 'What's new in Laos?' "

Jackie used her passion for interior decoration to build interest in the Kennedy White House. Dismayed by the White House's appearance—she compared it to "a hotel that had been decorated by a wholesale furniture store during a January clearance"—she set out to improve it. Just a month after the inauguration, Jackie created the White House Fine Arts Committee to oversee a White House restoration and to provide authenticated fine antiques for the rooms, to be purchased with private funds. Spooked by the memory of the uproar Truman caused by adding a balcony to the

White House, Jack initially opposed Jackie's project, but she managed to place her initiative in a scholarly framework that won both the respect and interest of the public.

At the same time that Jackie improved the White House as a historic public institution, she made it more gracious. She replaced Eisenhower's formal state dinners with a younger, more elegant style: black tie replaced white tie; intimate tables replaced the formal banquet table; fireplaces were lit; the Marine Band played music as guests arrived. As White House Chief Usher J. Bernard West noted, "It took much more planning to achieve that appearance of spontaneity."

Also, to identify the administration with artistic achievement, Jackie arranged frequent White House performances, and almost all her 175 public appearances outside the White House were at cultural events.

Despite Jackie's reluctance to become first lady, she shot to stardom in that role. Young, lovely, with adorable children and a distinctive personality, Jackie excited tremendous interest. A craze for the "Jackie look"—simple, sophisticated, with clean lines, a few oversized details, and luxurious fabrics—swept the nation. Jackie hit the "best dressed" list her first year in the White House, and Hollywood designer Edith Head declared her "the greatest single [fashion] influence in history." Jackie said, "All the talk over what I wear and how I fix my hair has me amused, but it also puzzles me. What does my hairdo have to do with my husband's ability to be President?" But nevertheless, she spent an enormous amount of time, attention, and money on her appearance.

Curiosity about Jackie was so great that, for the first time, newspapers assigned full-time reporters to cover the first lady. She soon topped the list of "most admired women" (where she'd stay for years), and magazine sales shot up 5 percent every time she was on the cover. She was even featured in movie magazines because, as *Modern Screen* observed, "Mrs. Kennedy is living a role that few actresses could play, and she brings to that role a 'star quality' which has transformed the White House into the most exciting home in America." Interest in Jackie and the children helped win Jack ubiquitous and flattering coverage in places most politicians never penetrated: social pages, magazine back-of-the-book coverage, women's magazines, and television programs.

Before the White House, Jackie hadn't played a significant role in Jack's political career, but the public's intense interest made her politically important. Lawyer and adviser Clark Clifford recalled that Kennedy's "respect and regard" for his wife increased steadily as she "performed flawlessly." Her appearance, accomplishments, and most of all, her ability to attract crowds and cameras made her a critical asset.

Jackie's contribution became obvious during the Kennedys' Paris visit in 1961. She created a sensation larger than the president's, with her elegant wardrobe and jewelry, her dramatic hairstyles (one even had its own name, "Fontanges 1961"), her knowledge of French language and culture, and her exercise of feminine charms to enchant the notoriously difficult de Gaulle. She was popular everywhere she traveled. Communist students at the Central University of Caracas waved a sign: "Kennedy—No; Jacqueline—Yes." In Colombia, a sign read, "Yankees Go Home, Jackie Come Back."

A shared goal—creating a glorious Kennedy White House—brought Jack and Jackie closer together, as each respected the contribution of the other. But tensions did exist.

First, they fought about money. Jackie spent an extraordinary amount; nagged by Jack, she made occasional efforts to economize, but she never managed to cut her expenditures on clothes, art, antiques, and horses. When a front-page *New York Times* story repeated *Women's Wear Daily*'s estimate that in 1960, "together with her mother-in-law," Jackie spent $30,000 a year on clothes from Paris, she retorted, "I couldn't spend that much unless I wore sable underwear." In fact, according to the secretary who kept the Kennedy accounts, Jackie's clothing bill for 1961 was slightly more than $40,000 (which would be more than $250,000 in 2004). In 1962, she spent $121,461.61 (which would be more than $759,000 in 2004) on personal and family expenses. Jack often complained about her free-spending ways, but he reaped the benefits of the ecstatic press she generated.

Jack was also annoyed by Jackie's frequent refusal to fulfill her obligations as first lady; she didn't want to meet with representatives from the Girl Scouts of America or the Muscular Dystrophy Association. She often used her health as an excuse to skip events, only to have newspaper reports reveal that she was perfectly fit. She claimed that fatigue prevented her from meeting Brazil's president, but photographers caught her water-skiing with astronaut John Glenn. She used her pregnancy to excuse missing a congressional wives' brunch, but everyone knew she'd attended a performance of the Royal Ballet in New York the night before. "The boss can't do a thing with her," Dave Powers admitted.

Another serious source of tension in their marriage was Jack's infidelity. From their marriage's first days, he'd had affairs. Longtime friend Lem Billings recalled that Jackie wasn't "prepared for the humiliation . . . when she found herself stranded at parties while Jack would suddenly disappear with some pretty young girl." Moving to the White House allowed the Kennedys to spend more time together than they had when Jack was campaigning, but it did nothing to change Jack's behavior.

Despite these conflicts, Jackie began to revel in her position. Noting that when Mrs. Joseph Kennedy called, White House operators would say, "Mrs. Joseph is on the line," Jackie remarked, "At the beginning I didn't know how it would be. I am *the* Mrs. Kennedy. I am the First Lady." Jackie as first lady became a star in her own right, and she used her power to benefit her husband. She was Jack Kennedy's greatest partner.

9

KENNEDY AS HUSBAND

Two Views

JACK KENNEDY WAS
A LOVING HUSBAND

Jack and Jackie Kennedy had an extraordinary marriage, a partnership of two people of exceptional gifts and personal charisma.

Mutual friends brought them together at a small Georgetown dinner party, and then, Jack said, "I leaned across the asparagus and asked her for a date." Because they both had such busy schedules, their dating had a slow start. Nevertheless, Jack's brother Ted recalled, "My brother really was smitten with her right from the beginning. . . . He was fascinated by her intelligence: they read together, painted together, enjoyed good conversation together and walks together."

Their engagement was announced on June 24, 1953, and they were married just a few months later, on September 12, in a beautiful ceremony in Newport.

Their marriage's early days were darkened by Jack's severe

back problems. He tried to shield Jackie from the seriousness of his condition and told his doctor, "It's best if you don't go into my medical problems with Jackie. I don't want her to think she married either an old man or a cripple." When Jack required two operations, Jackie nursed him during his long recovery. During that difficult time, she also helped him work on his book *Profiles in Courage,* and in it, he wrote, "This book would not have been possible without the encouragement, assistance and criticisms offered from the very beginning by my wife Jacqueline, whose help during all the days of my convalescence I cannot ever adequately acknowledge."

Refined and reserved, the Kennedys seldom displayed their affection in public. After the inaugural ceremony, Jackie recalled, "I was so proud of Jack. . . . But I could scarcely embrace him in front of all those people. So I remember I just put my hand on his cheek and said, 'Jack, you were so wonderful!' "

The frantic pace of Jack's campaigning was hard on their marriage. Clark Clifford acknowledged that their marriage was seriously strained in the late 1950s, but Jack's election as president drew them together. During the White House years, Jack no longer traveled constantly, they at last had the children that both had wanted so much, and Jackie had her own important role to play in support of her husband.

Jack was very proud of Jackie's beauty and intelligence. On their way to the inaugural gala, as people on the streets cheered the presidential car, Kennedy said, "Turn on the lights so they can see Jackie." Arthur Schlesinger Jr. recalled how Kennedy would brighten when he talked about Jackie or when she stopped by his office. Jackie, for her part, enjoyed planning special evenings or treats for her husband, to lighten his burdens.

Although rumors of Jack's infidelities surely hurt Jackie, their respect and love for each other grew. Also, in their public, mutually reinforcing roles, Jack increasingly realized his wife's unusual talents as first lady and the political asset she'd become. The demands of their position required them to spend a good deal of time apart; away from the White House, Jackie wrote her husband a long letter: "I loved you from the first day I saw you. . . . But ten years later I love you so much more." She added, "I am just sorry for Caroline—all I will tell her to put into and expect from marriage—but if she doesn't marry someone like you what good will it do her."

The Kennedys' relationship deepened, too, after the loss of their newborn son Patrick in August 1963. Many observers commented that they grew closer and more affectionate after his death. For a tenth-anniversary present, Jack gave Jackie a gold ring with emerald chips to wear in Patrick's memory.

In the summer of 1963, Kennedy told his friend Red Fay that of all the attractive women he'd known, "there was only one I could have married—and I married her."

JACK KENNEDY WAS NOT A LOVING HUSBAND

Jack Kennedy was a longtime and notorious ladies' man. "I only got married," he once explained, "because I was thirty-seven years old and if I wasn't married and in politics, people would think I was queer."

Jackie had the right background to be the ambitious politician's wife: Catholic, young, beautiful, well educated, an equestrian champion, winner of a prestigious writing award, listed in the *Social Register,* and "debutante of the year" for 1947–1948. Lem Billings recalled that after he heard Joe Kennedy remark that Jackie "probably has more class than any girl we've ever seen around here," he expected to hear of their engagement any day. Even Kennedy's doting secretary Evelyn Lincoln admitted, "I think old

Joe had a lot to do with their marriage. . . . There was no love there. That I'm sure."

Jack needed the respectability of a fiancée, but he wasn't romantic about the process. He never wrote Jackie a love letter before they were married, he proposed by telegram, and he left the selection of the engagement ring to his father. And Jack wasn't sentimental about the wedding. Jackie's wedding band was intended for a man; Jack had bought it in a hurry just before the ceremony. Jack was bored on their Acapulco honeymoon, so they left several days early to visit his navy friend Red Fay.

Jack was no more attentive as a husband. Not only did he travel often for political reasons, he also took vacations away from Jackie. After losing his 1956 vice presidential bid, Jack abandoned Jackie, then eight months pregnant, to go on a two-week Mediterranean yachting trip with friends and a changing cast of women. While he was gone, Jackie, who had already had one miscarriage, went into premature labor. A baby girl was stillborn. Jack couldn't be reached for three days, and when he finally learned what had happened, he told his father, "I suppose this means the end of the trip."

Of the four children to whom Jackie gave birth, she and her husband were in the same city for the birth only of Caroline. Just weeks after Caroline was born, in 1957, while Jackie was still recovering from her cesarean section, Kennedy went to Cuba on vacation. After his election as president, Jack spent most of the transition period in Palm Beach and left behind Jackie, who was eight months pregnant and unable to leave Washington. On Thanksgiving 1960, Jack spent only a brief time with Jackie and Caroline before returning to Palm Beach. Reporter Helen Thomas recalled that as photographers snapped holiday pictures, Jackie didn't try very hard to hide her anger. Two hours after Jack left, Jackie began hemorrhaging. By the time he'd returned, she'd given birth to John F. Kennedy Jr. Even Jack admitted, "I'm never there when she needs me."

Before becoming president, Jack had dismissed Jackie as an unimportant prop. When a journalist writing a Kennedy profile asked to speak to Jackie, Jack said, "What do you want to talk to my wife about? She's out of it. You're doing a piece on me." Publisher Dorothy Schiff recalled, "I had a feeling he had very little interest in her except as she affected his campaign." In conspicuous breaks with tradition, Jack didn't mention Jackie's name when he accepted the nomination and, even at the inauguration, didn't kiss her after the swearing-in ceremony.

In the White House, however, things changed. The two had separate bedrooms at night, but Jack couldn't ignore Jackie during the day; as first lady, she was too conspicuous. Jack worried about the public reaction to Jackie, with her horseback riding and designer dresses, and probably no one was more astonished than he at her transformation into a star.

Although bored by the cultural performances Jackie staged, Jack happily accepted credit for being an intellectual, sophisticated president. For her part, Jackie wasn't interested in politics or policy. As presidential aide Ralph Dungan commented, "She didn't understand things, mostly, and they didn't interest her. I think that probably contributed to the weakness of their marriage. . . . After a while, when you are living it, you really have to talk to someone."

High office did nothing to curtail Jack's adultery, and women shuttled through the White House whenever Jackie left town. Jackie obliged her husband by leaving for months at a time and spending most weekends, from Thursday until Monday afternoon, away from Washington.

A clue to the weakness of the Kennedys' marriage is the eagerness of the loyal Kennedy circle to insist that, just before his death, Jack had finally begun to change. Many echoed Deputy Defense Secretary Roswell Gilpatric: "There was a growing tenderness. . . . You could see now that he liked being with her. . . . I think their marriage was really beginning to work at the end."

This vaunted new closeness is frequently ascribed to their new-born son Patrick's death, but in fact, the activities of Jack's last days don't reflect long anguish about Patrick or much new tenderness for Jackie. Patrick died in August 1963. The Kennedys spent two-thirds of the days of September, October, and November 1963 apart. While Jackie went on a Greek cruise, spending her time swimming, shopping, and dancing in nightclubs, Jack took advantage of her absence to indulge in his own favorite diversion. Although together in the motorcade on that fateful day in Dallas, of the last fourteen days, they'd been apart for seven. And where did Jack Kennedy spend the last weekend of his life? In Palm Beach, with two of his regular White House women. Once Jack was dead, however, his supporters could safely claim that before he died, he had changed.

10

KENNEDY THE FOX
His Nature

Many figures in history take their significance from the power of a single idea. Abraham Lincoln: "Government of the people, by the people, for the people, shall not perish from the earth." Winston Churchill: "Never surrender."

Other great figures don't represent one towering principle; they embody—or invoke—many ideas. Kennedy sought to present himself as a man with a driving vision, but his legacy can't be summed up in one supreme idea. He was many-sided and worked toward a variety of goals.

"*The fox knows many things, but the hedgehog knows one big thing.*" In a famous essay, British philosopher Isaiah Berlin uses this fragment from the Greek poet Archilochus to explore a fundamental distinction that, he argues, divides intellectual and artistic personalities: *hedgehogs* are those "who relate everything to . . . a single, universal, organizing principle in terms of which alone all that they are and say has significance," while *foxes* are those "who pursue many ends, often unrelated and even contradictory . . . Their thought is scattered or diffused, moving on many levels, seizing upon the essence of a vast variety of experiences and objects."

This distinction can also be applied to great leaders. Hedgehog-leaders are those driven by a single purpose. Fox-leaders have shifting, sometimes contradictory, goals; they hold much in reserve; they appear different to different people.

Kennedy can be compared in this way to his great hero and model, Winston Churchill. And clearly, Churchill was a hedgehog, and Kennedy was a fox.

Churchill had one embracing vision that ordered all his actions and drove him until the end of his life: "*I want to see the British Empire preserved . . . in its strength and splendor.*" At times, he was lionized for what he did in the empire's name and, at other times, abused, but he never wavered from his purpose.

Kennedy was different. One of his most striking features was his many-sidedness—in the people he knew, in the ideals he embodied, in the actions he took, in the personality he presented. Although the public associated him with ideas of good government and self-sacrifice, his values and goals can't easily be more specifically characterized. When Martin Luther King Jr. said, "I have a dream," everyone knew what his dream was. When Kennedy said, "Let us begin anew" or "We can do better," people understood these phrases in different ways.

During Churchill's long life, his vision of imperial England often put him out of step with his countrymen. Churchill never changed, but the values of the world did. Kennedy, by contrast, guarded his ability to change course. He was never identified with any great controversial issue and was never the outspoken champion of a particular group or philosophy. He resisted efforts to tag him with an ideological label; although he's remembered as a great liberal, he strove not to be perceived that way. Soon after being elected senator, he told an interviewer, about constituents who chided him for not being a "true liberal," "I'd be very happy to tell them I'm not a liberal at all. . . . I'm not comfortable with those people." "The fear of making too much of a commitment, of going off the intellectual deep end, is locked in Kennedy's character," wrote James MacGregor Burns in an election-year biography. "To him, to be emotionally or ideologically committed is to be captive."

Churchill had the same personality at all times. He would declaim to his secretary from his bathtub as easily as to a full House of Parliament and would weep in front of the war cabinet as readily as in front of his wife. He labored to preserve the strength and splendor of the empire in 1945 just as in 1895, even though, by that time, the world and Britain, too, had accepted the principle of self-rule and rejected many of his beliefs. Kennedy, by contrast, presented himself differently to accommodate different circumstances. Even his name changed form to reflect his many-sidedness: the imposing and dignified "John Fitzgerald Kennedy"; the forthright, manly "John Kennedy"; the casual "Jack Kennedy"; and "JFK," a familiar nickname that anyone could use.

Kennedy refused to be pinned down. While the precision of words limited him, photographs allowed him to convey many ideas, even contradictory ideas, at the same time. He could present himself as modern, on the forefront, new; and yet also traditional, rooted in the past, respectful. He could offer an austere vision of duty and sacrifice next to pictures of comfort, relaxation, and glamour. He could refuse to be corny or sentimental but allow himself to be photographed in cloyingly heartwarming situations. Images are not arguments, but although they prove nothing, people crave them—and they use them as evidence.

Kennedy's fox quality can be seen most clearly in his compartmentalized personal relationships. Paradoxically, although Kennedy always seemed to be utterly himself, he embodied many things to many people: dozens of members of his circle wrote their memoirs, and each one presents a remarkably different portrait of Kennedy. He was extraordinary in his ability to strike so many notes. He could charm with his refined intellect and wit; he could also cuss and whore.

People saw in him what they admired most, and what they identified with. Recalling the campaign, the brilliantly capable Ted Sorensen sees in Kennedy the same kind of brilliance: "We had not only the best candidate there, but the best campaign manager, too. He knows the facts, who likes him and who doesn't . . . He has this incredible memory of places, names, dates." The joint memoir of "Irish mafia" members Kenneth O'Donnell and Dave Powers emphasizes Kennedy's Irish Catholic side. During the presidential campaign, when Powers reminded Kennedy that a Catholic can make three wishes when he enters a church for the first time, Kennedy said, "New York, Illinois and California." During the Cuban missile crisis, Powers recalled, Kennedy stopped to pray at St. Matthew's Cathedral on his way to an embassy lunch. According to O'Donnell and Powers, "Kennedy was a more deeply religious man than he appeared to be, or wanted to appear to be."

By contrast, gossipy rake Ben Bradlee's *Conversations with Kennedy* depicts Kennedy as a gossipy rake. Their conversations included such topics as "why none of us had women friends with large bosoms" or discussion of someone's confession that he hadn't slept with his wife in sixteen years, about which Bradlee remarked, "This kind of dirt, the president of the United States can listen to all day long." Worldly John Kenneth Galbraith played to the same side of Kennedy, by spicing up his envoy reports with the kinds of tidbits he knew Kennedy enjoyed. In one cable, he wrote, "I do note one redeeming feature: the more underdeveloped the country the more overdeveloped the women." Galbraith knew his audience well; Kennedy said, "Ken's memos are great."

To guard his various identities, Kennedy successfully kept elements of himself hidden, even from those who believed they knew him well.

For example, although Kennedy flaunted his sexual exploits in front of many of his associates, others knew little or nothing about them. Although Jackie in 1963 confided to Bradlee that he and his wife "really are our best friends," Bradlee insists he never knew about Kennedy's sexual exploits; so does Galbraith. Similarly, after reading accounts of Kennedy's behavior in Seymour Hersh's *The Dark Side of Camelot,* Arthur Schlesinger Jr. said, "The notion that there was a bunch of bimbos parading around the White House is ridiculous. I worked at the White House. No doubt, some things happened, but Hersh's capacity to exaggerate is unparalleled." On the other hand, Bobby Baker's visits to the White House often ended with Kennedy's regaling him with some "amazingly frank recitations" of his latest sexual exploits.

In July 1973, when the Senate Watergate hearings revealed the existence of the White House taping system under President Nixon, some former Kennedy aides expressed their outrage. Schlesinger dismissed the idea of secret recordings by Kennedy as "absolutely inconceivable." "It was not the sort of thing Kennedy would have done," he said. "The kind of people in the White House then would not have thought of doing something like that." Dave Powers said he knew of no similar system in the Kennedy White House. "If it had been done, I would have known it. I was in the president's office every day."

After their public comments, however, the John F. Kennedy Library's director, Dan H. Fenn, told these aides that in fact Kennedy had taped some meetings and phone conversations. Fenn issued a brief public statement but provided few details. Then, in 1982, the *Washington Post* created a shock when it published a log showing that from July 1962 until his assassination, Kennedy had secretly taped some six hundred meetings and telephone conversations in the Oval Office, the Cabinet Room, and elsewhere, with family members, cabinet members, White House aides, civil rights leaders, two former presidents, congressmen, and world leaders. His aides struggled to come to grips with the revelation. Sorensen said, "I'm dumbfounded." They thought they had known him so well.

After the Cuban missile crisis, aides insisted that Kennedy wouldn't consider trading the removal of Jupiter missiles from Turkey for the removal of Soviet missiles from Cuba. Decades later, the truth emerged: Kennedy had made a secret arrangement with Khrushchev to do just that. Only a few top-level advisers knew, and they were sworn to secrecy.

Most significant of Kennedy's foxlike qualities was his ability to embody different ideals to different people. Although he appeared sharp, crisp, and individual, he projected an image that voters could fill in as they wished. One of his greatest political assets was his warmth, which made voters feel that he shared their beliefs. He inspired people to an extraordinary degree—but as to what, they differed. Liberals agreed with the aspirations Kennedy voiced and the vocabulary he used; conservatives saw that his actions, for the most part, were in line with the Eisenhower administration's.

Kennedy also voiced contradictory views—as in two of his greatest speeches, given within sixteen days of each other in June 1963. On June 10, at American University, he made a stirring call for peace and a reexamination of relations with the Soviets; on June 26, in West Berlin, he delivered some of the most provocative Cold War rhetoric of his presidency. Similarly, in September 1963, he gave two TV interviews in which he explained what he believed to be the appropriate course in Vietnam. Both those who urged a stronger American commitment and those who advocated ending American intervention heard Kennedy support their view. Just days before his death, at a November 14, 1963, press conference, he explained his intention with this kind of ambiguity: "Now, that is our object, to bring Americans home, permit the South Vietnamese to maintain themselves as a free and independent country, and permit democratic forces within the country to operate."

In private, Kennedy said little about his beliefs or intentions; he listened, waited, and acted when public opinion was ready. Because Kennedy listened well, people assumed he shared their views. Many believed, for example, that Kennedy's apparent lack of passionate commitment hid an inner fire. Harris Wofford noted that Kennedy "made it difficult for anyone to be sure of the depth of his understanding or the extent of his vision. About the most important things, he was a man of few words—even with those closest to him"; nevertheless, Wofford concluded, "I do not doubt that John Kennedy felt much that he did not put into words." Dr. Janet Travell agreed: "He showed little emotion, not because he felt it lightly, but because he felt so deeply." Did Kennedy really feel deeply, or did those around him just assume he was hiding the qualities they wished to see in him?

Kennedy's fox nature enlarged the place he could occupy in the public mind; he and his memory could be invoked by many people, toward many ends.

11

KENNEDY REVISED
A Closer Look at the Evidence

Our impressions of others are shaped by what we see and what we don't see, and therefore, Kennedy and his supporters were able to influence the popular conception of John Kennedy by controlling the evidence that reached the public.

With time and with deeper probing, however, new information about JFK has come to light to alter our interpretations.

1.

In the 1959 campaign biography written by James MacGregor Burns:

He graduated [from Choate] sixty-fourth in a class of 112. But to his classmates, if not to his teachers, he must have shown some glimpse of his potential ability and later drive, for they voted him "the most likely to succeed."

————

According to Choate friend Ralph Horton:

In our senior year we had elections for the handsomest, the best dancer, the wittiest, and so on. Jack wanted to be voted the most likely to succeed. So we campaigned and traded votes back and forth . . . Jack secured approximately fifty percent of the vote for most likely to succeed.

2.

Rose Kennedy wrote of Jack's 1940 book Why England Slept:

> The professors at Harvard thought so highly of the thesis,
> in fact, that they suggested Jack expand it somewhat and
> interest a book publisher in it.

———

*The Harvard professors did not even award Kennedy's thesis the highest
grade. Joe Kennedy nevertheless labored to get it published as a book, then
sent a copy to renowned professor Harold Laski. Laski responded:*

> In a good university, half a hundred seniors do books like
> this as part of their normal work in their final year . . . I
> don't honestly think any publisher would have looked at
> that book of Jack's if he had not been your son, and if you
> had not been ambassador. . . . Do believe that these hard
> sayings from me represent much more real friendship than
> the easy price of "yes men" like Arthur Krock.

3.

According to John Hersey's 1944 piece "Survival," in The New Yorker, *Kennedy wrote a crucial note that led to the rescue of the men of the* PT-109:

> Some natives appeared from nowhere in a canoe, rescued Kennedy, and took him to Nauru. . . . Kennedy picked up a coconut with a smooth shell and scratched a message on it with a jackknife: "ELEVEN ALIVE NATIVE KNOWS POSIT AND REEFS NAURU ISLAND KENNEDY." . . . One of the natives seemed to understand. They took the coconut and paddled off.

———

After the wreck of the *PT-109,* an Australian naval coast watcher had spotted its hulk and sent out native islanders to find any survivors. Kennedy was off exploring when two of these scouts found most of the *PT-109*'s crew. The senior officer in Kennedy's absence, Lennie Thom, gave the scouts a detailed note asking for help. It wasn't until the next day that the Solomon Islanders discovered Kennedy and accepted his crude message, but in later accounts of the adventure, Kennedy's picturesquely carved coconut received much attention, while Thom's earlier and more comprehensive note, written with prosaic pencil and paper by an unknown navy man, was never mentioned.

4.

According to Ted Sorensen's 1965 biography Kennedy:

The responsibility for recording or not recording him on the censure vote [of Joseph McCarthy] . . . fell on me. I knew, had he been present, that he would have voted for censure along with every other Democrat. . . . I guessed that my failure to record him would plague him for years to come. . . . But his failure to be recorded at the time of the vote, which was persistently raised against him in some quarters, was due to my adherence to basic principles of civil liberties and not his indifference to them.

———

In 1977, Sorensen said he believed Kennedy "was sufficiently conscious in that hospital to get a message to me on how he wanted to be paired. I think he deliberately did not contact me."

5.

From Theodore White's The Making of the President, 1960*:*

For the crowds that erupted to greet Kennedy in the streets . . . in the last few weeks of the campaign were, and remain, unbelievable. . . . It was not their numbers that made them spectacular . . . but their frenzied quality. One remembers being in a Kennedy crowd and suddenly sensing far off on the edge of it a ripple of pressure beginning, and the ripple . . . would grow like a wave . . . until it would squeeze the front rank of the crowd against the wooden barricade, and the barricade would splinter.

————

From Jerry Bruno and Jeff Greenfield's The Advance Man, *a 1971 account of the advance work done for Kennedy's campaign appearances:*

The crowd began to push forward. They knocked down the snow fence and swarmed all over Kennedy, cheering and reaching out to shake his hand.

"My God," Kennedy said afterward, "I can't believe that crowd. How did you do it?"

. . . It looked so good on film and in the press that from then on we made sure that crowds surged over Kennedy. I'd have two men holding a rope by an airport or along a motorcade; then, at the right time, they'd just drop the rope and the crowd would rush close to Kennedy.

6.

According to Norman Mailer, at his first meeting with Kennedy, at Hyannis Port in August 1960:

As we sat down for the first time, Kennedy smiled nicely and said that he had read my books . . . "Yes," he said, "I've read . . ." and then there was a short pause . . . and then he said, "I've read *The Deer Park* and . . . the others," which startled me for it was the first time in a hundred similar situations, talking to someone whose knowledge of my work was casual, that the sentence did not come out, "I've read *The Naked and the Dead* . . . and the others." If one is to take the worst and assumes that Kennedy was briefed for this interview (which is most doubtful), it still speaks well for the striking instincts of his advisers.

———

According to magazine editor Clay Felker:

Peter Maas had told [press secretary Pierre Salinger] that Norman's favorite book was *The Deer Park,* Salinger told Kennedy, and of course at the lunch Kennedy very cleverly said that his favorite book of Norman's was *The Deer Park* too. In fact there was some doubt about whether Kennedy had ever read anything by Norman—nobody really knows; he was being a politician, and remember too, at that point Jack Kennedy was very aware of the power of magazines.

7.

According to Theodore White, on the day of the West Virginia primary:

He had flown to Washington on the morning of primary day, addressed a women's group at lunch, retreated to his Georgetown home and invited two friends [Ben and Tony Bradlee] for dinner with himself and his wife. . . . Kennedy calmly invited his two friends to sneak out with him to see a movie—the returns would be late coming in, and they might as well relax.

———

According to William Manchester:

Unfortunately they were too late to get in [to see *Suddenly Last Summer*], so they walked across New York Avenue to the Plaza, which showed X-rated movies . . . *Private Property* was nasty enough, starring one Katie Manx as a horny housewife who spread-eagled for every milkman, newsboy, and iceman who could identify a woman in heat.

8.

According to Kennedy aide Harris Wofford:

Late on election night, with Nixon still not conced-
ing . . . John Kennedy walked across Bob Kennedy's
lawn. . . . In the dark his companion [journalist Theodore
White] thought he said, "I'm angry." In the original manuscript he showed me, Theodore White pegged *The Making of the President 1960* on that incident. What finally broke
the calm of this cool, contained Kennedy and caused him
to display such heat? To answer this, White (in his first
draft) flashed back over all the miles traveled, talks given,
hands shaken, and deals made . . . culminating in that out-
burst in the early hours of Wednesday, November 9, 1960.

———

Wofford continues his story:

"Even if Kennedy said that, don't build your book on it,"
I advised White. Irony, gaiety, grace, restless curiosity, an-
tipathy to ideology, concern for the common good, a
thirst for power, and a respect for reason were [Kennedy's]
dominant qualities, I contended. . . .

While I was making the case against marring an excellent book with such an uncharacteristic anecdote, White
stopped me. "Don't worry," he said. "When Kennedy
read the manuscript that was the only thing he said I had
to change."

"That's not what I said," the President-elect told
White. "What I said was 'I'm hungry.' "

9.

A conversation, according to Ted Sorensen:

His wife, remembering his contentment in [the Senate], once asked Ted Kennedy at dinner whether he would give back Jack's seat when the time came, and Teddy loyally said that of course he would. But the President was upset, and sternly told Jacqueline later never to do that to Teddy and not to worry about his future.

————

A conversation, according to William Manchester:

Later, though, another exchange with Teddy [Kennedy] was one of those rare occasions when Jack disappointed you. After eight years in the White House, he said, he might like to return to the Senate. Would Teddy resign so he could regain his seat? Ted said yes, of course, although he was understandably upset. Bobby wasn't ruthless. But Jack could be, and this seemed to be an example of it.

10.

According to Arthur Schlesinger Jr.:

> No one who knew John and Robert Kennedy well be-
> lieved they would conceivably countenance a program of
> assassination. . . . They were Catholics.

———

According to Ben Bradlee, Kennedy said:

> He was all for people solving their problems by abortion
> (and specifically told me I could not use that for publica-
> tion in *Newsweek*).

According to Ralph Dungan:

> He was no hotshot Catholic by a long shot: On birth con-
> trol—like many Catholics in those days—he rejected the
> Church's teaching; he would go to mass on Sunday if
> somebody was watching, but he was not orthodox.

Henry James, a Kennedy friend from Stanford, observed:

> Religion didn't interest him. . . . He wasn't going to drop
> his religion. He liked the way it made him special, differ-
> ent in a Protestant world.

Jackie said to Arthur Krock:

> I think it's so unfair of people to be against Jack because he
> is a Catholic. He's such a poor Catholic.

11.

According to Hugh Sidey's 1961 Life *article "The President's Voracious Reading Habits":*

> Just how fast Kennedy reads has not been precisely determined, but his speed is at least 1,200 words per minute and sometimes more than that (the average person reads 250 words per minute).

According to Sidey's 1963 biography John F. Kennedy, President:

> [Kennedy] read from 1,200 to 2,000 words a minute, maybe faster when the going was light.

According to Red Fay's 1966 memoir The Pleasure of His Company:

> When I first came to Washington, my reading speed was about 400 words a minute. I took a speed-reading course, and I got it up to about 800 words a minute, with about 90 percent comprehension. But I knew that the President read around 2,200 or 2,400 words a minute, with almost total comprehension.

———

In his oral history at the Kennedy Library, Sidey admitted he'd allowed Kennedy to negotiate the 1,200-per-minute number. The speed-reading institute where Kennedy had taken his course couldn't confirm such a high rate of speed and suggested that, given that the average person reads 250 words per minute, 700 or

800 words was a likely estimate. "The president didn't like that one bit," said Sidey. After discussion, Sidey and Kennedy agreed that Sidey would report a reading speed of 1,200 per minute. "I noted for months and years after," Sidey said, with an apparent lack of a feeling of responsibility, "that this became the real gospel on his reading speed."

12.

Of Kennedy's statement about the administration's efforts to force U.S. Steel to rescind its price increase, Sorensen wrote:

Each new version reflected more strongly the President's by then wholly unemotional determination to impress upon the industry and the public the seriousness of the situation.

———

According to Ben Bradlee, Kennedy said:

[U.S. Steel] kicked us right in the balls. . . . The question really is: are we supposed to sit there and take a cold deliberate fucking.

13.

According to Pierre Salinger's memoir, With Kennedy:

> The brunt of [the press's] criticism fell on Mrs. Kennedy's young and beautiful Press Secretary, Pamela Turnure. Pam Turnure had never had any experience in dealing with the press prior to taking over the post with Mrs. Kennedy. But, despite this, Pam was ideally suited for her job. She had the confidence of both Mrs. Kennedy and the President.

———

Pamela Turnure and Kennedy were longtime lovers whose affair had begun in 1957, when Turnure was working in Kennedy's Senate office. Kennedy's indiscreet visits to Turnure's apartment were spotted by her landlady, Florence Kater, a Catholic who became obsessed with Kennedy's adultery. Kater pressed a dogged campaign to make the affair public, but although several reporters interviewed and believed her, they never reported the story. Kennedy may have insisted that Jackie hire Turnure in the hopes that Turnure's position would end the rumors about the illicit relationship.

14.

According to Kenny O'Donnell and Dave Powers's memoir of their time with Kennedy:

It was understood that Dave would be available to keep him company in the mansion. . . . During the summer months, when Jackie and the children were at Hyannis Port and the President faced solitary confinement in Washington in the evenings from Monday until Thursday, Dave stayed with him until he went to bed. Their nightly routine was always the same. The White House kitchen staff would prepare a dinner . . . that would be left in the second floor apartment . . . so that they could eat it late in the evening alone, without keeping any of the staff waiting to serve them. Then they would watch television, or sit outside on the Truman Balcony, or the President would read a book and smoke a cigar. . . . Around eleven o'clock, the President would get undressed and slip into the short-length Brooks Brothers sleeping jacket that he wore in preference to pajamas. Dave would watch him kneel beside his bed and say his prayers. Then he would get into the bed, and say to Dave, "Good night, pal, will you please put out the light?"

———

According to presidential kennel keeper Traphes Bryant:

[Kennedy] did enjoy having beautiful women around him at the White House and he did entertain them when Jackie was away. . . .

After Jacqueline would leave on one of her numerous outings, he would tell the kitchen help to prepare some food and drinks and just leave them. Then he would tell the waiters they could go home. "I can take care of it," he'd say. . . . When he wanted to be alone with his female company, JFK passed the word that the private family quarters on the second floor were off limits.

12

KENNEDY'S MYSTIQUE

What Made Him Interesting

What made Kennedy Kennedy? What accounts for the extraor-dinary hunger for any information or photograph of him or for the astonishing prices now commanded by his most inconsequential possessions? As naïve and simplistic as it sounds, Kennedy was interesting. *He was one of the most dramatic political personali-ties in modern history.*

He sparked people's imagination and conversation; he lived a life of adventure and accomplishment; he was surrounded by fasci-nating people. He could interest people on many levels. Policy makers, celebrity watchers, political junkies, gossip hounds, men who liked to read about battles, women who liked to read about child rearing—all found much to engage their attention.

This capacity, he knew, was his critical gift as a politician. Because he was able to interest the public, he was able to influ-ence them; as he himself said, "Law alone cannot make men see right."

Jack Kennedy had a single quality that lifted him into triumph; that most distinguished him from other political leaders; and that others often try, and fail, to copy: *he captured the interest and admiration of the public.* The entire world was excited by his personality. This quality, which seems straightforward and almost frivolous, is the foundation of Kennedy's historical importance, and it explains why his legacy is so enduring.

Kennedy understood he was playing a role in a public drama and communicating through the mass media, and he worked on his performance the way an actor rehearses. He had many advantages: he had the money to pay for staff and publicity; he came from a well-known family; he had a prominent office; and far more important, his character and circumstances fascinated the public. There was something about Kennedy that made him more interesting than others who might be *expected* to be equally interesting or who also received heavy publicity.

Kennedy had an excess of neither modesty nor vanity, and he tried to understand the secret of his own power. Chuck Spalding recalled that after the 1946 election, although talking about whether he did or didn't have "magnetism" made Kennedy "terribly self-conscious," the two would spend hours discussing it. Shrewd and self-aware, Kennedy recognized that his public appeal was a commanding weapon in the service of his political goals. While campaigning in the midterm elections, Kennedy said, "The question really is, can we interest enough people to understand how important the congressional election of 1962 is? And that is my function." Kennedy knew, as he said, that the public "won't listen to things which bore them. That is the great trouble."

He, Jack Kennedy, was so interesting to the public that he captivated white people, in both the North and South, and black people as well. Civil rights leader Roy Wilkins wrote, "The Kennedy Administration has done with Negro citizens what it has done with a vast number of Americans: it has charmed them. It has intrigued them." Interest in Kennedy wasn't just an American phenomenon. When he visited Mexico, his welcome was so enthusiastic that Ambassador Thomas Mann said, "I've never seen anybody making such an impression on the people of another country—anytime, anywhere."

Kennedy realized that his own personality was the most powerful instrument he possessed to shape public opinion, and he was supremely successful at capturing the public imagination. How did he do it?

For one thing, Kennedy encompassed intriguing contradictions. He combined the aristocratic traits of wit, graciousness, and urbanity, and the democratic traits of energy, toughness, and fair-mindedness. He was relaxed and fun-loving, yet he radiated discipline and deliberation as he presided over the cabinet or studied a memo. He was casual and natural without sacrificing the dignity suitable for a president. His public remarks showed both an ironic, puncturing humor and lofty ideals. As the first "Irish Brahmin," Kennedy combined Catholic and WASP traditions, so that those wary of a Catholic were reassured by his establishment connections and those resentful of wealth and privilege identified with his immigrant, Catholic heritage.

But to be consistently interesting to the public, it's not enough to have a sympathetic and attractive personality; there must be a stream of material to feed the public's interest.

By accident and by design, episodes of high suspense and mortal danger starred Kennedy's life. He almost died with his men in the Pacific. Few believed he could win the 1952 Senate race against popular incumbent Henry Cabot Lodge, but he did—by just seventy thousand votes, or 51.5 percent. His unexpectedly strong showing as a potential vice presidential candidate in 1956 kept millions glued to their television sets during the Democratic National Convention. In 1960, he and Nixon fought a close, tough race.

The 1960 presidential debates, unlike anything seen on TV before, were dramatic head-to-head contests, and people were as interested in the candidates' performances as in their policies. The election was a cliff-hanger: CBS News projected Nixon as the winner, then switched, and the outcome remained in doubt until the day after the election.

Throughout Kennedy's presidency, journalist James Reston recalled, Kennedy "always seemed to be striding through doors into the center of some startling triumph or disaster." Public fascination with Kennedy was unprecedented. Reporter Maxine Cheshire recalled that "suddenly, the whole world wanted to read about them. . . . The average housewife and her husband began to care more about what was happening in Washington than in Hollywood." Not just his policies and actions but his most trivial preferences were discussed. No detail was too trifling: one reporter inquired about Kennedy's bandaged finger (he'd cut it while slicing bread).

Interest in Kennedy was magnified by the interest in the family that framed him. After Kennedy's election swelled the demand for information, the numerous Kennedys proved a bonanza for reporters, because there was always a story to write, a photograph to print. Dwight Eisenhower commented, "Every day you'll find one of the Kennedys somewhere in the papers. It's Robert or Teddy or Jackie and, if they can't get anybody else, well, they get young John or somebody." Kennedy's children, still small and sweet, were a trove of colorful stories: Caroline emerging during a news conference wearing pajamas and her mother's high heels, Caroline in the West Lobby answering a reporter's question about what her father was doing ("He's upstairs with his shoes and socks off, not doing *anything*"), John Jr. crying when he couldn't board *Air Force One* with his father. Demand for the tiniest detail about private life in the White House was so strong that the escape of the hamsters Debbie and Billie from their cage was covered in the *New York*

Times, and a reporter once called Kennedy's press secretary at 3:00 a.m. to check an AP report that one had died. Kennedy stories filled the newspapers and television; Kennedy photographs appeared on countless magazine covers; images of the Kennedys were made into dolls and mannequins; their activities inspired Vaughn Meader's comedy album *The First Family,* the fastest-selling album of its time.

Just as the public was interested in Kennedy's presidential activities, they were fascinated by details from his life of wealth and privilege: Jackie's riding in hunts, Caroline's pony Macaroni, the White House's French chef. Moreover, the Kennedys were surrounded by celebrities, such as brother-in-law actor Peter Lawford, singer and actor Frank Sinatra, poet Robert Frost, actress Marilyn Monroe, and astronaut John Glenn. These elements interested people who wouldn't have bothered to read about politics or policy.

And there was the physical attractiveness of JFK and his family. It wasn't precisely great beauty; it was an entrancing quality that made people want to look again. One of his first volunteers in his 1946 campaign recalled, "My first impression . . . was that I was more interested in watching him than I was in listening to what he said." His voice, too, with a harsh but distinctive Boston accent, was interesting. Jackie wasn't conventionally pretty, with her broad shoulders, square face, wide-set eyes (so far apart that glasses had to be specially ordered for her), and stiff, dramatic clothes, but her odd proportions made her the more captivating. (Perfect beauty often has a generic quality, a tendency to drift into a mundane prettiness, as the very handsome John Jr. would demonstrate in adulthood.) And as inevitably happens, the more the Kennedys were photographed and studied, the more the public wanted to look at them.

Although Kennedy tried to avoid stirring up controversy, minor flurries of protest helped him by keeping the country engaged. Whether it was the White House decision to serve liquor at a reception, the length of young John's hair, Jackie's swim in shark-infested waters, or the parties at Bobby and Ethel's house where guests in evening clothes got shoved into the pool, the public loved to discuss and cluck. One concerned citizen wrote, "Mrs. Kennedy is . . . a wonderful example to hold up to our growing daughters. Therefore, I consider the picture of her seated on a swing in India with her dress hiked above her knees in very poor taste." These pseudo-issues were of no importance, but they gave people something to talk about and so tied the people and the president together.

And while his life's air of optimism and possibility captured the public's interest, Kennedy's assassination absorbed the country with its atmosphere of violence, grief, and mystery. His shocking murder and its aftermath, with its odd cast of characters, melodramatic unfolding of events, heartbreaking poignance, and hints of conspiracy, continues to grip the public.

Some commentators marvel that, despite the explosive information about JFK that has emerged since the 1970s, he remains one of the most popular figures in American history. But these observers misunderstand the dynamic: these revelations don't diminish interest in Kennedy, they *feed* it. Fortune turns everything to the advantage of her favorites. It's ironic, but true, that facts that would have destroyed Kennedy's presidency—his assignations with Marilyn Monroe, the secretly taped conversations, the affair with his White House intern—now help keep him, and his legacy, in public sight. Somehow, for most people, these details don't tarnish Kennedy's brilliant reputation but merely make him more interesting.

A key to maintaining a vital legacy is holding people's attention, and certainly, Kennedy's darker exploits have sharpened the public's curiosity. Reputation often tracks the amount of coverage given a president, and each new revelation about Camelot spurs TV documentaries, books, and a flurry of commentary. The controversies have kept JFK's presidency in full view, and although the public eagerly greets each new tidbit, disclosures about the "real" Kennedy do nothing to diminish his legend.

13

KENNEDY IN HIS OWN WORDS
What He Said

One of Kennedy's greatest strengths was his brilliant use of language—both in the high rhetoric of his prepared speeches and in the quick wit of his spontaneous remarks.

As with many beloved figures, books of Kennedy quotations, speeches, writings, and table talk have sprung up to preserve his words. These collections are carefully edited to reinforce the reverential picture of the subject's life.

Kennedy wrote his parents about his *PT-109* adventure, in a letter received September 12, 1943, "On the bright side of an otherwise completely black time was the way that everyone stood up to it. Previous to that I had become somewhat cynical about the American as a fighting man. I had seen too much bellyaching and laying off. But with the chips down—that all faded away. . . . For an American it's got to be awfully easy or awfully tough."

In a letter from the South Seas in 1944, Kennedy wrote to his seventeen-year-old brother Bobby, who had joined the navy, "The folks sent me a clipping of you taking the oath. The sight of you there, just as a boy, was really moving, particularly as a close examination showed that you had my checked London coat on."

Renowned journalist John Hersey wrote a piece for *The New Yorker*, "Survival," which described Kennedy's heroic actions in the South Pacific. The piece later was used extensively in Kennedy's campaigns. Kennedy wrote to Lem Billings, "What you said about the break I got when Hersey did the article is extremely true I guess . . . It was such an accident that it rather makes me wonder if most success is merely a great deal of fortuitous accidents. I imagine I would agree with you that it was lucky the whole thing happened if the two fellows had not been killed which rather spoils the whole thing for me."

Of Vietnam in 1951, he declared, "I am frankly of the belief that no amount of military assistance in Indochina can conquer an enemy which is everywhere and at the same time nowhere."

In 1958, when Joseph Alsop predicted to Kennedy that he'd be offered the vice presidential nomination, Kennedy smiled and said, "I am completely against vice in all forms."

As he discussed with aides whom he should name to be his vice presidential running mate, Kennedy said, "I'm forty-three years old, and I'm the healthiest candidate for President in the United States. . . . I'm not going to die in office. So the Vice-Presidency doesn't mean anything."

Kennedy remarked that peaceful civil rights demonstrations weren't "something to be lamented, but a great sign of responsibility, of the American spirit. It is the American tradition to stand up for one's rights—even if the new way to stand up for one's rights is to sit down."

"Sam Rayburn may think I'm young, but then most of the population looks young to a man who's seventy-eight . . . I do not recall that I have demonstrated any lack of judgment under the heat of the past four years. The test is not in the age but in the man himself."

"Democracy is the superior form of government because it is based on a respect for man as a reasonable being."

When Nixon said that unemployment wouldn't become a significant issue unless it climbed above 4.5 million unemployed, Kennedy responded, "I would think it would become a significant issue to the 4,499,000."

In his powerful address to the Greater Houston Ministerial Association, Kennedy said, "If this election is decided on the basis that 40 million Americans lost their chance of being President on the day they were baptized, then it is the whole nation that will be the loser."

After he was elected, Kennedy greeted Jackie and Tony Bradlee, both pregnant, "Okay, girls, you can take out the pillows. We won."

Kennedy's inaugural address is one of the most famous political speeches in American history. It's also one of the shortest inaugural addresses. "I don't want people to think I'm a windbag," Kennedy said, and he spoke for only sixteen minutes.

> Let the word go forth from this time and place, to friend and foe alike, that the torch has been passed to a new generation of Americans—born in this century, tempered by war, disciplined

by a hard and bitter peace, proud of our ancient heritage—and unwilling to witness or permit the slow undoing of those human rights to which this nation has always been committed, and to which we are committed today at home and around the world.

Let every nation know, whether it wishes us well or ill, that we shall pay any price, bear any burden, meet any hardship, support any friend, oppose any foe to assure the survival and the success of liberty. . . .

So let us begin anew—remembering on both sides that civility is not a sign of weakness, and sincerity is always subject to proof. Let us never negotiate out of fear. But let us never fear to negotiate.

Let both sides explore what problems unite us instead of belaboring those problems which divide us. . . .

All this will not be finished in the first one hundred days. Nor will it be finished in the first one thousand days, nor in the life of this Administration, nor even perhaps in our lifetime on this planet. But let us begin. . . .

In the long history of the world, only a few generations have been granted the role of defending freedom in its hour of maximum danger. I do not shrink from this responsibility—I welcome it. I do not believe that any of us would exchange places with any other people or any other generation. The energy, the faith, the devotion which we bring to this endeavor will light our country and all who serve it—and the glow from that fire can truly light the world.

And so, my fellow Americans: ask not what your country can do for you—ask what you can do for your country.

Of his invitation to Robert Frost to speak at the inauguration, Kennedy said, "I felt that he had something important to say to those of us who were occupied with the business of government; that he would remind us that we were dealing with life, the hopes and fears of millions of people, and also tell us that our own deep convictions must be the ultimate guide of all our actions."

When asked at a press conference about the failed Bay of Pigs invasion, Kennedy said, "There is an old saying that victory has a hundred fathers and defeat is an orphan. I am the responsible officer of this government."

When a reporter observed, "Businessmen seem to have the attitude, 'Now we have you where we want you,' " Kennedy joked, "I can't believe I'm where big business wants me."

At the April 29, 1962, dinner that included forty-nine Nobel Prize winners, Kennedy opened his remarks by denying a report "that this is the President's Easter egg-head roll on the White House lawn."

In his speech at Yale on June 11, 1962, Kennedy said, "The great enemy of the truth is very often not the lie—deliberate, contrived, and dishonest—but the myth—persistent, persuasive, and unrealistic."

When asked at a press conference, "How is your aching back?" Kennedy replied with a smile, "Well, it depends on the weather—political and otherwise."

In the summer of 1962, during a visit with Mexican president López Mateos, Kennedy admired López's watch. In keeping with Mexican custom, López insisted on giving it to Kennedy. When Jackie appeared soon after, López expressed his admiration for her stunning dress, and Kennedy told him, "You had better take back your watch."

During the Cuban missile crisis, Kennedy commented that the "brass hats" had an advantage: "If we listen to them, and do what they want us to do, none of us will be alive later to tell them that they were wrong."

During a White House performance of *Brigadoon* for the king of Morocco, the fuses blew. After a long moment in complete darkness, Kennedy said, "Your Majesty, it's part of the show, you know."

In a December 1962 interview, Kennedy said, "It is much easier to make the speeches than it is to finally make the judgments, because unfortunately your advisers are frequently divided. If you take the wrong course, and on occasion I have, the president bears the burden of the responsibility quite rightly."

Of Ted Kennedy's race against Eddie McCormack for the U.S. Senate, Kennedy said, "We'd rather be Ted than Ed."

"In politics nobody gets everything, nobody gets nothing, everybody gets something."

Kennedy's June 10, 1963, speech at American University was one of his greatest. Coming from Kennedy—who had long emphasized the threat of the Soviet Union—the unexpected call for cooperation and peace was striking.

> Our problems are man-made; therefore they can be solved by man. And man can be as big as he wants. . . . Man's reason and spirit have often solved the seemingly unsolvable—and we believe they can do it again. . . .
>
> Let us reexamine our attitude toward the Soviet Union. . . . As Americans, we find communism profoundly repugnant. . . . But we can still hail the Russian people for their many achievements. . . .
>
> Our most basic common link is that we all inhabit this small planet. We all breathe the same air. We all cherish our children's future. And we are all mortal.

On June 11, 1963, after the Alabama National Guard was needed to enforce a court order mandating the desegregation of the University of Alabama, Kennedy decided he wanted to address the nation that evening.

> I hope that every American, regardless of where he lives, will stop and examine his conscience about this and other related incidents. This Nation was founded by men of many nations and backgrounds. It was founded on the principle that all men are created equal, and that the rights of every man are diminished when the rights of one man are threatened.
>
> Today we are committed to a worldwide struggle to promote and protect the rights of all who wish to be free. And when Americans are sent to Viet-Nam or West Berlin, we do not ask for whites only. It ought to be possible, therefore, for American students of any color to attend any public institution they select without having to be backed up by troops. . . .
>
> It is better to settle these matters in the courts than on the streets, and new laws are needed at every level, but law alone cannot make men see right.
>
> We are confronted primarily with a moral issue. It is as old as the scriptures and is as clear as the American Constitution.
>
> The heart of the question is whether all Americans are to be afforded equal rights and equal opportunities, whether we are going to treat our fellow Americans as we want to be treated. If an American, because his skin is dark . . . cannot enjoy the full and free life which all of us want, then who among us would be content to have the color of his skin changed and stand in his place? Who among us would then be content with the counsels of patience and delay? . . .
>
> Now the time has come for this Nation to fulfill its promise. The events in Birmingham and elsewhere have so increased the cries for equality that no city or State or legislative body can prudently choose to ignore them. . . .

We face, therefore, a moral crisis as a country and as a people. It cannot be met with repressive police action. It cannot be left to increased demonstrations in the streets. . . . It is time to act in the Congress, in your State and legislative body; and above all, in all of our daily lives. . . . A great change is at hand, and our task, our obligation, is to make that revolution, that change, peaceful and constructive for all.

In West Berlin, on June 26, 1963, Kennedy spoke to the largest crowd he ever addressed: 1.5 million out of a population of 2.2 million. Kennedy declared:

There are many people in the world who really don't understand, or say they don't, what is the great issue between the free world and the communist world. *Let them come to Berlin.* There are some who say that communism is the wave of the future. *Let them come to Berlin. . . .*

Freedom has many difficulties and democracy is not perfect, but we have never had to put a wall up to keep our people in, to prevent them from leaving us. . . .

Freedom is indivisible, and when one man is enslaved, all are not free. . . . All free men, wherever they may live, are citizens of Berlin, and, therefore, as a free man, I take pride in the words *Ich bin ein Berliner.*

At the dedication of the Robert Frost Library at Amherst College, Kennedy said, "A nation reveals itself not only by the men it produces but also by the men it honors, the men it remembers."

In Texas on November 21, 1963, Kennedy told one of his favorite campaign anecdotes, about a boy who threw his cap over a wall that looked too high to scale, so he would have to climb it. Kennedy explained, "This nation has tossed its cap over the wall of space, and we have no choice but to follow it."

In the speech prepared for November 22, 1963, but never given, Kennedy's prepared remarks concluded:

> We, in this country, in this generation, are—by destiny rather than choice—the watchmen on the walls of world freedom. We ask therefore that we may be worthy of our power and responsibility, that we may exercise our strength with wisdom and restraint, and that we may achieve in our time and for all time the ancient vision of "peace on earth, goodwill toward men." That must always be our goal, and the righteousness of our cause must always underlie our strength.

14

KENNEDY'S USE OF THE MEDIA
How He Reached the Public

Reporters of every kind were Kennedy's principal interpreters and amplifiers, and by winning their admiration, he was able to enlist them to make his case to the public. Flattered and cooperative, journalists—in print, on television, and in photography— permitted Kennedy a striking freedom to construct his image and to hide his secrets.

Kennedy's brilliant handling of the media made him a new kind of political hero. As Norman Mailer predicted in November 1960, Kennedy's ascent meant that "America's politics would now be also America's favorite movie, America's first soap opera, America's best-seller." Kennedy's stellar media performance would establish the standard against which all future leaders would be judged—and found wanting.

Kennedy in Print

As candidate and president, Kennedy made an enormous effort to cultivate reporters, editors, and columnists. Kennedy genuinely enjoyed the company of journalists, but that wasn't his only reason for befriending them; he recognized their importance in shaping public opinion.

Kennedy won the trust of reporters, in part, by showing trust in them. During the 1956 convention, Kennedy began to walk into his hotel living room in his underwear. "You can't go out there in your shorts," an aide warned, "there are reporters and photographers there." Kennedy answered so the reporters could hear, "I know these fellows. They're not going to take advantage of me."

During the presidential campaign, Kennedy made reporters' work as easy as possible. Not only did the campaign take steps such as timing news releases to meet press deadlines and providing instant transcripts, but Kennedy made himself available for endless interviews, press conferences, and "backgrounders." A rotating trio of pool reporters accompanied him on his personal plane; he explained his strategies and his vision; he gave the press an inside view. Nixon did just the opposite. The vice president only occasionally allowed reporters to ride on his plane, rarely explained his thoughts or tactics, and treated the press with open suspicion. He believed reporters were hostile to him, and by his behavior, he succeeded in making them hostile.

Kennedy did more than provide material for writers' convenience. He confided in them, teased them, quoted from their work, and paid close attention to their gossip. A good way to make a friend is to ask a favor, and Kennedy would borrow journalists' combs, pencils, and money as well as ask for their advice. In this way, Kennedy implicated the journalists in his success, and his obvious interest helped secure their loyalty.

Kennedy's wooing of the press continued after the election. *Life* called Kennedy "the most accessible American president in memory," and during the first year, Kennedy met individually with more than fifty White House reporters. Within a month of taking office, he permitted a *New York Times Magazine* photographer to shadow him for an entire day—an effort that resulted in an hour-by-hour portrait of a dynamic, highly engaged president. He invited the White House press corps to state dinners and social functions and gave dozens of exclusive interviews. He invited publishers and editors from other parts of the country to the White House and cooperated with books on his presidency.

Kennedy knew how to charm. When he spotted senior White House correspondent Merriman Smith in the crowd the day after the 1960 election, he said, "If you're here, Smitty, I guess I've really been elected." Reporter Helen Thomas "practically lived" at the hospital while covering the birth of John Jr. When Kennedy one day spotted her on N Street, he exclaimed, "You've deserted my child!" He went out of his way to congratulate reporters on pieces he thought particularly good.

Another of Kennedy's effective techniques was giving reporters the impression of unguarded candor. The press loved hearing his indiscreet remarks and outspoken judgments, and faithfully kept his secrets. Even his unprintable words were seen as a sign of directness and trust, as when candidate Kennedy told several editors, "Well, for openers, I am going to fucking well take Ohio." He never seemed to be posing or editing his comments.

Kennedy used his good relationships with journalists to steer their reporting. He called Gore Vidal to tell him, "I hear Rovere is writing about my health. I do not have Addison's disease." Vidal reflected later, "He was lying. Of course he had it." Kennedy's friend *Washington Post* publisher Phil Graham kept *Newsweek* and the *Washington Post* from criticizing Kennedy too harshly about the Bay of Pigs disaster. When rumors of a Kennedy–Marilyn Monroe

affair began surfacing in gossip columns, Kennedy instructed former journalist and Peace Corps Inspector General William Haddad: "See the editors. Tell them you are speaking for me and that
it's just not true." (Haddad later said, "He lied to me. He used my
credibility with people I knew.") Kennedy was so well liked, and
reporters were so eager to stay on good terms, that he was able to
defuse their instinct to report aggressively. Writers frequently submitted material to Kennedy or his surrogates for comment before
publication. "That's a great thing, that right of clearance," Kennedy
said. In general, the press accepted the Kennedy rules, as when he
didn't want the public to know that Jackie was a chain smoker or
that his bad back prevented him from picking up his children.

Kennedy cultivated friendships with many journalists, particularly Phil Graham, columnist Joseph Alsop, the *Chattanooga Times*'s
Charles Bartlett, and columnist Rowland Evans. *Newsweek*'s Ben
Bradlee was Kennedy's closest journalist friend and, perhaps not by
coincidence, the most useful. Bradlee checked with Kennedy whenever he wrote about him and forewarned him when *Newsweek* prepared to criticize the administration. The two men spoke regularly,
and the Bradlees had dinner at the White House each week.
Bradlee noted, "The setting of these contacts was predominantly
social . . . [I saw] a president off duty, a president trying to relax, a
president in search of personal contact." But although Bradlee may
have *believed* that Kennedy was relaxing—that he was seeing
Kennedy in unguarded moments—it appears that, in fact, Kennedy
was working, in his seemingly casual, effortless way. Kennedy himself said, "I don't tell anything to the press, on any basis, that I don't
expect to see in print. When you're president, you are president
twenty-four hours a day."

Kennedy had his own view of the terms of their friendship,
and when Bradlee violated those terms, Kennedy struck back. An
August 1962 *Look* article, "Kennedy vs. the Press," catalogued the
administration's efforts to manage the news. "Never before have so

few bawled out so many so often for so little." The article quoted Bradlee as saying, "It's almost impossible to write a story [the Kennedys] like. Even if a story is quite favorable to their side, they'll find one paragraph to quibble with." In a reaction that proved Bradlee's observation, a furious Kennedy broke off all contact with his friend.

Before long, however, Kennedy needed a reporter to help bury a persistent rumor that he'd been married to socialite Durie Malcolm before Jackie. He and Bobby warned reporters off the story—"I'll wind up owning your magazine," Kennedy told *Look*'s Laura Bergquist—but it refused to die. Bradlee agreed to work with the White House to debunk the secret-marriage rumor. Kennedy sat down briefly with Bradlee and gave him access to family files and FBI reports, and in return, Bradlee gave Kennedy veto power. But even after this effort, Bradlee endured three months of exile before Kennedy relented. Properly chastened, Bradlee never again risked banishment.

Later, in 1963, Kennedy again seemed to have been laying careful groundwork in his journalist friend's mind. Just as Bradlee had quieted talk of a secret marriage, now, perhaps, he could squash rumors swirling around Ellen Rometsch, a "party girl" at Bobby Baker's Quorum Club who was a familiar White House visitor and a suspected spy. The timing of the Rometsch rumor was particularly dangerous, because Washington was abuzz about a sex-and-spy scandal involving the recent resignation of British war minister John Profumo after revelations of his affair with prostitute Christine Keeler, who was also the mistress of a Soviet deputy naval attaché.

On the evening of November 5, Kennedy invited Bradlee to dinner later that night and, when Bradlee demurred, changed the dinner's time to ensure Bradlee's presence. There, Kennedy mentioned he'd seen FBI chief J. Edgar Hoover a few days before. "Boy, the dirt he has on those senators," Kennedy said. "You wouldn't believe it." Kennedy soon steered the conversation to Rometsch. "He described a picture of Elly Rometsch that Hoover had brought with him. Her name had popped up in and out of print as one of the women who frequented the Quorum Club." As if he'd never met her, Kennedy said the photo showed she was "a really beautiful woman." Kennedy and Bradlee speculated about "who might be the hidden Profumo in the Kennedy administration."

Bradlee assumed their conversation was mere gossip, but Kennedy was adept at making comments to throw people off dangerous subjects. Almost surely, he was raising sensitive issues to show himself unconcerned. Of course, Kennedy knew exactly what Rometsch looked like, and he knew the hidden Profumo's identity, and he knew the dirt in Hoover's files didn't just concern senators.

Kennedy's relationships with reporters, and his deep understanding of the press's demands, allowed him to reach the public through print with unprecedented success.

KENNEDY ON TELEVISION

Kennedy was a remarkably telegenic man at the very time television was transforming the American scene. His outstanding TV performances—enhanced by the audience's fascination with the new medium and its lack of critical sophistication—set expectations for all future leaders. To this day, Kennedy remains one of the most appealing people ever to appear on television. "Kennedy has box office," one TV producer commented.

Kennedy's rise in power corresponded to the rise of television as an influence in American life. In 1950, 11 percent of American families owned a television, and only ten years later, that number had mushroomed to 88 percent—while only 78 percent had a telephone. Kennedy grasped the enormous significance of TV for politicians and how his own particular qualities suited the small screen. "We wouldn't have had a prayer without that gadget," he said.

Kennedy appeared younger on-screen than he did in person, and his easy, engaging manner perfectly suited the new medium. Theodore White observed that, in contrast, television gave Nixon's deep-set eyes and heavy brows a grim aspect that he didn't have in person. Norman Mailer described how Kennedy would look older than his age, and not remarkably handsome, but when TV cameras

July 15, 1960.
Senator John Kennedy
faces photographers as
he accepts the
Democratic Party's
nomination for the
presidency.

began to roll, he'd again look "like a movie star, his coloring vivid, his manner rich, his gestures strong and quick, alive with the concentration of vitality a successful actor always seems to radiate."

Writing about television's influence on politics, Kennedy emphasized the importance of a politician's "creating a television image people like and (most difficult of all) remember." He recognized that the TV camera's unflattering gaze made it more important to look attractive, and he was the first candidate or president to diet frequently, to use a sunlamp, and to change clothes several times a day. To prepare for the first televised debate, he consulted his movie star brother-in-law, Peter Lawford, who coached him to look directly into the camera. After the first debate, radio listeners thought Nixon had won or tied with Kennedy, but TV viewers disagreed: on television, Kennedy, with his cool, handsome, and confident demeanor, beat the sweaty, uneasy Nixon.

Kennedy's TV appearances gave him a dramatic boost. It's one of the curious characteristics of television that, in a kind of cynosure effect, no matter how lofty or insipid the context, the mere sight of a face on TV significantly increases an audience's interest, and the more the image is repeated, the more attractive it becomes. After Kennedy's appearance at the 1956 Democratic National Convention, female college students surrounded his car shouting, "We love you on TV!" "You're better than Elvis!" Kennedy returned from the 1960 Democratic National Convention to a surprisingly enthusiastic crowd; his new "star quality" was attributable, all agreed, to the unprecedented convention TV coverage. In the same way, Kennedy's crowds swelled tremendously in size and fervor after the first debate aired. It was then that the adoring "jumpers" and "screamers" appeared.

As president, Kennedy exploited his exceptional TV skills by introducing live televised press conferences—an innovation strenuously opposed by officials afraid he'd make dangerous misstatements and by print reporters worried about losing their competitive advantage. The TV press conference became an ideal showcase for Kennedy, as people saw for themselves his ability to field tough questions with an easy wit and a striking command of the facts. Although Kennedy seemed natural, he and his staff prepared thoroughly and directed the staging, down to the white cardboard placed on the lectern to reflect light onto Kennedy's face. The press conferences were dramatic performances as well as exchanges of information, and public interest was so great that the TV networks gave up millions of dollars in commercial time to carry them. As always, Kennedy benefited from his pioneer status. The sessions were friendly, with reporters asking softball questions and laughing at Kennedy's jokes.

Kennedy found other ways to reach TV viewers. Cameras twice followed him through his day, and he held several successful television interviews. In December 1962, he gave an unprecedented interview to the three networks' White House correspondents, broadcast by all three networks to a huge audience. Kennedy understood how to exploit the format: during shooting, if he didn't like a question, he gave a rambling, dull answer, which he knew would be edited out. Also, as in so many aspects of his presidency, Jackie's efforts fortified her husband's. Her Emmy Award–winning White House "tour" was broadcast in February 1962, without commercials, to 56 million viewers.

Kennedy was the most astute critic of his own TV performances. Before one appearance, he instructed, "The monitor is all right, but the camera should be brought up." He watched reruns of his press conferences: "I could have done better with that one," "That's lousy lighting," "That camera angle murders me."

Kennedy's spectacular TV success blazed him in the public mind. Aide Burke Marshall pointed out, "He was a president who was filmed, so people who weren't alive then still see him. . . .

There were three generations of people who said, 'That's what I want my politicians to be like.' "

KENNEDY IN PHOTOGRAPHS

Kennedy was the first president to realize photography's power, and his brilliant use of pictures was as critical to his success as his mastery of print and television. Because television was still in its early stages, glossy, large-format picture magazines such as *Life, Look,* and *The Saturday Evening Post* remained influential sources of visual information for the public.

Many famous Kennedy images appear spontaneous, and viewers assume that these unguarded pictures are evidence of the *real* Kennedy. In fact, by controlling photographers, their access, and—most of all—himself as subject, Kennedy ensured that the photographic record supported his idea of John F. Kennedy. Viewers didn't perceive Kennedy's role, however; he appears as the unguarded subject, not the author, of the skillfully crafted images.

Kennedy's first step was to choose who shot the pictures. In a then-unusual move, the 1960 campaign hired the gifted Jacques Lowe as a semiofficial campaign photographer. "Most politicians were fearful of letting journalists into their smoke-filled rooms," Hugh Sidey recalled. "The Kennedys were not frightened by 35-millimeter intimacy. Indeed . . . they loved the art form and understood that those honest images enhanced their own fast-moving story." Honest images, but not just anyone's images. Reliable Lowe continued to receive special access after the election, as did acclaimed and trusted photographers such as Mark Shaw and Richard Avedon. These men were not typical newshounds but exceptional photographers of the celebrated, fashionable, and beautiful.

The abundance and apparent artlessness of the Kennedy pictures make them look like casual snapshots of a glorious family; in fact, master photographers used techniques of camera angles, lighting, and composition to take the best pictures and, from those, selected the most successful. The result, for the public, is the impression that Kennedy's day-to-day life looks better than the average person's best photograph.

Kennedy's natural advantages made the photographers' job easier. He was surrounded by the glamorous trappings of the White House and wealth: the trips on the presidential yacht, the khakis and sunglasses, the private talks on the White House promenade. Kennedy was attractive, his wife was striking, and his children were adorably young—not yet sulky eight-year-olds or homely teenagers. While Jackie tried to limit the photographs taken of Caroline and John, Jack often circumvented her. "He knew damn well his image would be burnished by good, heartwarming pictures," observed reporter Laura Bergquist.

Kennedy frequently allowed his picture to be taken in situations that juxtaposed his imposing public role with the casual intimacy of his family role. These kinds of pictures—which show the common humanity of the great—are always pleasing to the public. But such pictures also surreptitiously emphasize Kennedy's unique stature. Who but the president himself would dare allow his children to interrupt the business of the Oval Office?

Just as Kennedy offered pleasing tableaux for photographers, he avoided any situation that might make him look ridiculous. *Look*'s Stanley Tretick remembered that Kennedy avoided being photographed doing anything—such as eating or wearing a funny hat—that might result in an undignified picture. On November 22, 1963, in Fort Worth, he was given a cowboy hat—but he refused to put it on, despite the urgings of two thousand Texans.

For although Kennedy never appeared to pose, he was acutely aware of the camera's recording presence. From childhood, just as he was accustomed to the watchful presence of servants, he was accustomed to being photographed, because his father had always

1962. President Kennedy claps while watching his daughter, Caroline, and his son, John, dance in the Oval Office.

worked to get maximum publicity for the Kennedys. Jackie, too, with her background as "debutante of the year" and her job as the "inquiring photographer," appreciated photography's demands.

Kennedy understood the elements of a great photograph, and when the February 1961 *New York Times Magazine* picture essay "A Day with John F. Kennedy" included a small photo on the third page of Kennedy leaning over a table to read, Kennedy pointed it out: "This should have been on the cover." Now the photograph is one of the best-known Kennedy pictures. Watching the dog Pushinka climb a ladder, then ride down Caroline's slide, Kennedy asked for a photographer: "That's worth six million votes right there." He held up a picture of himself with Douglas MacArthur and suggested, "How about that for a magazine cover?" At the

*March 28, 1958. At home in Georgetown, Senator Jack Kennedy
leans down to smile at his daughter, Caroline.*

onset of the terrifying Cuban missile crisis, he didn't neglect to
summon a photographer to take pictures of his meeting with his
advisers.

People accept JFK pictures at face value. Unlike fine-art photographs—which, in inviting viewers to make critical judgments,
cause them to consider the photographer's shaping presence—the
journalistic-style Kennedy photographs don't provoke analysis.
Cameras often catch Kennedy in what appear to be unguarded
moments, and viewers, forgetting the photographer's necessary
participation, believe they are seeing the private man. As a result,
these "candid" photographs draw authority from both the validity
of the spontaneous and the artfulness of the staged.

Some pictures seem affected and almost silly if a viewer acknowledges that a photographer was present. Somehow, seeing the
Life cover "Senator Kennedy Goes A-Courting," viewers don't

consider the artificiality of a man's taking a *Life* photographer on a small boat with his date. Although the couple appears to be enjoying a private moment, they were in close quarters with a camera. When a friend saw the cover, he remarked that Jackie must enjoy sailing. "No," said Jackie. "They just shoved me into that boat long enough to take the picture."

Picturing Kennedy tossing stones into the surf while a camera

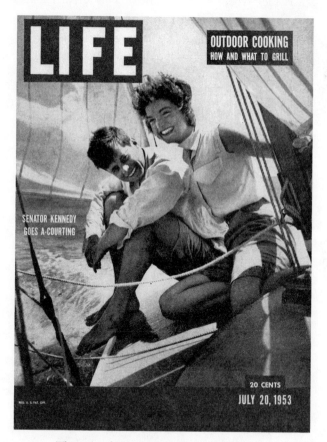

The cover of Life *shows Senator John Kennedy
and his fiancée, Jacqueline Bouvier, enjoying a casual sail.*

clicks away changes a scene of private fun into one of pose. What we can appreciate *now* is that when Kennedy appeared to be relaxing or utterly absorbed in his work—playing with his children, meeting with advisers, talking on the phone, or entertaining at the White House—he was also, in fact, building his image.

There are so many Kennedy photographs that it seems that *everything* was photographed. With so much revealed, the viewer doesn't consider what's cropped out or why a particular photograph was chosen or what episodes *aren't* being captured.

But Kennedy made sure that while certain moments were witnessed, his truly unguarded moments remained hidden. The pub-

July 1963. Jack Kennedy skips stones across the water near his family's Hyannis Port summer house.

lic must see enough to *feel* able to judge but can't be given full knowledge.

What was not photographed?

Palm Beach, for one thing. The Kennedy clan was always identified with Hyannis Port, even though Palm Beach had been Joe and Rose's legal residence since 1941. And although Kennedy often went to Palm Beach (he spent seventeen days there during his last Christmas), vacation photos were always taken at Hyannis Port. Hyannis Port carried associations of bracing winds, wholesome exercise, and traditional values; Palm Beach was too luxurious, too openly rich, to suit the Kennedy image. Photographer Slim Aarons recalled that Joe would allow her to photograph him in Florida only if the picture had no dateline. "He wanted people to think he lived year-round in Hyannis Port. . . . Palm Beach was a downer for anyone whose son wanted to be President." Kennedy would never have allowed himself to be pictured, as David Ormsby-Gore remembered seeing him, "sitting by the pool at Palm Beach . . . having a manicure [with] the manicurist sitting beside him."

Photographs of Kennedy football games and sailing excursions were ubiquitous, but Kennedy hid his passion for golf. He didn't want to be associated with rich men's country clubs or the golf-addicted Eisenhower, and he steered clear of holes visible to spectators or photographers. In the ten weeks between the election and the inauguration, Kennedy played more than twenty times—but he forbade photographers to take his picture on the golf course.

Once his presidential campaign started, Kennedy didn't allow any photographs to be taken of him with his controversial father. As soon as he'd safely won the election, however, he insisted that Joe appear in family photographs.

There are almost no photographs of Kennedy wearing glasses, although he wore them to read, and of course, Kennedy hid his crutches, his back brace, and other signs of ill health. Jackie was never shown with a cigarette, though she smoked three packs a day, or wearing pants, although the White House chief usher recalled that she never wore a dress in the White House unless she had company.

Thousands of pictures show Kennedy in his role as loving father and husband, but none catch him in his more sordid pursuits. Photographers did manage to take pictures of Jack and Bobby Kennedy with Marilyn Monroe at the party after Monroe sang her infamous "Happy Birthday, Mr. President," but the party's hosts later revealed that Secret Service agents confiscated all the film. Only a single photograph survived.

May 1962. Actress Marilyn Monroe stands between Bobby and Jack Kennedy at a party after a Democratic fund-raiser.

Kennedy knew exactly the image of himself he wanted to present: energetic, dignified, thoughtful, courageous, full of good humor, a loving family man. In this, he was hardly unusual—what politician wouldn't seek to be associated with these attributes? Kennedy was fortunate, and unusual, in his ability to convey these qualities with his appearance. His family, his circumstances, and his pastimes set him in surroundings that suggested these qualities, and his very countenance seemed proof of his good character.

Joe Kennedy had emphasized, "It's not what you are that counts, but what people *think* you are." By controlling the media, Kennedy knew that he could prove himself in the public mind—and in this, he succeeded beyond measure.

Kennedy's successors were infuriated by the press's refusal to grant them the kind of admiring attention and protection lavished on JFK. Johnson berated his press secretary—why couldn't he win

A thoughtful President Kennedy takes a quiet moment in the Oval Office in his signature rocking chair.

for Johnson the kind of press Pierre Salinger had gotten for Kennedy? Much in Kennedy's record—his health, his education, his wartime experiences, his sexual escapades, and rumors that he'd stolen the 1960 election—wasn't suitably investigated. Vietnam, Watergate, the rise of Washington's prosecutorial culture, and greater media competition meant the press would never again be so tractable for those who followed Kennedy.

15

KENNEDY'S CIRCLE
His Associates

Fascination with great figures provokes curiosity about their associates. The people around Kennedy throw light on his character, because they show what he wanted and needed from others.

Kennedy prized achievement, brains, and toughness, and he was able to attract a circle that was exceptionally brilliant and accomplished; he also had associates who filled other, darker needs.

Kennedy had a rare ability to cultivate a wide range of people—school friends, members of the jet set, journalists, academics, Hollywood stars, and political cronies. Without being demonstrative, he gave his companions a feeling of deep connection. "Kennedy had an extraordinary knack for capturing people and changing them," observed Joseph Alsop. "To me, this was his most inexplicable quality."

Most of the people in Kennedy's circle fell into distinct groups, and each group fed a different part of Kennedy's personality and fulfilled some specific purpose—whether they recognized it or not.

The innermost circle held his father, Joe, and his brother Bobby. Joe worked tirelessly for his son, and although Kennedy kept his controversial father's role hidden for strategic reasons, Joe remained an important influence until his incapacitating stroke. By the middle of 1961, Bobby was his brother's most influential adviser and his closest confidant. "There was a connection between them that transcended passion," said Bobby's aide John Seigenthaler. "I think it was as close to one heartbeat, one pulsebeat, as you could get."

Another group were the old friends from Choate, Harvard, the navy, and the early days in Congress. Choate roommate Lem Billings, who gave himself the title "first friend," later bragged, "I was at his house every single weekend he was president. . . . Jack was the closest person to me in the world for thirty years." Friend Torbert Macdonald, later a Massachusetts congressman, had been Jack's Harvard roommate. Paul "Red" Fay had been Jack's fellow PT boat officer. Jim Reed was another friend from navy days. Senator George Smathers had been a freshman congressman with Kennedy.

A parallel group of old friends was the "Irish mafia" of Dave Powers, Larry O'Brien, and Kenny O'Donnell (O'Donnell had been captain of the Harvard football team on which Bobby played), who had worked on Kennedy's early campaigns and followed him to the White House.

Of these longtime relationships, Billings wondered "why Jack wanted to keep all those friends, since his mind and interests did grow, let's face it, at a much faster clip than any of his contemporaries." Kennedy seemed to need the comfort and trust, and perhaps the easy domination and outlet for bullying, that these familiar relationships offered. Some old friends played the role of court jester, performing their tricks on command: personal aide Dave Powers, with his sports statistics and constant jokes; Lem Billings, the perpetual weekend house guest who accepted Kennedy's orders and pranks with adoring patience; Red Fay, with his willingness to belt out "Hooray for Hollywood" whenever Kennedy demanded a performance.

Others found these relationships puzzling or even unseemly. Schlesinger described Billings as "a mystifying relic of JFK's youth." Press aide Barbara Gamarekian described Powers as "a perennial jokester. It was almost demeaning to the President to find solace with someone like that." (Sorensen, by contrast, described Powers as Kennedy's "only one really close friend" besides Bobby.) Kennedy friend Henry James said he lost Kennedy's friendship because "I wasn't going to be his toady like Lem Billings. . . . I envied people like Billings for their continuing close relationship to Jack, but I didn't respect them for it."

Outside this tight circle, Kennedy befriended many journalists. He enjoyed their conversation and their gossip—and their help. He invited them to the White House swimming pool, projection room, presidential bedroom, and dinner parties, in situations that blurred the line between reporter and friend.

He was particularly close to three journalists. Charles Bartlett, the *Chattanooga Times*'s Washington correspondent, was a longtime friend who had introduced Jack to Jackie. Bartlett acknowledged that "it was not possible to be a good newspaper man and be a close friend of the President"; he preferred the role of friend. Columnist Joseph Alsop was a frequent White House guest, and his was the only private house the Kennedys visited regularly. He later acknowledged that Kennedy was "adept at flattery, and I suppose I, as a member of the press, was at times . . . a target of his considerable and manipulative charm." Kennedy's closest relationship, however, was with *Newsweek*'s Ben Bradlee.

Yet another group reflected Kennedy's interest in policy. His chief issues adviser and speechwriter, Ted Sorensen, had worked beside him during the rise from senator to president. Intense, a true liberal, utterly dedicated, Sorensen helped give Kennedy his distinctive voice. When someone said Sorensen was becoming more like Kennedy than Kennedy himself, Kennedy defended him: "Don't—he gets that from all sides." However, the two men never became social friends; Sorensen himself described their relationship as "close in a peculiarly impersonal way." Kennedy did become personally friendly with cabinet members Robert McNamara and Douglas Dillon, for whom he felt great admiration and personal regard.

One group stood secret and apart: the procurers. Chief among them was Dave Powers, who trawled for women for Kennedy in California, Florida, and the White House. Traphes Bryant recorded in his diary: "Dave Powers once asked the President what he would like to have for his birthday. He named a TV actress from California. His wish was granted." Actor "brother-in-Lawford" Peter Lawford was a steady source of Hollywood girls—most famously, Marilyn Monroe. Dean Martin's ex-wife recalled, "I saw Peter in the role of pimp for Jack Kennedy. It was a nasty business—they were just too gleeful about it, not discreet at all." *Washington Post* publisher Philip Graham and Kennedy had a friendship based partly on swapping sex partners, and Graham friend Jean Friendly described the situation as a "scandal": "The pair of them were sleeping around with the same people." Bobby Baker also got girls for Kennedy, as did railroad lobbyist Bill Thompson, whom Bartlett described as a "pimp for Jack" and "the dark side of Jack Kennedy."

Kennedy's dazzling personality overwhelmed his circle. Journalist Gloria Emerson wrote that men wanted "to win his favor, but even more important, they seemed to love him. People wanted to please Jack." The allure of intimacy was so irresistible that few dared to jeopardize his friendship. A Kennedy observer argued that men such as Robert McNamara, McGeorge Bundy, and Arthur Schlesinger "could have stretched their minds more if they hadn't gotten so tangled up in competing for his favor and his time. They wanted to hang out, as well as to think about public policy."

The men in his circle strove to impress him. They wanted to be just as witty, just as cool, just as tough. Advisers on the Bay of Pigs invasion hesitated to voice their doubts, partly from fear that Kennedy would think them soft. Old friend Jewel Reed noted that even men "who were older, wiser, more senior than he were very, very much drawn into his thinking."

Desperate to hold his attention, Kennedy's circle feared his boredom. "Either you informed him or you amused him," said reporter Mary McGrory. "Otherwise he turned away." Everyone knew his warning signs: tapping his teeth, drumming his fingers, swinging his foot. Bartlett recalled, "He could not stand to be bored. . . . It made him rather exhausting to be around for a long period of time. As you got to know him, you went to some pains not to bore him." Kennedy's desire not to be bored distorted administration councils. As aide Harris Wofford noted, "Brutal analysis and covert action were not boring. Lectures about morality, legality, and principles were. . . . The witty, rough, sardonic language that Kennedy liked was stimulating, but the degree to which this style dominated the White House . . . was self-defeating. . . . There was the same hesitation about saying anything unless it was amusing." Successful aides shared his qualities of irreverence, gaiety, sardonic wit, and toughness, while the boring, long-winded, or preachy—whatever their other merits—fell out of favor.

Despite many close relationships, Kennedy remained remote; one aide described him as a "rather detached, friendly but essentially impersonal leader." He left many things unsaid, turned inward, and chose to reveal only a part of himself. Somehow, this reserve only increased others' attraction to him. A cabinet member reflected, "Jack Kennedy was never really outgoing in a sense with people that you felt close to him, but yet he had that peculiar quality that so endeared him and commanded such loyalty and devotion . . . until I could almost say that you love that man [despite] his somewhat taciturn New England attitudes." In fact, the memoirs written by the Kennedy men seem in many cases to be attempts to establish a relationship with JFK deeper than they'd had during his life.

Kennedy's death devastated his circle. Their grief was so staggering that Joseph Alsop described them as "male widows." "It was a shattering sensation," he recalled, "to discover quite abruptly that one had lived the best years of one's life . . . I had never known I loved the president (for one does not think of this kind of relationship in those terms) until I felt the impact of his death." He added, "Why I should so irrationally mind the president's loss, and mind it much more than the loss of my own father, I cannot say." McGeorge Bundy also said he was struck more deeply by Kennedy's death than by his own father's. Roswell Gilpatric said that when Kennedy died, "I suddenly realized that I felt about him as I've never felt about another man in my life." Bobby Kennedy Jr. recalled of Lem Billings, "In many ways Lem thought of his life as being over after Jack died."

The fierce devotion and affection of his circle was one of the most striking facts about Kennedy. Most presidents command loyalty, particularly in their closest advisers, but few inspired the intense love that Kennedy roused.

16

THE IDEA OF JOHN F. KENNEDY
How He Presented Himself

Kennedy blazed himself so brilliantly in the public mind that he remains vivid today, long after his death. He knew how he wanted to be understood by the public, and he had a rare skill for presenting himself through symbols, language, and gestures that could reach everyone. He didn't, however, accomplish this alone. His father and his wife amplified his efforts far beyond what he could have achieved himself.

Ironically, Kennedy, who exercised perfect control over the idea of John F. Kennedy, was trusted partly because he appeared so unguarded and natural. His image was carefully constructed, and yet—was the idea of John F. Kennedy artificial?

Kennedy's greatest achievement was the *idea* of President John F. Kennedy—brilliant, witty, idealistic, practical, cool, aristocratic, and kind. He embodied many virtues and was associated with many great institutions—Harvard, the navy, Congress, the Pulitzer Prize, the United States itself. His character and goals penetrated the imagination of Americans with unique intensity. But Kennedy didn't do this alone. Three masters of imagery came together to build the idea of John Kennedy: Jack, Joe, and Jackie Kennedy.

All three were highly theatrical personalities, skilled in presenting themselves and one another with dramatic gestures and gorgeous images. With conscious effort, some instinct, and some luck, the three Kennedys loaded on symbols and ideas that made the idea of Jack Kennedy enormously abundant and powerful. Nothing seemed calculated, and yet every detail contributed to the whole.

The first, and by far the greatest of the three, was John Kennedy himself. He saw himself with a detached eye and never ceased to try to make himself both appear, and actually become, greater. Walking through the White House grounds, Kennedy reflected, "A politician is a dream merchant." After a moment, he added, "But he must back up the dream." Kennedy was far too sophisticated to leave the creation of that dream to chance; projecting his character was as important to his success as deciding the right policies. His detachment allowed him to recognize how he impressed other people and how he might enhance that impression.

Kennedy appreciated that, to stamp himself in the public mind, he must fill a distinct and memorable place; through the glitter of wealth and eminence, his outline must be clearly visible and admirable. He accomplished this by repeatedly associating himself with the ideas of beauty, intellect, energy, family, and courage. He showed himself through words and photographs: with his wife and children, he was a picture of youth, sophistication, and playfulness; in the Oval Office, he was a model of firmness, resolve, rationality, and cool. Every gesture worked—not even his name was overlooked. His aides asked reporters to refer to him as "JFK" to associate him with FDR and, as soon as he was elected, told the newspapers that he must be "John" Kennedy, never "Jack."

Kennedy considered every aspect of the idea of John F. Kennedy, even at the most superficial level. He never underrated the importance of physical attractiveness. Appointments secretary and old friend Kenny O'Donnell recalled, "All of the Kennedys, and especially Jack, judged people by their appearance." During the transition period, when press secretary Pierre Salinger appeared on television wearing shorts, Kennedy ordered, "Get into long pants. You haven't got the legs for shorts." Kennedy was just as hard on himself. Particularly weight-conscious because cortisone puffed up his face, he dieted frequently. He brought his scales when he traveled so he could weigh himself every day. Kennedy was horrified by a photograph showing him looking fleshy in a bathing suit: "It shows the Fitzgerald breasts." Because he often woke with his face puffy, three-inch-high blocks were placed under his bed legs, to keep his head elevated as he slept. Secretary Mary Gallagher hints broadly that he dyed his hair, and he constantly worked on his tan.

More important, Kennedy surrounded himself with signs of intellect and accomplishment. His writing two books was no lark; "There's something about being an author," he told Richard Nixon, "which really builds the reputation of a politician." His aides emphasized how much he read, and how quickly. He surrounded himself with people of the highest quality: astronauts, artists, military heroes, professors.

Kennedy radiated vigor, an extraordinary accomplishment considering his chronic pain. Somehow, despite poor health and a fragile back, he associated himself with touch football, fifty-mile hikes, and sailing. He set the tone during his inaugural address, where he spoke without a hat or an overcoat, despite the frigid weather— a sharp contrast to Eisenhower, who huddled in coat and scarf. (JFK wore thermal underwear under his clothes.) When riding through Paris, Kennedy insisted on sitting in an open car, in the pouring rain, despite agonizing back pain.

A happy family was equally vital to the idea of John F. Kennedy. American families, increasingly fractured and transient, were drawn to the loyalty and closeness of the Kennedy clan. Kennedy was lucky that his extended family was photogenic, hardworking, and cooperative; he wasn't burdened by the indiscreet wife, scalawag brothers, or rebellious children that vex many politicians. The fact that Jackie became pregnant in 1960 reinforced the idea of family and youth—not since 1895 had a child been born to a sitting president—as did the fact that Kennedy's own parents were still alive and active and that he had so many siblings and nieces and nephews.

At the same time, Kennedy reinforced his image as a tough fighter. From his first campaign, he emphasized ideas such as challenge, battle, and courage. He scattered tie clips in the shape of the *PT-109,* encouraged his navy buddies to campaign for him, and kept the famous coconut shell message encased in plastic on his desk. Cigar-smoking Kennedy advised a pipe-smoking military aide, "No politician ever wins an election smoking a pipe. It's not aggressive-looking enough. A cigar gives you a positive and aggressive look, so if you ever run for office, switch."

Just as he knew how to convey his personality to the public, Kennedy had an unerring instinct for identifying policies that carried the right symbolic freight. He chose a brilliant theme for his administration—the "New Frontier," with its pioneer associations of self-sufficiency, toughness, cooperation, and daring. He used signature policies to project his image of himself and the country. Two initiatives under Kennedy's special sponsorship, the Peace Corps and the Green Berets, used bold action and heroic involvement to revitalize the American identity. His challenge to the United States to send a man to the moon by 1970 ignited the imagination and competitive spirit of the country.

Part of Kennedy's genius, too, was to include some jarring notes in his self-presentation. Quoting poetry, sitting in a rocking chair, appointing his brother to be attorney general—these unexpected, potentially unpopular actions proved his sincerity. The public is suspicious of too obvious a concern with "image," and Kennedy's gestures were all the more winning for being not perfectly worked out.

Jack Kennedy had exceptional support from his father, Joe, who, with his fortune and unflagging cultivation of good press, gave his son a tremendous boost. Joe's film-industry experiences had taught him the importance of public relations and image building, and he sought to apply such methods to his son's campaigns. He didn't have any sentimental notions about the "real" Jack Kennedy. Hubert Humphrey warned primary voters, "Beware of these orderly campaigns. They are ordered, bought and paid for. We are not selling corn flakes or some Hollywood production." Joe boasted about doing exactly that: "We're going to sell Jack like soap flakes." By the time of the 1960 campaign, the public already knew all about JFK, the Kennedys, and their adventures: Joe's post as ambassador, the weddings, the sad deaths of Joe Jr. (a war hero!) and Kick (a future duchess!). The *New York Times* sports pages had even reported when seven of the nine Kennedy children won most of the prizes in a 1940 sailing contest.

But there was even someone else to build the idea of John F. Kennedy: Jackie Kennedy. It was only after Jack's election—and even more, after his death—that her gifts became apparent. Jackie worked constantly to buttress the vision of President Kennedy as a paragon of excellence. Without mixing in politics, she built a prestige for her husband he couldn't have achieved without her.

Jackie understood that the Kennedy household must contribute to the idea of John F. Kennedy. She put it simply: "I just think that everything in the White House should be the best." Her restoration project lifted the White House to the level of quality and historical significance worthy of John F. Kennedy. She also made it a showcase for great artists, and their presence gave the administration its air of sophistication and gaiety. Metropolitan Opera stars, Shakespearean actors, the Joffrey Ballet, the Scottish Black Watch Regiment—all came to the Kennedy White House.

But Jackie's most important contribution to the idea of John F. Kennedy was *herself* as his perfect wife: glamorous, intelligent, dedicated to the traditional feminine occupations of motherhood, housekeeping, and entertaining. The renowned "Jackie style" of dress was a visual manifestation of the "Kennedy style": regal but not fussy, stylish yet dignified, distinctive but not eccentric. Like her husband, she seemed to do everything beautifully. If she wasn't speaking French to General de Gaulle, she was doing the Twist with Defense Secretary Bob McNamara or waterskiing with astronaut John Glenn or convincing André Malraux to lend the *Mona Lisa,* over the protests of the Louvre, to the United States.

Jackie's dedication to the idea of John F. Kennedy shaped the magnificent ceremony of his funeral. Determined that its dignity be worthy of her husband, Jackie modeled it not on Roosevelt's (the last president given a state funeral) or on McKinley's (the last president assassinated) but on Lincoln's. She sent people to the darkened Library of Congress, where, armed with flashlights, they searched for illustrations that depicted the 1865 Lincoln funeral. Jackie used ceremony to establish JFK as Lincoln's equal and heir and to give historic import to the proceedings. She excelled at the inclusion of dramatic details that seared the day in public memory: the black translucent veil that made her instantly identifiable in the crowd, the riderless horse, the walking procession of mourners, the muffled drums, her whispered instruction to John Jr. to salute the casket. "John, you can salute Daddy now and say good-bye to him."

Most presidents are buried in their native states, and almost everyone—the Kennedy siblings, the Irish mafia, the White House staff, and the State Department—wanted Kennedy to be buried in Massachusetts. Jackie, however, decided that her husband should be buried in Arlington Cemetery, at a national, rather than parochial,

*November 1963. Members of the Kennedy family gather
at the funeral of the assassinated president.*

location. Almost at the last moment, she insisted on adding an eternal flame to his grave. Brother-in-law Sargent Shriver cautioned, "I want to be sure you're not subjecting yourself to criticism. Some people might think it's a little ostentatious." But Jackie was certain that the idea of John F. Kennedy was imposing enough to justify the gesture. The stately funeral ceremony that she directed—and that was witnessed by tens of millions on television—further strengthened the legacy Kennedy had worked so hard to build during his life. By permitting Kennedy to be memorialized as a fallen hero, his death lifted his acknowledged virtues into the legend of Camelot.

Kennedy and his father and wife so successfully established the idea of John F. Kennedy that his memory has never faded. The glittering parties—the air of intellect and culture—the exultant visits abroad—the bold stands in the Cold War—the endearing photographs—the witty and commanding press conference performances—the solemn grandeur of his funeral—all etch him unforgettably in the public mind.

17

KENNEDY REMEMBERED
How Others Saw Him

A key to the enduring legacy of great figures, and an important venerative form, is the collection of people's recollections and impressions. Almost always, such testimony is carefully chosen to glorify the subject; a collection that's not conventionally edited to support a glowing portrait may startle readers who expect to see only the usual flattering entries.

Jane Suydam first met Kennedy in the late 1930s. "He was unbelievably handsome. He had this remarkable animal pull. The impact on me was overwhelming."

Johnny Iles, Kennedy's hut mate in the South Pacific, said, "He was going to be something big. He just had that charisma. You could tell just by his nature, by the way people would stop by and visit with him. . . . It was obvious that politics was in his blood."

A close friend and fellow officer in the South Pacific, James Reed, recalled, "There was an aura about him that I've never seen duplicated in anybody else. . . . He was several steps ahead of all of us. He'd had the opportunity to be exposed to people in high places . . . plus the fact that he had such a marvelous sense of humor."

Ted Sorensen wrote, "No attribute he possessed in 1953 was more pronounced or more important than his capacity for growth, his willingness to learn, his determination to explore and to inquire and to profit by experience. He had a limitless curiosity about nearly everything. . . . He hated to bore or be bored."

In 1956, Eleanor Roosevelt condemned Kennedy as a man "who understands what courage is and admires it, but has not quite the independence to have it." But in an August 1960 letter, she wrote, "I liked him better than I ever had. . . . My final judgment is that here is a man who wants to leave a record (perhaps for ambitious personal reasons, as people say) but I rather think because he really is interested in helping the people."

Jewel Reed, later the ex-wife of Kennedy's old friend Jim Reed, recalled, "Jack would frequently ask Jim to parties—but not me! It was a male prowling thing and Jack couldn't understand why Jim couldn't leave me behind and prowl with him."

Kennedy's doctor Janet Travell observed, "Senator Kennedy never lost the air of innate dignity that was the product of personal reserve, self-respect, style, and a distaste for ostentation."

Jackie Kennedy described her husband as a "curious inquiring mind that is always at work. If I were drawing him, I would draw a tiny body and an enormous head."

To Tip O'Neill, Joe Kennedy said, "Never expect any appreciation from my boys. These kids have had so much done for them by other people they just assume it's coming to them."

Jackie Kennedy wrote in 1959, "I see, every succeeding day I am married to him that he has what may be the single most important quality for a leader—an imperturbable self-confidence and sureness of his powers."

Gore Vidal wrote, "There were few intellectuals in 1960 who were not beguiled by the spectacle of a president who seemed always to be standing at a certain remove from himself, watching himself with amusement at his own performance. He was an ironist in a profession where the prize usually goes to the apparent cornball."

Betty Spalding, wife of Kennedy's friend Chuck Spalding: "He was nice to people, but heedless of people, heedless about his clothes, and heedless about money."

Aides Kenny O'Donnell and Dave Powers wrote, "As casual as he seemed, President Kennedy was always striving for perfection in everything he did."

After Kennedy's inaugural address, House Speaker Sam Rayburn said, "That speech he made out there was better than anything Franklin Roosevelt said at his best—it was better than Lincoln. I think—really think—that he is a man of destiny."

Just a few days after the inauguration, after dinner, Kennedy and his friend Charley Bartlett set off to explore the Executive Office Building. Bartlett recalled, "It was probably the happiest moment of Jack Kennedy's life, and Jackie's too. There was this wonderful and exhilarating sense that all things were possible. He was just bursting with all the things he could do."

Time editorial director Hedley Donovan wrote a memo to his colleagues in February 1961: "I am evolving a theory that it is rather pointless to analyze whether Kennedy is at heart 'conservative' or 'liberal.' Kennedy is Kennedy. Either the least ideological of our 20th Century Presidents, or the inventor-to-be of a new ideology cutting across the traditional right-left patterns of U.S. politics."

Joseph Alsop recalled, "He liked people to be good looking and hated people who let themselves go. He was snobbish about courage, and he was snobbish about experience. He didn't want us to be ordinary and routine. . . . He wanted experience to be intense."

Close friend Lem Billings observed of the Kennedy brothers, "They were all oriented toward their kids far more than toward their wives."

When a former member of the Joint Chiefs was asked why that group hadn't argued more against the Bay of Pigs, he answered, "You won't believe this but the fact is we were so in awe of this bright, young, charismatic hero, that we were waiting to speak when we were spoken to. We were old enough to be his father; and he never asked us."

Around the time of the Bay of Pigs, President Eisenhower reflected that Kennedy viewed the presidency as "not only a very personal thing, but as an institution that one man could handle with an assistant here and another there. He had no idea of the complexity of the job."

Press secretary Pierre Salinger recalled, "Our faith in him and in what he was trying to do was absolute, and he could impart to our work . . . a feeling that he was moving, and the world with him, toward a better time. We could accept without complaint his bristling temper, his cold sarcasm, and his demands for always higher standards of excellence because we knew he was driving himself harder than he was driving us."

Critic Alfred Kazin wrote, "His most essential quality, I would think, is that of the man who is always making and remaking himself. He is the final product of a fanatical job of self-modeling. . . . Even now there is an absence in him of the petty conceit of the second rate, and a freshness of curiosity behind which one feels not merely his quickness to utilize all his advantages but also his ability to turn this curiosity on himself."

British ambassador David Ormsby-Gore, of Kennedy's handling of the Cuban missile crisis: "I think that everybody who worked with him during that week conceived this fantastic admiration for him; the way he kept his humor, the way he could make decisions at the exact time they were needed, the way he could listen to a vast quantity of contradictory advice and come out with what everybody at the end of the day decided was exactly the right action."

Norman Podhoretz observed of those in the Kennedy administration, "They were very, very arrogant, very cocksure of themselves. . . . What made them so sure that they knew not only how to fight a war in that country [Vietnam] but how to reshape that society? They knew nothing about it, yet this didn't bother any of them at all."

Joseph Kennedy's nurse Rita Dallas wrote of Kennedy, "I realized that a part of him had been manufactured by a slick advertising campaign. . . . The smile was flawless. Every physical motion was carried through with the studied precision of a dancer. The voice was used with studied inflections to evoke just the right response. . . . He was also friendly, perceptive, inquisitive, tender, and powerful."

Budget Director David Bell said, "Kennedy was a magnificent natural leader. . . . Everyone had the natural feeling they'd follow him anywhere. He was quick and funny, and committed to all the right purposes."

James MacGregor Burns observed, "Kennedy accumulated tremendous personal popularity. The trouble is, popularity is not power. . . . I don't think Kennedy ever found the secret of translating his personal popularity into fundamental legislative power or administrative power."

Norman Mailer observed, "Jack Kennedy is somewhat more and considerably less after all than a hero or a villain—he is also an empty vessel, a man of many natures."

Roger Hilsman said, "Camelot was an invention of my good friend Teddy White, using Jackie's romanticism after the president's death. If Jack Kennedy had heard this stuff about Camelot, he would have vomited."

"That poor President talked of Lincoln in a way that struck me," remarked Charles de Gaulle in 1969. "He was hoping to follow his path in life; and he followed it in death."

18

KENNEDY'S HIGH IDEALS
What He Represented

"He is greatest," wrote Samuel Butler, "who is most often in men's good thoughts." The public saw Kennedy, with his extraordinary personal gifts and accomplishments, as the embodiment of everything that made America exceptional. Not only did he articulate a vision of a braver, better nation, but his own life seemed to exemplify its promise. And far more difficult than merely embodying the American dream, Kennedy actually inspired people to meet the challenge of a country that could begin anew.

The 1950s had left people with a feeling of complacency, stagnation, and loss of higher vision, and Kennedy thrilled them with his challenge: "This is a great country. But I think it can be greater. I think we can do better. I think we can make this country move again."

The public saw Kennedy as the model of the American dream, which so many wanted and strived for: he was educated, brave, athletic, dedicated to public service, rich but hardworking, ethnically identified yet assimilated, churchgoing yet broad-minded, with a strong family and traditional values. He lived the life that people wanted for their children.

And yet his origins were still visible: from the potato farm in Ireland, the saloon in Boston, he had traveled the entire way, all the way to the Harvard Spee Club, the sailboat races on the Cape, the English nanny for his children. It was right that such a man should talk about what we *owe* to the country. It was appropriate that a great figure such as the president should be rich, that his wife should dress well, that he should have habits and interests that ordinary people didn't share.

The glamour and excellence that Kennedy himself embodied played an important role in inspiring people, because these attractions helped his ideas catch fire. Just as his example prompted people to stop wearing hats or to wear their hair longer, Kennedy's inaugural address inspired them to commit themselves to a larger vision. Kennedy opened people's minds to new ideas; he raised their expectations of themselves and their country.

Kennedy drew on the American impulse toward sacrifice and self-improvement. His most famous sentence was a challenge: "*Ask not what your country can do for you, but what you can do for your country.*" Kennedy understood the desire of many to dedicate themselves to an ideal. Aide Edward McDermott recalled, "There was an exhilaration that a lot could be done and that this was a group of people collectively, led by the president, that could inspire the American people to do things that they hadn't done before. It was Camelot."

Kennedy had a tremendous ability to inspire despite the fact— or more likely, *because* of the fact—that even with his persuasive elegance, his vision wasn't quite clear. Harris Wofford admitted that during the transition, aides had a difficult time evaluating potential administration appointees according to their "devotion to Kennedy's programs" and "principles," because no one on Kennedy's staff knew exactly what those programs and principles were. Kennedy's vagueness, however, allowed many more people to identify with him. They poured their own content into his words; they saw what they wanted to see.

While there's nothing unusual in politicians giving speeches about high ideals or the American dream, Kennedy actually stirred people to action. James Meredith, a black air force veteran from Mississippi, was so moved by hearing Kennedy's inaugural address on the radio that, the same night, he wrote to Old Miss to apply for admission—the first step in a long struggle that would stand as a great civil rights landmark. Sometime after Kennedy gave a university commencement address, when an applicant for the law school was asked, "Why do you want to study law?" he answered, "I heard Senator Kennedy make his address at the commencement, and I want to prepare myself seriously to be of service in our government." Cellist Pablo Casals had refused to perform in the United States to protest U.S. recognition of Franco, but he played at the White House out of admiration for Kennedy. So many people took up Kennedy's challenge to march fifty miles that doctors' groups issued health warnings.

Kennedy enjoyed a special rapport with young people, who found it easy to identify with him—the youngest man ever elected president, surrounded by young aides and a young family. Kennedy tapped into their desire to take an active role in improving the world, and the response to his proposal for a Peace Corps was overwhelming. It's a sign of Kennedy's personal power that, although Hubert Humphrey and Congressman Henry Reuss had also proposed a Peace Corps–like program, the idea didn't ignite until Kennedy mentioned it in his extemporaneous remarks in the middle of the night at the University of Michigan. Although he made only a general proposal, it met with terrific enthusiasm.

Ironically, although he provoked passionate emotions, Kennedy himself remained cool and detached. He became the focus of an idealism that he—with his pragmatic view of the world—didn't share. His force was so great, in fact, that he unleashed passions and energy far beyond what he intended, or wanted: he exhorted the country to move, and it *did* move. The country was superenergized from its eight years of peace and prosperity; millions of people were graduating from college; millions of black people were moving to the cities and becoming organized. Kennedy gave shape to the energy that began to erupt out of traditional forms. The expectations he aroused unleashed a determination to bring about change.

Although one of Kennedy's favorite quotes was Lord Falkland's "When it is not necessary to change it is not necessary to change," he sparked drastic action by others. For example, Kennedy wanted the Freedom Riders to stop their dangerous push through the South and didn't understand his role in inspiring that kind of initiative. Civil rights leader James Farmer reflected, "I adored . . . how he had encouraged our movement by his rhetoric. He hadn't intended to do that, I guess, but he had: 'Ask not what your country can do for you; ask what you can do for your country.' Ah, 'What I can do for my country is to wipe out segregation,' we answered." When Louis Martin, Kennedy's one black adviser, told him, "Negroes are getting ideas they didn't have before," Kennedy asked, "Where are they getting them?" Martin answered, "From you! You're lifting the horizons of Negroes."

In the same way, though Kennedy was no feminist, he helped ignite the women's movement. Nancy Dickerson, a White House reporter who also dated Kennedy, observed that Kennedy "was the complete male chauvinist. He saw women primarily as sex objects, and . . . he thought it ridiculous to pay them the same as men." Ben Bradlee explained, "I don't think he saw equality of the sexes as a viable option." In a 1963 interview, Kennedy noted that "by carrying out her primary responsibility to back up her husband and care for her children well, [Jackie] is doing her real job as a woman." But his inspiring rhetoric stirred women to action, and by establishing the President's Commission on the Status of Women, Kennedy unintentionally encouraged the women's rights movement by spotlighting injustice.

Kennedy found his own powers unsettling. After his discouraging summit with Khrushchev in Vienna, he gave a speech that touched off national hysteria over civil defense. When he spoke in West Berlin in 1963, the crowd's response was so fervent that Kennedy felt first exhilarated, then alarmed. German chancellor Konrad Adenauer was also troubled by the frenzy inspired by Kennedy: "Does this mean Germany can one day have another Hitler?"

Although it's true that Kennedy's rhetoric at the microphone was not always matched by his actions in the Oval Office, somehow, whatever his personal limitations, he raised the moral climate of the country. Texas senator Ralph Yarborough remembered, "It was a special time; I was there. Lord, I've never had such a feeling before or since then. It was marvelous; without living it, you can't express it. It gave the country a lift; it gave the world a lift. People cried in the dusty streets of Africa when he died." Not only Americans, but people all over the world, found in the ideals articulated by Kennedy the values they wished to associate with the United States.

19

KENNEDY AS CIVIL RIGHTS LEADER

Two Views

PRESIDENT KENNEDY WAS SINCERELY COMMITTED TO CIVIL RIGHTS

Kennedy energized the nation with hope for a better future, and in particular, he inspired the black community with his vision of a freer, fairer country. In the summer of 1961, when Freedom Riders traveled through the South to challenge segregated bus facilities, their leader, James Farmer, explained he'd been inspired to action by Kennedy's words about change and liberty. Civil rights leader John Lewis recalled, "There was something about the Kennedy presidency—about the man—that touched the black people immediately."

Kennedy won significant black support during the campaign when, after Martin Luther King Jr. was sentenced on a thin pretext to four months' hard labor, Kennedy called the distraught, pregnant Mrs. King to offer his support. His brother Bobby called the judge to argue for King's right to make bail, and the judge agreed to release him. Word of Kennedy's concern swept through the black community, which then voted overwhelmingly for Kennedy; many analysts argue that Kennedy's sympathetic gesture decided the election.

Initially, it's true, Kennedy didn't recognize the depth of the civil rights problem. But with time and experience, he began to understand the issues and see that he must provide moral leadership. Several times during his presidency, Kennedy told his appointments secretary, "I want to clear this desk. No foreign visitors for a month. I have to concentrate on civil rights."

The composition of Congress limited Kennedy's options. The coalition of conservative southern Democrats and Republicans could defeat most controversial legislation, and Kennedy didn't want to pitch a battle for civil rights legislation that he would almost certainly lose, when that fight would jeopardize southern Democratic support for other legislation, also important to black people.

Although stymied in Congress, Kennedy did take advantage of the power of dramatic, symbolic acts. During the campaign, Kennedy moved his entourage out of a Kentucky hotel when the manager refused to give a room to a black reporter. Angered by the inauguration parade's all-white coast guard unit, Kennedy pushed for its immediate desegregation as well as a special effort to attract black recruits. Far more than any president before him, Kennedy invited black people to the White House to attend meetings and social functions, and he dramatically increased their number in high government positions. In 1961, his interior secretary, Stewart Udall, refused to permit the Washington Redskins to use D.C. Stadium unless the team ended its ban on black players. Several members of Kennedy's administration resigned from Washington's Metropolitan Club after a member was censured for bringing George Weaver, a black man and an assistant secretary of labor, to lunch.

Kennedy recognized that he must shape public sentiment to create an environment that would make bold statutes and decisions possible. Schlesinger explained Kennedy's effectiveness: "His actions, his remarks, the concern for Negro rights and scorn for racism implicit in his personality and bearing—all had subtly entered and transformed national expectations and attitudes. He had quietly created an atmosphere where change, when it came, would seem no longer an upheaval but the inexorable unfolding of the promise of American life. Yet he did not call for change in advance of the moment."

Despite his commitment to civil rights, Kennedy hesitated to push Congress and the country too far in advance of popular sentiment. For example, he worried that the planned March on Washington would give Congress an excuse to refuse to act, but when he realized the organizers' determination, he did everything he could to help. Afterward, civil rights leader Roy Wilkins told the president, "You gave us your blessings. It was one of the prime factors in turning it into an orderly protest to help our government rather than a protest against our government." Kennedy was willing to risk his popularity to take a strong stand and, in the fall of 1963, when his stance on civil rights dropped his approval rating to a low of 57 percent, said, "Well, if we're going down, let's go down on a matter of principle."

Kennedy looked forward to a second term, when he hoped to have a working majority in Congress. Referring to a list of difficult civil rights actions, he promised his aide Harris Wofford, "You will see, with time I'm going to do them all." The assassination destroyed these plans. "Unhappily," Wofford writes, "we will never know how well Kennedy would have followed up his own great—and late—initiative in civil rights. Was it really so late? I thought so then, but looking back across two decades the whole of Kennedy's thousand days seems almost like a flash of lightning. . . . It may well be that the President was right, in the long run, to let things ripen as they did."

Kennedy knew the country must overcome its divisions. When asked whether he believed the country might split along racial lines, he said, "I think the American people have been through too much to make that fatal mistake. . . . Over the long run we are going to have a mix. This will be true racially, socially, ethnically, geographically, and that is really, finally, the best way."

Jackie, with her gift for grasping the essential, recognized the importance of civil rights for her husband's legacy, and that it was the issue for which he would have chosen to be martyred. After hearing about Lee Harvey Oswald, Jackie told her mother, "He didn't even have the satisfaction of being killed for civil rights—it had to be some silly little Communist."

Although Kennedy at times frustrated activists by failing to move more quickly, he was popular with the larger black community, who judged him a powerful force on their behalf. In mid-1963, in a poll asking black people who'd done the most for Negro rights, the top choices were the NAACP, Martin Luther King Jr., and John Kennedy. Kennedy is remembered for his contribution more than others whose accomplishments appear greater. As journalist Tom Wicker observed, "John F. Kennedy is revered today; you will find his picture and Robert's in black households that don't think anything of Lyndon Johnson, who you would have thought would be the great hero." After Kennedy's death, Martin Luther King said, "I think historians will have to record that he vacillated like Lincoln, but he uplifted the cause far above the political level."

PRESIDENT KENNEDY WAS NOT
SINCERELY COMMITTED TO
CIVIL RIGHTS

Kennedy wasn't deeply dedicated to the cause of civil rights. He acted with reluctance, and only when the press of events left him no choice.

Black Americans, like white Americans, had been thrilled by Kennedy's promises and expected great things from him. They were disappointed. One black activist said, "We've gotten the best snow job in history. We lost two years because we admired him." Kennedy's lack of commitment can be heard in his famous inaugural address. When the speech draft failed to address civil rights, Kennedy's civil rights adviser Harris Wofford protested. In response, Kennedy added a mere two words: "those human rights to which this nation has always been committed and to which we are committed today *at home* and around the world" (emphasis added).

With his background of wealth and privilege, Kennedy failed to comprehend the depth of the racial problem. As civil rights leader James Farmer observed, "Jack Kennedy was particularly ignorant on civil rights in particular and blacks in general at the time he became president. He had had no contact with blacks." When, as president, he learned that restaurants on the highway between New York and Washington refused to serve African diplomats, Kennedy's response was worthy of Marie Antoinette: "Tell these ambassadors I wouldn't think of driving from New York to Washington. Tell them to fly!" Asked to attend a commemoration of the Emancipation Proclamation's hundredth anniversary, Kennedy sent a taped message and went sailing instead.

Kennedy didn't approve of racial injustice, but he wanted to fight it on his own terms. He and his brother preferred to focus on enforcing voter registration laws in the South—an incremental and less confrontational approach that would, incidentally, bring more Democrats to the polls. Kennedy refused to take political risks on behalf of civil rights and deferred to southerners on issues involving race. For example, at the same time he urged black people to seek justice in the courts, he appointed several segregationist judges in southern federal districts to placate southern congressmen.

Kennedy hoped that with modest steps, he could keep the support of both black people and southern Democrats as the racial issue gradually resolved itself. He underestimated the force of both the movement and its opposition. In fact, for most of his presidency, Kennedy treated the civil rights battle as a distraction from what he considered his real work: foreign affairs. In early 1963, Louis Martin said, "The fact is, the President cares more about Germany than about Negroes, he thinks it's more important."

Kennedy's own stirring rhetoric, ironically, helped inspire actions that he would later try to discourage. The Freedom Riders of 1961 angered Kennedy, partly because he believed that the Freedom Riders were embarrassing him as he prepared to meet Khrushchev. He told Wofford, "Can't you get your goddamned friends off those buses? Stop them." He opposed the August 1963 March on Washington, then, when he wasn't able to stop it, and after it proved to be a success, he took credit as its sponsor.

For the first two years of his presidency, Kennedy didn't undertake any major civil rights initiatives. During the campaign, Kennedy had criticized Eisenhower for failing to end discrimination in federal housing programs with a simple "stroke of his pen"; as president, Kennedy began to receive pens by mail from those impatient to see him use his *own* pen for that task. It took him two years.

Finally, in February 1963, he submitted legislation to Congress, but, reflecting Kennedy's usual preference for a gradual approach, it focused solely on voting rights; civil rights leaders were deeply disappointed. It was only in the spring of 1963 that Kennedy took action. Acknowledging at last that "a great change is at hand," he introduced a comprehensive civil rights bill.

In his private life, Kennedy failed to show a deep commitment to the principle of racial equality. Kennedy needled McGeorge Bundy for joining the all-white Metropolitan Club but didn't mention the fact that, since 1957, he himself had been a member and visitor of the Brook, an exclusive New York men's club, and although it had no black members, Kennedy didn't resign. Kennedy spent much of his time in Palm Beach, where no black person was permitted to own a house.

Despite his poor record, Kennedy's early, shocking death allowed him to be associated, in memory, with admirable goals he only halfheartedly supported and accomplishments for which he wasn't responsible.

20

VENERATION FOR KENNEDY
The Emotion He Inspired

Kennedy aroused feelings of near adoration both in those who knew him well and in the wider public. People wanted to please and impress him, to live up to his ideals, to draw near him.

We have only a few names to describe extraordinary individuals: saints and stars and geniuses. Whatever the name, veneration takes the same forms, with the collection of relics—the wish to touch—the attempts to memorialize in personal testimony as well as in art, poetry, and biography—the imitation of dress and manner—the desire to serve and sacrifice—the attribution of miracles.

To a striking degree, people venerated Kennedy. Those who saw Kennedy's picture in magazines or on television were drawn to his good looks and energy, his inquisitive mind, his ideals, and his self-deprecating humor. Those close to him felt his charisma even more strongly; women melted, men vied to win his attention. People longed to dedicate themselves to his service, as a way to become closer to him.

Kennedy was a man worthy of veneration—this, everyone around him agreed, was true. Others had written books, he'd won a Pulitzer; others had served in the war, he was a lifesaving hero; he was a millionaire; he was a TV star; he was married to a fashion icon who could speak several languages; he knew Hollywood celebrities, British aristocrats, Harvard professors, Boston-Irish politicians, and European playboys. He was brighter, wittier, more confident, and more disciplined than anyone else. If only he had the time, he would be his own best secretary of state, press secretary, chief of staff, or campaign manager. Other politicians recognized Kennedy's gifts. As local politicians watched Kennedy with obvious envy, a JFK aide observed, "They can't understand this. They think he has a trick. They're listening to him because they think if they learn the trick they can be President, too."

Kennedy's heroic image wasn't just a matter of good press. Jacques Lowe noted that "no man is a hero to his photographer" but that nevertheless he'd become "something of a hero-worshiper" of Kennedy. Theodore White wrote that after the assassination, "I would never again, after Kennedy, see any man as a hero." Charley Bartlett explained, "We had a hero for a friend. . . . He had uncommon courage, unfailing humor, a penetrating, ever curious intelligence, and over all a matchless grace."

His faults, no less than his virtues, inspired love. The fact that he hated to be bored and loved gossip; that he, a rich man, never carried cash and instead borrowed money from low-paid staffers; that he expected someone else to clean up his messes and run his bath; that he demanded heroic last-minute efforts from his speechwriter; that he expected the best from all who served him—all this was part of his allure. He had a large vision and made tremendous demands, and he took what he wanted. Raised with great wealth

and privilege, he had an air of command that others found en-
nobling.

Kennedy was remarkable in his ability to arouse the dedication
of a large and varied group of people. Many of his most fervent admirers were prominent people in their own right, with a wide range
of temperaments and abilities, and often of enormous ego themselves—men as diverse as John Glenn and Norman Mailer, Oleg
Cassini and Robert Frost, and David Ormsby-Gore and Bobby
Baker. Joseph Alsop admitted to an admiration of Kennedy that was
"this side of idolatry—and not much this side." White House aide
Mike Feldman said, "I've never met anybody with . . . that special
ability to attract people to him and his ideas, and do it with all
kinds of people."

In his oldest friends, Kennedy inspired a veneration that far exceeded ordinary affection. In 1955, during his long convalescence
after back surgery, Red Fay joined him for ten days; Lem Billings
stayed for a month. Billings had repeated his senior year at Choate
to have an extra year with Jack and even pretended to have been
born the same year, and after the presidential election, quit his job
to be free to be Kennedy's companion. Billings later said that
Kennedy "may have been the reason I never got married. . . . Do
you think I would have had a better life having been Jack
Kennedy's best friend . . . having had the best friend anybody ever
had, or having been married . . . ?"

Two of Kennedy's most improbable admirers were Richard
Nixon and Frank Sinatra. In the first TV debate, for example, Nixon
underscored the similarities of their views, and while Kennedy referred to Nixon as "Mr. Nixon," Nixon referred to Kennedy as
"Senator Kennedy." By the campaign's end, Nixon had adopted
many of Kennedy's themes for his own speeches: "So I say, yes,
there are new frontiers, new frontiers here in America, new frontiers all over the universe in which we live." Henry Cabot Lodge,

Kennedy's opponent in the 1952 Senate race, had a similar experience. He recalled that Kennedy was an "extraordinarily likable man. In fact, I liked him. So often in a campaign, you look for a man's faults and then campaign on them. Well, in his case, you didn't do that."

World-famous, selfish, domineering singer Frank Sinatra had an almost abject devotion to Kennedy. During the 1960 convention, he and his Rat Pack—which Sinatra renamed the "Jack Pack"—mingled with the crowd to try to influence delegates, and after Kennedy's victory, Sinatra worked furiously to stage a star-studded preinaugural gala. At the end of that evening, Kennedy thanked Sinatra onstage, and Sinatra later bored friends by playing a recording of the tribute over and over. Sinatra even mounted a plaque to mark the room in his house where Kennedy had slept, and he remodeled his house extensively to outfit it for a presidential visit.

Kennedy seemed to have an invisible measuring rod in his head, and friends and colleagues pressed themselves to be their most witty, their most daring, their most cool in his presence. For many, their praise became so exaggerated—so far exceeding ordinary admiration—that it tipped into mawkishness. Theodore White slipped into biblical phrases to describe the "enchanting man" eating his dinner. "Then the plane was aloft again, and he was somber in the dark. . . . The stewardess brought him a steaming bowl of hot tomato soup . . . He stirred in a thick glob of sour cream and supped." At another point, White's account reads like teenage poetry: "Kennedy loped into the cottage with his light, dancing step, as young and lithe as springtime." William Manchester explains any possible failing as a virtue in disguise; every comparison is heroic. Kennedy's lousy performance in school? "Intellectuals are often nonconformists. Their early school records may be unimpressive because as children they were indifferent to curricula—this was true of Jack." His appalling spelling? "[Intellectuals] are inclined to be impatient of details; *e.g.,* orthography. Kennedy, like Fitzgerald, became a popular author without mastering this elementary skill ["litary," "peciliar"]." His "reluctance to enter into meditative penumbrae"? "Some see this trait as a weakness. It need not be. Caesar and Napoleon shared it." Manchester also fell under Kennedy's physical spell and described him rising naked from the bathtub: "six feet tall, with tousled hair, a straight mouth, skin coarsened by the sea . . . and those extraordinary eyes, which, if he felt hostile or betrayed, could be riveting, even intimidating. His shoulders and arms were muscular, his legs solid."

None, however, was as effusive as Schlesinger, who saw Kennedy as nothing less than a new founder of the nation: Kennedy "reestablished the republic as the first generation of our leaders saw it—young, brave, civilized, rational, gay, tough, questing, exultant in the excitement and potentiality of history." (Fellow Kennedy aide Harris Wofford commented, "Kennedy would surely have laughed at Schlesinger's unmitigated romanticism about him.")

Kennedy seemed to bewitch his companions; to illustrate his charms, they relate incidents that put him in a bad light. When, in front of Jackie, Kennedy described a reporter as a "Charlie-Uncle-Nan-Tare," Bradlee was captivated. "He used 'prick' and 'fuck' and 'nuts' and 'bastard' and 'son of a bitch' with an ease and comfort that belied his upbringing, and somehow it never seemed offensive." Joe Kennedy visited after his stroke, and Kennedy summoned his father's nurse at 10:30 p.m. to report on Joe's condition. Rita Dallas was ushered into Kennedy's bathroom. "He was stretched out full length in the tub," she wrote. "All I could really think of was what in heaven's name does one say to a naked President. . . . So I took a washcloth off the rack, tossed it in the tub, and said, 'For heaven's sake, cover up.' He splashed the water with his hands like a gleeful boy, then . . . made a fair attempt to cover up by ceremoniously draping the cloth over himself." Kennedy's followers ignored evidence that seemed directly to contradict their claims. Schlesinger observed Kennedy with his aides: "Rambling made him impatient, but his courtesy was unshakable; there were only those drumming fingers." Kennedy managed to show "unshakable courtesy" as he drummed his fingers while someone was talking. Reporter Nancy Dickerson knew that Kennedy "did entertain other women" when Jackie was away, but she maintained that "he was extremely discreet about it." How discreet could he have been if Dickerson, a reporter, knew about his exploits?

As excessive as this praise appears, it nevertheless points to some rare quality in Kennedy. What *was* it about Kennedy that made these grown men and women gush?

Power, wealth, fame, and beauty each inspire the desire to serve—even the impulse for subservience—and Kennedy possessed all four of these qualities. His associates took pride in their exertions, however humble, on his behalf and, by their labors, sought to claim his loyalty; memoirs by Kennedy friends and aides recount the sacrifices—often hardly noticed, the reader suspects—that they happily offered. Sorensen recalled that while he worked for Kennedy, Kennedy "was the only human being who mattered to me." After his marriage broke up, he said, "It was very sad, but I don't regret what I did for Jack Kennedy." Because of Kennedy's severe allergy to dog and cat fur, Caroline's cat was sent to live with Jackie's secretary. She recalled, "Ray and I decided to take the opportunity for a nice, long vacation. We didn't quite succeed— because Tom Kitten died. . . . We rushed right home . . . I never dreamed we would give up a vacation for a cat—but this, of course, was a White House cat!"

Kennedy continued to inspire self-sacrifice, even after his death. When Jackie called Theodore White and invited him to Hyannis Port to talk about how JFK should be remembered, White immediately left to visit her—despite the fact that not only was there a near hurricane over New England but his mother was literally having a heart attack. "If the widow of my friend needed me and my mother needed me, what should I do?" White made his decision, and he called periodically from the road to Hyannis Port to check his mother's condition.

It's not surprising, perhaps, that Kennedy aroused admiration among his close friends and colleagues, especially once he assumed the loyalty-inspiring office of the presidency. But he inspired veneration not only among those close to him but, more remarkably, in journalists, artists, and intellectuals. Skeptical and proud, this group is usually hard to impress.

One reason writers, artists, and scholars respected Kennedy, admittedly, was that he took them seriously and, by lending his cachet to their work, made it seem glamorous and masculine. Adlai Stevenson had been intellectual but ineffectual; Joseph Alsop called Kennedy "Stevenson with balls." Also, this group rarely had the opportunity to bask in presidential glory, and their excitement in being included surely accounts for some of their enthusiasm. But mere self-interested gratitude can't account for their fervor. Ernest Hemingway wrote, "It is a good thing to have a brave man as our President in times as tough as these are for our country and the world." E. B. White wrote Kennedy, "One of the excitements of American citizenship is a man's feeling of identity with his elected President. I never had this feeling hit me so hard as on January 20, 1961." Thornton Wilder said Kennedy had roused "a whole new world of surprised self-respect" in the arts. The swaggering, volatile Norman Mailer became preoccupied with Kennedy and described him as "a true existential hero." Norman Podhoretz, an arrogant and trenchant Kennedy critic, had to admit Kennedy's powerful effect on him: "I was quite taken aback by my reaction to shaking his hand and exchanging a word with him. That was true of several of the people who were there that day."

Even poets mustered to Kennedy's side. Robert Frost, who detested New Deal principles, was a passionate Kennedy supporter. Robert Lowell was invited to the inauguration and wrote a friend,

"With a lot of reservations, I feel like a patriot for the first time in my life. I wrote in the Kennedy guest-book, *Robert Lowell, happy that at long last the Goths have left the White House.*"

It's true that while paying tribute to Kennedy, many of these people also hoped to make a place for themselves in the enchanted circle. But it's also true that their admiration wasn't merely flattery. Kennedy somehow stood for a standard of excellence to which they responded.

What's more, Kennedy was venerated as well by those who knew him only through the mediation of the press. The public devoured articles, books, and photographs on Kennedy and his family. Every aspect of his history, character, family, and circle was celebrated and studied. After his death, the flood of material only increased.

Kennedy inspired surprisingly raw and primitive forms of crowd worship—forms familiar from the adoration of saints and movie stars. People struggled to get near him, and a campaign worker said, "We've never seen people so enthusiastic. People were fighting to get near enough to touch him." Congressman Roman Puchinski noted how often people wanted to kiss Kennedy's hand. Kennedy's barber was deluged with requests for locks of Kennedy's hair, and he admitted he'd taken home one himself. The Kennedys had bookkeeping problems, because people wanted to keep their checks instead of cashing them. Kennedy's image was placed in sacred company. An acquaintance wrote Rose Kennedy to report that almost every Irish cottage displayed a picture of the Sacred Heart, the Blessed Virgin, and President Kennedy. In remote villages in India, his picture was hung beside pictures of Gandhi and Nehru.

People aped his dress and mannerisms. *Time* noted that just twenty-nine months into his term, Kennedy had had far more influence on style and taste than had Eisenhower, Truman, or Roosevelt, and *Esquire* named Kennedy as practically the first fashion-setting president of the twentieth century. In imitation of his habits, cigar sales soared and hat sales fell. Dozens of men in Washington, Manchester noted, "have unconsciously adopted the Kennedy pause, the Kennedy walk, and the Kennedy habit of disciplining a shock of unruly hair—even when they haven't got unruly hair or, for that matter, hair." Kennedy's family was imitated, too. Jackie's style of curved dark sunglasses, pillbox hats, and sleeveless sheaths swept the country. Hostesses copied her dinner parties, and vacationers took up waterskiing. The infant-shoe industry complained because baby John was so often photographed barefoot.

The veneration for Kennedy, worthy of a saint, continued after his death. No one begrudged him the extraordinary pageantry of a funeral modeled after Abraham Lincoln's. An exhibition of Kennedy relics—his rocking chair, golf cart, paintings, letters, the famous coconut shell, and other items—toured the country and Europe. Ted Kennedy's wife Joan observed of the visitors, "It was almost as if they were in church, the way they were hushed and the way they examined each of the objects." Coins, stamps, and medals memorialized Kennedy, and countless roads, schools, bridges, and other facilities were named for him. Long after Kennedy's death, when visiting distant villages in his travels as World Bank president, Robert McNamara would see Kennedy's photograph, torn from a magazine or newspaper, on the wall. Kennedy sites, such as his grave in Arlington National Cemetery, the John F. Kennedy Library and Museum, and the Sixth Floor Museum at Dealey Plaza have attracted millions of visitors. Any object, however mundane, associated with Kennedy is infused with his magic. At auction in 1996, for example, his golf clubs sold for $1.16 million. People will pay extraordinary amounts to own something that belonged to him or Jackie.

But Kennedy's treatment as a kind of saint went beyond pilgrimage, collection of relics, and the offering of sacrifice; after his death, he was even credited with *miracles.*

When the casket team was moving his coffin up the steps into the Capitol, the eight men were "near panic" for fear they'd falter beneath its unexpected weight. Although the undertaker estimated that it couldn't weigh more than five hundred pounds, and although usually six men could easily lift a casket, the men carrying Kennedy's body thought that even an estimate of twelve hundred pounds was absurdly low—and these men had participated in more than a thousand Arlington funerals. They spent the night rehearsing with a sandbag-filled casket, with men sitting on top to add additional weight, until they knew they'd be able to handle Kennedy's coffin without incident the next day. But in the morning, when they picked it up, "The fantastic weight of yesterday was gone. The coffin seemed incredibly light . . . It seemed that way to each of the eight bearers . . . They withdrew in wonder." Jackie asked friend and White House garden designer Bunny Mellon to fix a flower basket from the Rose Garden to send to Arlington. Because of the season, Mellon doubted she'd find many flowers, but she found "to her vast surprise" dozens of white roses blooming in late November. After hearing of Kennedy's death, writer and Kennedy friend Kay Halle cut three roses from her garden. "We brought them in, and I had a picture Jack gave me which I brought down here and I put the roses in front of it. You know that those roses lasted for three solid weeks. Couldn't believe it. Roses don't last."

For some, veneration twisted into resentment when they felt rejected by Kennedy. After Norman Mailer wrote the hyperbolically flattering article "Superman Comes to the Supermarket," to which he credited Kennedy's electoral victory, he took a proprietary attitude toward the presidency. He wanted to ingratiate himself with the Kennedys, to make them his audience, and when he wasn't welcomed in the golden circle, his praise turned to vitriol. In 1963, he described Kennedy: "It is true that we have a President with a face. And it is the face of a potential hero. But he embodies nothing, he personifies nothing, he is power, rather a quizzical power, without light or principle." Jackie's quasi sibling writer Gore Vidal was a Kennedy supporter until a fight with Bobby ended his White House visits and turned him into a caustic critic. Frank Sinatra desperately wanted his Palm Springs compound to become the Western White House. When Kennedy proposed to visit in March 1962, Sinatra installed a communications system, poured a concrete heliport, built cottages for the Secret Service, and even erected a flagpole to fly the presidential flag. But when Bobby insisted that Sinatra's well-publicized Mafia ties made it politically dangerous to be his guest, Kennedy canceled. Sinatra was so enraged that he grabbed a sledgehammer and chopped up the heliport's concrete landing pad. He later became a prominent Republican.

In others, the pervasive veneration for Kennedy fueled the urge to debunk; such unflattering accounts, no less than the admiring accounts, have found a wide audience. The first critical biography, Victor Lasky's 1963 *J.F.K.: The Man and the Myth,* became a national best seller. Many other observers, such as Seymour Hersh and Garry Wills, have sought to demythologize Kennedy. But even as they expose Kennedy's weaknesses, the passion of their criticism only confirms the strength of the larger faith.

Whether by gushing tribute or slashing attack, the attention to Kennedy demonstrates the tremendous impression that he made. Few leaders have so dominated the imagination of both their inner circle and the larger public; Kennedy—with his associations of virtue, power, and elegance—made himself an object of such esteem and affection that veneration for him persists until this day.

21

THE KENNEDY PHOTOGRAPHS
Why Pictures of Kennedy Fascinate

William Hazlitt, Winston Churchill, and others have observed, "Words are the only things that last forever." But photographs last, too. Although they lack the precision of words, they are more concise, more evocative.

Kennedy kept tight control over photographers and their pictures; nevertheless, his efforts can't wholly account for the power of the Kennedy photographs. What makes them so inexhaustibly interesting—even now, decades out of date?

The relentless grip of these photographs must be credited to something more than even the enormous interest generated by the subjects. The attributes of photography, coupled with the matchless history of the Kennedy family, come together to engage the viewer.

The demand for Kennedy photographs is greater than for any other American figure. Jack Kennedy and his circle presented themselves as subjects for a seemingly limitless supply of pictures, for which the public continues to have an insatiable appetite. Each year, volume after volume of slick-paged albums appear.

The fascination with these photographs is due, of course, to their subjects, but in addition, the Kennedy family's history interacts with many of the aspects of photography that give this medium its peculiar power. Density, meditation, familiarity, knowledge in the viewer, and dramatic irony join to give the pictures an unparalleled appeal.

DENSITY

A photograph's density gives it exceptional force. A potent photograph omits everything unimportant; every element contributes to its meaning; its power can't be explained in words. And a photo-

Density: January 1961. At the inaugural ball, a glowing Kennedy points the way.

graph doesn't require the effort of reading or the time to watch a moving image—it can be understood in a glance or studied with interest for hours.

Kennedy surrounded himself with photographers who masterfully shaped the Kennedy images to saturate them with meaning.

MEDITATION

Like the devout who gaze at a crucifix to bring Jesus vividly to mind, viewers pore over Kennedy's photographs as food for their imagination, to invoke his particular charisma. Kennedy is associated with exalted ideals—patriotism, sacrifice, cool, intellect, bravery—and looking at his picture is an exercise to pay tribute to them.

Meditation: January 20, 1961. President Kennedy delivers an inaugural address that exhilarates the country. As always, he is touched by light and less warmly dressed than everyone else, as if he carries his own sun with him.

FAMILIARITY

Another reason for the extraordinary power of the Kennedy photographs is the familiarity of the faces; they leap out at you like those of your own parents. It's most pleasing to look at well-known faces and scenes, and great familiarity with even a stranger's appearance—through photographs or, more effectively, film—creates a feeling of intimacy and curiosity. It's not easy for the public to identify new heroes—it's easier to recycle recognizable names and faces—and even before Kennedy became president, familiarity's pull was already at work, thanks to his father's habitual publicity seeking. Once Kennedy was president, the constant coverage amplified this effect.

Interest in the familiar Kennedy pictures might be expected to pall from overexposure, but surprisingly, they remain engaging. Not every likeness can sustain so much scrutiny; it is part of Kennedy's strange magic that interest in his photographs has never been exhausted.

Familiarity: 1960. Jack, Jackie, and Caroline relax on the lawn in Hyannis Port.

KNOWLEDGE IN THE VIEWER

Not only does the public recognize the faces of the Kennedys, but the public knows a great deal about their lives, and because the public brings more knowledge to the photographs, they find more in them. There is much to look for: tracing family resemblances, interpreting the nuances of posture and placement, criticizing clothes and waistlines, and recalling what happened between photographs.

Kennedy students look at the picture of the Kennedys gathered for Thanksgiving and know that Joe was a compulsive adulterer, that Rose spent a fortune on clothes, that Jack, now eldest son, has replaced his dead brother Joe Jr. as the object of his father's ambi-

Knowledge in the Viewer: 1948. The Kennedys gather for Thanksgiving. Their broad smiles and close embrace, the porch of the white house, their footballs and the Harvard sweater, all seem to illustrate the family's qualities.

tion. The family has grown smaller: Joe is dead, Kick is dead, and the retarded Rosemary, incapacitated by a failed lobotomy, has been exiled to a nursing home. Such knowledge, present in the viewer's mind, adds greatly to the interest of an otherwise unexceptional group picture.

DRAMATIC IRONY

In a related way, such photographs draw from the power of dramatic irony. We know what will happen to the Kennedy family; these photographs from their past are made more poignant by our disruptive glimpses into their future.

How pleased they look! The family is at a moment of extreme triumph. Those pictured know only that Jack has just been elected president; viewers, however, also know that soon Bobby will be named attorney general and Ted will be elected senator, and that later, Jean will be ambassador to Ireland, and Eunice will launch the Special Olympics.

And viewers also know what disasters await: Joe will be incapacitated by a stroke within months; and Jack will be assassinated in 1963, and Bobby, in 1968; and Teddy will be disgraced in 1969 when he drives his car off a bridge at Chappaquiddick. Jackie will shock the world in 1968 by marrying Aristotle Onassis, and she will die in 1994 of non-Hodgkin's lymphoma. Viewers' knowledge even extends past those pictured—to David Kennedy's fatal drug overdose, William Kennedy Smith's trial for rape, Michael Kennedy's death in a skiing accident and the accusations he had an affair with his children's teenage babysitter, and more.

For the same reason, later viewers are moved by the endearing 1963 photograph of two-year-old John holding his father's hand in one hand and a toy helicopter in the other.

Within a few months, Kennedy will be assassinated. John was

Dramatic Irony: 1960. President-elect John Kennedy stands with his family in Hyannis Port. Standing, left to right: *Ethel Kennedy, Steve Smith, Jean Smith, Jack Kennedy, Bobby Kennedy, Pat Lawford, Sargent Shriver, Joan Kennedy, Peter Lawford;* seated in foreground: *Eunice Shriver, Rose Kennedy, Joseph Kennedy, Jackie Kennedy, Ted Kennedy.*

young, but he understood what had happened. When Dave Powers told him, "Davy Crockett had a rifle," John answered, "A bad man shot my daddy in the head with a rifle." Many remarked on John's fascination with airplanes: "John, Jr. wanted to fly everywhere with his father. The President gave him a toy plane and said he would get him a real one when he grew up." Viewers know that the boy who loved airplanes will die in 1999, along with his wife and her sister, when the small plane he is piloting crashes into the ocean.

In these iconic photographs, the Kennedys appear to have their whole lives before them, but these pictures remind viewers of the progress of babies into old age, and of the capriciousness of fate.

August 1963.
President Kennedy walks
with his son, John, at
Hyannis Port.

The photographs will continue to gather power as the passage of time adds to their significance. As long as Kennedy and his family continue their hold over the American imagination, the pictures will only become more rich, more interesting.

22

KENNEDY AS HERO
How He Saw Himself

To understand Kennedy, we must understand his vision of himself as hero—as a courageous, energetic president who carried the American promise of liberty and prosperity to the world. And while we might scoff at his vainglory, there's the inescapable fact that much of the world did *perceive him to be a courageous, energetic president who carried the American promise of liberty and prosperity to the world.*

Kennedy's vision of himself as hero was so compelling that he persuaded the public to share it.

From childhood, Kennedy was enthralled by the idea of the hero— men like Marlborough and the Knights of the Round Table. "Jack had this hero idea of history," Jackie explained. In his twenties, Kennedy's idea of the hero was shaped significantly by two books he admired, each written by a British lord and published within a year of his own *Why England Slept:* John Buchan's *Pilgrim's Way* and David Cecil's *The Young Melbourne.* These books shaped his thinking and provided him with a model for himself.

Pilgrim's Way features character sketches of Buchan's circle; in particular, it celebrates the brilliance of comrades who died in the Great War. The portrait of Raymond Asquith, son of the prime minister, particularly interested Kennedy. He often mentioned Asquith, and Kennedy friend David Ormsby-Gore, later British ambassador to the United States, noted, "Whether Jack realized it or not, I think he paralleled himself after Asquith all the way, I really do." Certainly, Kennedy resembled Asquith, who was described as possessing a "careless good-breeding, an agreeable worldliness," and innumerable gifts, all later ascribed to Kennedy as well: "great beauty of person; the gift of winning speech; a mind that mastered readily whatever it cared to master; poetry and the love of all beautiful things; a magic to draw friends to him; a heart as tender as it was brave." The description continues: "One gift only was withheld . . . length of years."

Another of Kennedy's favorite books was Cecil's *The Young Melbourne,* a biography of William Lamb, Lord Melbourne. Cecil described Melbourne's character in terms that would be used for Kennedy's: "Educated without pedantry, informal but not slipshod, polished but not precious, brilliant without fatigue, it combined in an easy perfection the charms of civilization and nature." In fact, Cecil's description of Melbourne's circle even offers a hint at Kennedy's secret life: "Their circumstances did not encourage the virtues of self-control. Good living gave them zest; wealth gave them opportunity; and they threw themselves into their pleasures with an animal recklessness."

Kennedy's interest in studying heroes would continue. As senator, he wrote a book about heroic senators, and he later developed his ideal of the heroic president. "If this nation is to reassert the initiative in foreign affairs," he announced, "it must be presidential initiative. . . . If we are to regain progressive leadership on our domestic problems, it must be presidential leadership." Kennedy had been frustrated in Congress, where, with little patience for the tedious legislative process and with little regard for his colleagues, he hadn't been an effective member. But the presidency would be different.

Believing that Eisenhower had done little except play golf and cozy up to businessmen, Kennedy didn't expect much difficulty in triumphing as hero-president. If the bland, passive Eisenhower had managed to bring about peace and prosperity, imagine what Kennedy, with all his intellect and vigor, could accomplish. Once in office, however, Kennedy discovered that Eisenhower, like himself, had the gift of making the difficult appear easy. Governing was harder than it looked.

Dazzled by Kennedy's charisma, people expected great achievements. But he'd defeated Nixon by a razor-thin margin; the 1960 election had increased the number of congressional Republicans; and no crisis kindled support for sweeping changes and new programs. Once in executive office, he realized its limits. "When I was a congressman," he said as president, "I never realized how important Congress was. But I do now."

Kennedy was attracted to international affairs, where presidential authority and scope for action were greatest. Domestic issues—civil rights, education, taxes—with their lower stakes, niggling details, and squabbling constituencies, attracted him less. As he said, "Domestic policy can only defeat us; foreign policy can kill us."

In the men he chose for his administration, Kennedy looked for the heroic qualities of cool, toughness, and intellect. "There's nothing like brains," he often said. "You can't beat brains." Kennedy's admiration for "brains" didn't, however, give him a respect for experts. After the Bay of Pigs, he berated himself: "I know better than to listen to experts. . . . All my life I've known it, and yet I still barreled ahead." He expected his aides not to be specialists but brilliant generalists who could excel at any task. Kennedy often assigned a job to whoever happened to be in the Oval Office when a particular issue arose. Even a complete lack of expertise wasn't an obstacle. Without having met Robert McNamara, and despite McNamara's lack of any specific qualifications—besides which, he'd been president of Ford Motor Company for only thirty-four days and was a Republican—Kennedy first offered the forty-four-year-old McNamara the post of Treasury secretary, and when McNamara turned that down, Defense secretary. It was not the qualification, but the quality of the man himself, that counted. Kennedy distrusted bureaucracy and refused to burden himself with organizational charts and multistep processes but instead trusted the swift response of a few outstanding men, in whom experience wasn't as important as brains and "balls." This approach had disadvantages. Although, for example, the Kennedy circle later blamed the military for the Bay of Pigs, an investigation concluded that Kennedy's unsystematic approach largely excluded the military perspective and procedures that would have put plans in writing, established accountability, and exposed the plan's weaknesses.

Kennedy's attraction to heroes helps explain his fascination with the Green Berets, an elite group that epitomized the romance and dash of the Kennedy approach. This special forces group, set apart from regular army troops by name and appearance, specialized in guerrilla warfare and counterinsurgency tactics. Kennedy took a personal interest in their training and equipment—to the point of suggesting that their heavy combat boots be replaced with sneakers, reinforced with steel innersoles. When the Defense Department ordered an end to the wearing of the distinctive green berets, in the belief that visibly elite units undercut morale, Kennedy personally overruled the order. He enlarged their numbers from twenty-five hundred to ten thousand.

Because Kennedy cast himself in the hero's role, he viewed

himself as the central character in any confrontation. When the failure of the Bay of Pigs invasion became undeniable, Bobby—Kennedy's alter ego—said with fury, "We've got to do something! They can't do this to you!" Both Kennedy brothers became preoccupied with striking back at Castro. Kennedy felt personally challenged by Khrushchev and presumed that Khrushchev's foreign policy decisions stemmed from his reading of Kennedy's character. When Khrushchev announced he planned to sign a treaty with East Germany, Kennedy concluded that the action centered on him. "If he thinks I'm inexperienced and have no guts, until we remove those ideas we won't get anywhere with him. So we have to act." When Kennedy learned of the discovery of Soviet missile sites in Cuba, his first response was to say, "He can't do that to me!" In the same way, his advisers viewed the Soviet retreat during the Cuban missile crisis as a triumph for Kennedy the man, who had won a personal contest for world leadership.

Kennedy sought the leader's highest role for himself, and whether or not he deserved to be deemed a hero, he embodied the heroic ideal for much of the public.

23

KENNEDY'S LEGACY

His Purpose

What drove Kennedy? The desire to acquire raw power, to shape the policies of the country, to prove himself to his father, to win the adulation of the public. These played their part in his race toward the presidency, but once he achieved the great office, he had one compelling purpose: to win his place in the pantheon of leaders, beside his hero Churchill and the great presidents.

Kennedy recognized that to secure his place in history, he must direct the historians. Charming the public during life is one thing, when a leader wields the gifts of witty conversation, physical presence, and high office; leaving an admired historical legacy is far more difficult. For this, the evidence of the written record is crucial.

From the first, Kennedy was preoccupied with his legacy as president. Kennedy wasn't content with his popularity among contemporary voters; he cared deeply how he would be measured by historians. On the very night of his election, he wandered around with a paperback copy of *Sayings of Great Presidents*. Arthur Schlesinger Jr. recalled, "Kennedy felt individuals could make a difference for history . . . Churchill and Franklin Roosevelt were examples. He thought he would like to be like that."

Kennedy studied venerated figures from the past. He invited Lincoln expert David Herbert Donald to the White House and asked, "How do you go down in history books as a great president?" He asked Donald whether Lincoln would have been judged a great president if he hadn't been assassinated. Donald later wrote a friend, "His view of history, it is clear, is very largely in personal terms—great men and their influence. This is a man determined to go down in our history books as a great President, and he wants to know the secret."

But of course, it's impossible to anticipate the judgments of the future. Consider that Kennedy's favorability rating hit a very high 83 percent after the Bay of Pigs invasion, which today is considered his greatest failure; it hit its low of 57 percent in October 1963 largely because of his stand on civil rights, which today is considered one of his areas of greatest accomplishment. Events, as they unfold, have a far different significance than they have in history's eyes. Kennedy did all he could to shape his legacy, but it turned out very different from what he imagined, and influenced by factors he couldn't have foreseen.

Kennedy believed the struggle against communism was the great challenge of his time, and the opposition to Khrushchev was the kind of historic confrontation Kennedy relished; his other chief focus was Cuba and his attempts to bring down Castro. Kennedy certainly didn't anticipate the significance his actions in Vietnam would come to have. Schlesinger acknowledged that Kennedy would have recognized Vietnam as his great failure in foreign policy, but, he justified, Kennedy "had never really given it his full attention." Indeed, Kennedy never gave a speech about Vietnam or held a crisis meeting to discuss it.

It wasn't until almost the end of his days as president that Kennedy realized that the battle for civil rights would be a defining issue of his time; he'd discounted the movement as a distraction from the real work of his presidency. But looking back, the public is less interested in Kennedy's clashes with Castro than his clashes with Bull Connor.

The civil rights struggle wasn't the sort that attracted Kennedy. With civil rights, instead of a single, outside foe—a Khrushchev or a Castro—Kennedy had to struggle with homegrown sheriffs and segregationists who had a lot of pull in Congress. The heroes of the domestic battle were not glamorous counterinsurgents fighting in exotic lands but humble people sitting in coffee shops and bus stations. But by the end of his life—which wasn't even at the end of his first term—he'd recognized the importance of the struggle.

As it happened, something wholly out of Kennedy's control—his assassination—contributed most to his legend. His terrible death and magnificent funeral crystallized people's feelings of respect and affection, and the outpouring of grief around the world was extraordinary. His assassination solidified his place in history; because he died, he never had to keep his promises or fulfill the expectations he raised. Now Kennedy's short record is dwarfed by time and by the enormous actions, for good and for ill, of Johnson and Nixon, but instead of being forgotten, Kennedy's brief moment shines the more bright and pure.

But if Kennedy couldn't himself control the nature of his legacy, he could try to influence the people who would help shape it. "Some of us think it wise," Kennedy said, "to associate as much as possible with historians and cultivate their good will." Master of word and image, Kennedy was determined to shape his legacy by directing those who would write his record.

In 1961, Kennedy opened a speech by mentioning Churchill's prediction that history would be kind to his role in World War II, "Because I intend to write it!" Kennedy was determined to imitate his hero. When Sorensen conveyed a writer's request in 1962 for access to the Bay of Pigs files, Kennedy said, "This isn't the time. Besides—we want to tell that story ourselves." But while Churchill shaped history by writing his own accounts, Kennedy shaped history by controlling writers whom he directed, edited, and encouraged.

He'd planned to "write" a memoir of his administration with Sorensen. During the Cuban missile crisis, at one point, he told Sorensen, "I just wanted to make sure you got that down for the book we're going to write."

Kennedy also wooed the men he knew would write independent accounts. He cultivated Theodore White, who was writing a record of the 1960 election, and managed to win over White completely. As president, Kennedy made Pulitzer Prize–winning historian Arthur Schlesinger Jr. a special assistant. Although Schlesinger was unsure about his role—he told a friend he was "unhappy and uncertain concerning his White House assignment. He has a good address but no clear function"—Kennedy knew what *he* wanted from Schlesinger. "I'll write my own official history of the Kennedy administration," Kennedy said. "But Arthur will probably write one of his own, and it will be better for us if he's in the White House, seeing what goes on, instead of reading about us in the *New York Times* and *Time* magazine up in his office."

Kennedy recognized that even records of his table talk could help cement his place in history. As he knew, his friend, journalist Ben Bradlee, made nightly notes of their conversations. "He insisted that he was glad that someone was keeping some kind of a record of the more intimate details without which the real story of any administration cannot be told," recalled Bradlee. Along the same lines, in 1963, Kennedy told Red Fay, the navy buddy he'd appointed to be undersecretary of the navy, "Redhead, you've had an exposure of the Presidency that few people have had. You've got an obligation to write about it." Fay soon began to take notes—not for a history but for a "journal of a friendship" that would "reveal some aspects of the personality" of JFK.

Kennedy's strategy worked: these men, as well as many others, wrote admiring memoirs that burnished Kennedy's reputation. Only a handful of technicians and aides knew about Kennedy's provision for another kind of historical account: in the summer of 1962, Kennedy began secretly tape-recording hundreds of White House telephone conversations and meetings.

But although Kennedy may have expected professional men such as Sorensen, Schlesinger, and Bradlee to memorialize him, it was *Jackie* who, in the end, most brilliantly crafted the Kennedy legacy. With her gift for association, she established the Kennedy administration as "Camelot" in history.

Jackie understood, as she said, that "Jack's life had more to do with myth, magic, legend, saga, and story than with political theory or political science." A week after the assassination, she summoned Theodore White to Hyannis Port to talk about her dead husband; she had something to say to the country, and he was the one to write it. Jackie described how Jack liked to listen to records at night before going to sleep. The lines he loved to hear were: "*Don't let it be forgot, that once there was a spot, for one brief shining moment that was known as Camelot.*" She added, "There'll be great Presidents again . . . but there'll never be another Camelot again." White obediently wrote the famous *Life* piece that introduced the idea of the Kennedy era as Camelot.

The public seized on the symbol. Examined closely, the tragic legend of Camelot doesn't correspond well to the Kennedy story, but in its vague outlines, and with the overtones of the Broadway musical thrown in, "Camelot" suggests gaiety, idealism, a charmed circle of heroes, a world now sunk away.

But Jackie not only found the supreme metaphor to define her husband; she tirelessly guarded his place in history. As much as possible, she controlled the written record. Many memoirists allowed her to read drafts of their work, and she often demanded heavy edits; even in the "Camelot" piece she'd entreated White to write, she insisted on numerous changes. Some writers refused her edits, and she broke with many old friends when their accounts didn't correspond with her heroic vision.

Jackie was guided by a desire for glorification more than for accuracy. After Schlesinger sent her the manuscript of *A Thousand Days* for comments, she objected to his observation that Kennedy had entered the White House more versed in domestic than foreign affairs: according to Jackie, he "knew as much about foreign as domestic affairs & certainly more than any other American President coming into office." According to William Manchester, Ted Sorensen had to give way on numerous points, and weaken his book, to win her approval for his memoir *Kennedy*. Even the most affectionate accounts angered Jackie if the tone wasn't properly elevated. She objected to the "locker room humor" of Red Fay's lighthearted memoir, *The Pleasure of His Company*, and insisted the book would diminish Kennedy's memory. She pressed Fay for major cuts, and when Fay refused most of the edits, Jackie was so angry that she rejected Fay's three-thousand-dollar gift to the Kennedy Library. When Ben Bradlee published *Conversations with Kennedy* in 1975, Jackie was furious at his inclusion of personal details and, in particular, Kennedy's use of profanity; she never spoke to Bradlee again. Jackie tangled with secretary Evelyn Lincoln over *My Twelve Years with John F. Kennedy* and with Maud Shaw over *White House Nanny*, but she fought her most infamous battle with William Manchester, whom she'd enlisted to write the authoritative account of the assassination. She cooperated with Manchester but then demanded hundreds of deletions and eventually went to court to block publication of *The Death of a President*. Ultimately, the book was published with only minor changes, and the incident damaged Jackie's reputation.

Kennedy wanted to be remembered as a great president. Now

his place in history is tended by sentimental hagiographers, who supply readers who can't get enough heartwarming stories or glamorous photos; by dirt-digging tabloidists, who capitalize on the growing supply of salacious Kennedy details; and by historians, whose sober work greatly benefits from the energy and interest generated by the first two forces.

Would Kennedy be happy with his legacy?

It must be admitted that the Kennedy story—with its suspenseful showdowns, movie stars, sexual hijinks, true crime, fashion photos, and relatively light quantity of substantive policy history—is the "beach book" of presidential biographies. And Kennedy, who hated anything corny, is now surrounded by the great cult of Camelot, with its syrupy television tributes and melodramatic memorials.

And yet, somehow—despite revelations of infidelities and policy blunders—the public remembers John F. Kennedy more reverently than almost anyone else. With all his personal limitations, he continues to invoke a sense of optimism and rectitude. Kennedy's place in history is assured by his affirmation of the ideals of personal excellence and good government; he's remembered less for his acts as statesman than for the exalted standard he set. If it's true, as Samuel Butler wrote, that "he is greatest who is most often in men's good thoughts," Kennedy has rightly won the place in history for which he strove.

24

KENNEDY—BEGINNINGS AND ENDINGS

What He Offered

A great leader must offer more than logic; somehow, he or she must provoke emotions that go beyond intellect. For this, imagery and association are more powerful than arguments, however sound.

One reason for Kennedy's electric appeal was his ability to invoke certain ideas—not completely worked out—in people's imaginations. Whether by impulse or deliberation, Kennedy knew how to move the public.

Kennedy had an uncanny ability to tap into the desires and fears of the American people. Part of his genius was his ability to convey contradictory themes, and he invoked both *beginnings* and *endings*, fresh starts and last stands, with their dramatic appeal to the public.

Kennedy awakened feelings of hope and limitless possibility: "Let us begin anew," he proposed. The Eisenhower years, as peaceful and prosperous as they were, had given rise to boredom and complacency. Vice President Nixon was just four years older than

Kennedy, and the two had started in Congress on the same day, but Nixon seemed a generation older, and tied to Eisenhower; Kennedy represented something new. The vote was extremely close, but once Kennedy took office, the public welcomed his dashing style and his young family.

Kennedy identified his administration as "the New Frontier." That phrase—alluding to America's legendary origins, the greatness of the past, and the TV Westerns then so popular—caught people's eagerness to be challenged. Kennedy promised Americans a new beginning in which they would confront the future as tough and productive as ever. They would defend and spread the blessings of democracy. They would relieve world poverty. They would go to the moon.

But at the same time that he offered the allure of beginnings, Kennedy tapped into the apocalyptic longings in the American public. The very prosperity of the time bred a fascination with desperate hours; with his sensationalist talk, Kennedy allowed the public to enjoy this spectacle. He urged the nation to confront vital but obscure crises; he played to people's desire to believe that they, more than anyone in history, lived at the world's most dire hour. In his first State of the Union address, he warned, "Each day, the crises multiply. . . . Each day, we draw nearer the hour of maximum danger, as weapons spread and hostile forces grow stronger." When, in his speech of July 25, 1961, he urged the steps that "every citizen . . . can take without delay to protect his family in case of [nuclear] attack," people eagerly began to stockpile necessities, to build shelters, to buy firearms to protect themselves, and to debate the logistics of chaos and desperation. The public embraced the specter of Armageddon.

Kennedy emphasized that the perilous times demanded "sacrifice," and people welcomed his challenge—especially because Kennedy didn't actually require any heroic sacrifices. When asked exactly what average Americans could do for their country, Kennedy answered, "Restrain their wage demands." With his deep insight into human nature, Kennedy understood the public's appreciation of a play-crisis very well; he told a reporter, "The country rather enjoyed the Cuban quarantine. It was exciting; it was a diversion; and there was the feeling we were doing something. But that was an easy one. They didn't have to go." The threat of the Cold War was terrible and real, and Kennedy rightly feared nuclear war, and so did the country. But there was an element of titillation as well.

What Kennedy could never know was that, in hindsight, he would represent a very different kind of beginning and ending. Kennedy viewed himself as modern, forward-looking, a new kind of leader. In retrospect, his life and death stand instead as an end point.

Kennedy's assassination marks the time, in memory, when the old and new ways split apart. Before, the world seemed simpler and clearer—it wasn't better, but it was more straightforward. The United States and the Soviet Union divided the world; the United States was good, the communists were evil. Black people and white people lived separately. Men went to the office, and women stayed home or worked as secretaries. No one publicly admitted to being homosexual, although people had their suspicions about men such as Lem Billings, Joseph Alsop, Gore Vidal, and J. Edgar Hoover. People drank plenty of liquor and smoked cigarettes or cigars anywhere they liked; aides smoked during meetings in the Oval Office, for example, as did witnesses testifying before Congress, and Jackie smoked throughout her pregnancies.

Even during Kennedy's life, of course, the old simplicity had begun to slip away. By the end of 1962, a traveler could cross the country without seeing "White" and "Negro" signs in waiting rooms. Black people, women, young people—they felt that change was in the air.

Although cultural periods and generations don't really divide neatly, looking back, we detect fault lines. Theodore White explained that it seemed to him, later, that when Kennedy died, the country "passed through an invisible membrane of time which divided one era from another . . . Jacqueline Kennedy's farewell to Camelot was farewell to an America never to be recaptured." The three-year Kennedy presidency now seems its own brief era, a refreshing change from the complacent conformity of the fifties, but before the tumult of the youth decade, with its protests, drugs, strange fashion, and rebellion against traditional roles. Although Kennedy himself embraced social conventions, he helped prepare the way for this upheaval—but he died before the new ways erupted.

25

KENNEDY IN VIETNAM

Two Views

HAD HE LIVED, PRESIDENT KENNEDY WOULD HAVE PULLED THE UNITED STATES OUT OF VIETNAM

Given Kennedy's character—his prudence, his willingness to reconsider his positions, his distrust of the military's promises, and his concern for America's reputation in the Third World—it's inconceivable that, had he lived, he would have taken the same disastrous course in Vietnam as did Lyndon Johnson.

Although politically he couldn't reverse position before the 1964 election, he confided to several people that he intended to do so afterward. John Kenneth Galbraith explains that "just before his death he made clear his intention to bring our involvement in Vietnam to an end. . . . I do not doubt that he would have done it."

The record supports this contention. Not long before his death, in a September 1963 interview with Walter Cronkite, Kennedy observed, "In the final analysis, it is their war. They are the ones who have to win it or lose it." At a press conference on October 31, 1963, he announced a desire to reduce the number of American troops—at that time, 16,200—in Vietnam. After Diem's assassination, in November 1963, Kennedy asked Michael Forrestal, on the National Security Council staff, for a complete review of U.S. involvement in Vietnam: "what we thought we were doing and what we now think we can do . . . I even want to think about whether or not we should be there."

Ever since the Bay of Pigs disaster, he'd been increasingly skeptical of the hawkish advice of his military advisers. As Schlesinger pointed out, "He was a prudent executive, not inclined to heavy investments in lost causes. His whole Presidency was marked precisely by his capacity to *refuse* escalation—as in Laos, the Bay of Pigs, the Berlin Wall, the missile crisis." Clark Clifford argues that Kennedy wouldn't have followed the course later taken by Johnson, with escalation of the ground war and the bombing of North Vietnam; Kennedy, Clifford contends, would have sought either a negotiated settlement or a phased withdrawal.

Given all these factors, it seems certain that Kennedy wouldn't have permitted the United States to be drawn into an open-ended war.

HAD HE LIVED, PRESIDENT KENNEDY WOULD NOT HAVE PULLED THE UNITED STATES OUT OF VIETNAM

Given Kennedy's character—his persistent need to show his toughness, his love of crisis, his firm belief in the "domino theory," and his sensitivity to domestic political risk—it's inconceivable that, had he lived, he would have pulled American troops out of Vietnam without a demonstrable victory.

In a September 1963 interview with Walter Cronkite, Kennedy noted of South Vietnam, "I don't agree with those who say we should withdraw. That would be a great mistake." "We want the war to be won, the Communists to be contained and the Americans to go home. That is our policy. . . . We are not there to see a war lost." In the same month, Kennedy told television news broadcasters Chet Huntley and David Brinkley, "I think we should stay. We should use our influence in as effective a way as we can . . . We should not withdraw."

Kennedy was also acutely aware of domestic political considerations. Just as Johnson (who inherited his advisers from Kennedy) refused to preside over the loss of South Vietnam, Kennedy would have refused as well.

Kennedy excelled at giving people the impression he agreed with them, and it's true he told a few advisers he planned a withdrawal after the 1964 election. But consider the facts. Kennedy expanded the number of American advisers over the Geneva limit (16,200 Americans were in Vietnam when he died, up from 685 when he took office), began covert operations against the North Vietnamese, and escalated his rhetoric so that the public began to see the Vietnamese conflict as vital to American security interests. Secretary of State Dean Rusk insists that at no time did "Kennedy ever say or hint or suggest to me that he was planning to withdraw from Vietnam in 1965." Bobby Kennedy—Kennedy's closest confidant—agreed there had been no talk of withdrawal. In a 1964 oral history, Bobby said, "The President felt there was a strong, overwhelming reason for being in Vietnam and that we should win the war in Vietnam." Kennedy, he said, had concluded that "probably it was worthwhile for psychological, political reasons" to remain. If Kennedy had indeed decided to pull troops out of Vietnam after he'd safely won the 1964 election, his policy meant he'd kept Americans fighting and dying in combat merely to assure his own political victory.

The text of a speech he intended to give in Dallas on November 22, 1963, reflects Kennedy's continued commitment: "Reducing our efforts to train, equip, and assist their armies can only encourage Communist penetration and require in time the increased overseas deployment of American combat forces. . . . Our adversaries have not abandoned their ambitions, our dangers have not diminished, our vigilance cannot be relaxed." Kennedy would not have pulled the United States out of Vietnam without a victory.

26

EYEWITNESS TO KENNEDY
What We See

It shouldn't be true, but it is true: a picture is worth a thousand words. And it shouldn't be true, but it is true: seeing is believing.

July 1953.
Jack and Jackie Kennedy
relax at the Kennedy
summer house.

1960. Supporters surround John Kennedy during his presidential campaign tour.

1960. John Kennedy has a moment of reflection during the presidential campaign.

November 1960.
President-elect Kennedy
holds his daughter on the
morning he learns he's
won the presidency.

1961. President Kennedy and Mrs. Kennedy return to the White House.

*1961. President Kennedy talks on the telephone
in the Oval Office.*

27

KENNEDY IN CRISIS
How He Shaped His Image

"Great crises make great men," Kennedy observed in his book
Profiles in Courage. *As president, he applied this insight to
himself. He exploited crises to bolster his political authority and to
kindle an excitement and intensity that kept the country rallied
behind him.*

As president, Kennedy was preoccupied with securing his name in
the roster of great American leaders. Looking at his models of Lincoln, Roosevelt, and Churchill, it seemed to him that to be great,
a president must preside during a time of war. Kennedy didn't have
his war, but he was determined to build his name in history by
meeting great crises—and because he went looking for them, he
found them, when a more disinterested leader might not have.

Kennedy started this approach during the campaign. To contrast with Eisenhower's calm leadership style, Kennedy painted a
picture of a nation asleep while the world hovered near disaster. He
swore he was the man to "get the country moving again," and he

emphasized "the danger of the hour." But was this true? The economy was in something of a recession, but America was more prosperous than ever. While tensions lurked on the foreign scene, no threat seemed menacing. Kennedy charged Eisenhower with neglect of nuclear defenses and urged that the United States must close the "missile gap," even though, as Kennedy knew from his briefings by national security experts, no gap existed. Nevertheless, Kennedy made the missile gap a major campaign issue, and a Gallup poll showed that he'd convinced the public. By a 47 to 33 percent margin, the public believed Kennedy, not Eisenhower. (Three weeks into the job, Defense Secretary Robert McNamara showed remarkable political naïveté by confessing that Eisenhower was indeed right—there was no missile gap.)

Once in office, Kennedy again used high rhetoric to overstate the dangers facing the country. In his first State of the Union address, he announced, "Before my term has ended, we shall have to test anew whether a nation organized and governed such as ours can endure. The outcome is by no means certain." Kennedy used lofty goals and exaggerated dangers to build excitement that distracted attention from his lack of legislative success. For example, three key episodes in Kennedy's term are, in significant measure, self-inflicted and inflated crises.

Because he'd repeatedly attacked Eisenhower for failing to confront Cuba, President Kennedy felt pressure to act. He treated Castro as if he were a real threat to U.S. security, when in fact, as Senator J. William Fulbright, chairman of the Senate Foreign Relations Committee, would write him, "The Castro regime is a thorn in the flesh; but it is not a dagger in the heart."

After Kennedy won the election, Eisenhower informed him of a CIA-inspired plan to train a group of Cuban exiles for possible use against Castro and urged Kennedy to support them. As a candidate, Kennedy had enjoyed the luxury of being able to urge action without acountability. That Eisenhower himself might now enjoy making free with advice didn't occur to Kennedy. However, given Eisenhower's general record of nonintervention, and particularly his refusal to order a Cuba invasion before the election, despite the urgings of Vice President Nixon, who would have benefited at the polls, it seems very unlikely—despite his vague exhortations—that Eisenhower himself would have ordered an invasion. He certainly never *approved* an invasion plan.

A blow to Castro appealed to Kennedy, and after much discussion, he approved a plan to send fourteen hundred U.S.-trained Cuban exiles on a nighttime amphibious invasion, with a landing at the Bay of Pigs. The plan assumed that the United States wouldn't be held accountable, because the invasion force was Cuban; that the invasion would spark a mass uprising by the Cuban people—the only way the plan could succeed, because the invading force wasn't large enough to defeat Cuban armed forces; and that if all else failed, the invaders could melt into the mountains. The Kennedy style was to be audacious, to seek crisis—and if cautious Eisenhower backed this initiative, Kennedy could hardly demur. Also, Kennedy realized, cancellation would mean disbanding the exile army, who would have publicized the fact that Kennedy had refused to let them fight.

Kennedy approved the invasion but explicitly ruled out direct U.S. military intervention and, finding the plan "too spectacular," modified it to try to disguise the American role. He continued to tinker with the plan until the day before the invasion.

The operation was doomed. "Everybody wanted to show they were just as daring and just as bold as anyone else," journalist Hugh Sidey explained. "They didn't look at it close enough." But as Dean Acheson observed, it wasn't "necessary to call in Price, Waterhouse to discover that 1,500 Cubans weren't as good as 25,000 Cubans." Castro had fairly well-equipped forces of 200,000 men. Also, although security in Washington kept many knowledgeable officials from challenging the plan, it was an open secret. Several newspapers, including the *New York Times,* had reported on the invasion plans. If the U.N. ambassador, Adlai Stevenson, didn't know about it, Castro certainly did. And it was implausible to pretend that the United States had no role in an invasion force of that size.

The operation began on April 17, 1961, and ended two days later in defeat. The invading force was far too small to take on Castro's forces. The Cuban people had little stomach for an uprising, and anyhow, Castro had had enough notice to round up any possible participants—he ordered the arrest of as many as 100,000—and to ready his forces. While the original plan had called for a landing near mountains to which the invaders could escape, when Kennedy ordered a less conspicuous scheme, the landing was moved to the Bay of Pigs, where the invaders were trapped by swamps. Of the 1,400 men who landed, 114 died and nearly 1,200 were captured.

Why did Kennedy approve the operation? The only possible hope for success depended on American military intervention, and Kennedy had emphasized repeatedly that he wouldn't order it. Indeed, the plan was so obviously flawed that some speculate that Kennedy must have known about the CIA's plan to use the Mafia to assassinate Castro and therefore expected that Castro would be dead by invasion day. In any event, Kennedy's love for crisis and confrontation had led him to make a serious, and obvious, mistake.

On October 16, 1962, Kennedy learned that the Soviets had put missile sites in Cuba, and for the next several days, he and his advisers deliberated in secret about the proper course of action. On October 22, Kennedy addressed the nation about the threat and his response: he ordered a naval "quarantine" stopping offensive weapons headed to Cuba and demanded that the missiles be withdrawn. By delivering a dramatic public ultimatum with a tight deadline, without first using diplomatic channels, Kennedy put unnecessary pressure on Khrushchev—pressure that carried with it the risk of nuclear war. His direful speech was calculated to create shock and alarm, and it misled the public on key points.

Kennedy described the Soviet action as "a deliberately provocative and unjustifiable change in the status quo." He hid his own responsibility in triggering the crisis, however. Since the Bay of Pigs debacle, the CIA had stepped up its efforts to topple Castro—and although Americans didn't know about these actions, Castro and Khrushchev did. Believing that a U.S. invasion of Cuba was imminent, Khrushchev decided to place missiles in Cuba to deter an American invasion and also, by adding to the Soviet threat to the United States and deterring any U.S. first strike, to enhance his nation's position in the Cold War.

Furthermore, although Kennedy described the Soviet buildup in terrifying terms, he actually held a different view. He agreed with the memo that argued, "It is generally agreed that these missiles . . . do not significantly alter the balance of power—i.e., they do not significantly increase the potential megatonnage capable of being unleashed on American soil, even after a surprise American nuclear strike." When National Security Adviser McGeorge Bundy asked, "What is the strategic impact on the position of the United States of MRBMs [medium-range ballistic missiles] in Cuba? How gravely does this change the strategic balance?" Defense Secretary McNamara answered, "*Not at all.*" The missiles did enhance the Soviets' meager first-strike capacity, because the missiles from Cuba could reach the United States faster and more precisely, and by placing missiles in Cuba, Khrushchev was trying to ensure that neither side would have an incentive to attack first. Nevertheless, the overwhelming strategic advantage remained with the United States. McNamara said, "I'll be quite frank. I don't think there is a military problem here. . . . This is a domestic political problem."

Whatever the actual strategic consequences, for domestic and foreign political reasons, Kennedy couldn't permit the missiles to stay in Cuba, where they'd been introduced in secret, contrary to stated American interests. To rally the public behind him, Kennedy chose, however, to terrify them. The day after his speech, the stock market plunged, people in Florida rushed to buy rifles and shotguns, and in Los Angeles, people packed grocery stores after officials announced that stores would close for five days if war broke out.

After several days of negotiations and suspense, and a pledge by the United States not to invade Cuba, the Soviets agreed to dismantle the missile bases. For Kennedy, it was a public triumph. "It was this combination of toughness and restraint, or will, nerve and wisdom," Schlesinger wrote, "so brilliantly controlled, so matchlessly calibrated, that dazzled the world." Only a handful of advisers knew the truth: Kennedy had secretly agreed to Khrushchev's demand that the United States remove its missiles in Turkey, on the Soviet border.

Kennedy misled the public by failing to explain why the Soviets felt provoked; he contrived the situation unnecessarily to the brink of nuclear war; he whipped the public into panic by exaggerating the actual danger; then miraculously saved the world with his seeming firmness—while keeping secret his actual compromise. Had the trade been known, it would have dimmed his glory for having faced down Khrushchev. Even Kennedy loyalist Ted Sorensen admitted later that the Cuban missile crisis represented an "unwise, unwarranted, and unnecessary" showdown. It's true that the missiles would have had an important impact in *appearing* to change the balance of power, but Kennedy was willing to gamble everything for that. The public would have been in an uproar if the missiles had remained in Cuba. But it was Kennedy, in large part, who had inflamed public opinion. It was he who, as a candidate in 1960, had made such a huge issue out of Cuba and the communist presence so close to the United States; as president, he couldn't permit his opponents to turn the issue against him.

Domestically, too, Kennedy sought crisis and personal confrontation. In the steel crisis, he went head-to-head with big business.

Because of the economic impact of steel prices on inflation, in 1962, the Kennedy administration helped negotiate a contract between labor and management that held down wage increases. A few days after the contract had been signed, however, U.S. Steel chairman Roger Blough announced a price hike.

Kennedy had reason to be furious. If the steel industry prevailed, he would look weak, and organized labor felt betrayed. But Kennedy and his administration reacted to the crisis by taking extreme measures that pushed acceptable boundaries. Kennedy denounced the steel companies at a press conference: "Some time ago I asked each American to consider what he would do for his country and I asked the steel companies. In the last 24 hours we had their answer." Bobby sent FBI agents to seize documents from steel company executives and to call journalists in the middle of the night to question them about statements by steel officials; the Defense Department began to move contracts to companies that hadn't raised prices; and the Justice Department's antitrust division and the Federal Trade Commission began investigations. Kennedy said, "Do you know what you're doing when you start bucking the power of the President . . . ? I don't think U.S. Steel . . . wants to have Internal Revenue agents checking all the expense accounts of their top executives. . . . Too many hotel bills and night club expenses would be hard to get by the weekly wives' bridge group. . . ." "It was a tough way to operate," Bobby admitted, "but under the circumstances, we couldn't afford to lose." After a week, the industry backed down.

Kennedy's actions shocked the business community. Although this group had always been cool to Kennedy, his overreaching earned their permanent distrust. Soon after the confrontation, the stock market plummeted, and many viewed Kennedy's dramatic measures against steel as one factor. What's more, when the steel companies raised prices a year later, Kennedy didn't object, which suggests Kennedy was more concerned with his reputation than with the actual economic effect of a steel price hike.

With these and other episodes, Kennedy sought to build an image of himself as the tough president capable of courageous action. In truth, however, he had little stomach for real conflict—say, with southern Democrats, over civil rights issues—or for politically daring actions or innovative proposals. He refused fights he thought he might lose. One friend remarked, "Jack was attracted to a mythic persona. He liked the idea of being a streamlined version of FDR. The only problem was that with Roosevelt the reputation had been the result of some fairly bold acts. Jack would have liked to be seen in those heroic terms, but he was basically very cautious in his approach to the presidency." Although Kennedy's embrace of crisis seemed to show his cool and determination in the face of great challenge, it was a posture he adopted to engage the public, not an actual approach to governing.

28

KENNEDY'S PROMISCUITY
His Most Explosive Secret

During Kennedy's life, his integrity, candor, and loyalty to his family seemed plainly in evidence. Considering what we now know to be true shows how easily image can mislead.

His promiscuity seems to undercut everything that made Kennedy Kennedy. That behavior shouldn't be disregarded, however, because it sheds light on other important aspects of his character: his irresistibly attractive personality, his assumption that he was entitled to whatever he wanted, his competition with other men, his refusal to allow ill health to interfere with his activities.

Kennedy, we now know, was wildly promiscuous. Although the presidency made conquests easier, his behavior didn't depend on the prestige of high office; he had dozens of girlfriends as a youth and was involved in a serious sex scandal by age twenty-four. Actor Robert Stack recalled, "I've known many of the great Hollywood stars and only a very few of them seemed to hold the attention for women that JFK did, even before he entered the political arena."

Marina Sulzberger described Kennedy as "the sexiest and most irresistible man on earth . . . I would have given my right hand to seduce him. . . . Just to listen to him talk is irresistible."

Kennedy's father realized that JFK's longtime habits could threaten his political career. In 1957, when Lem Billings made a joke about Kennedy's sexual adventures, Joe glared at him: "You're not to speak like that any more. There are things that you just can't bring up any more, private things." But as noted by Adlai Stevenson during the 1960 campaign, Kennedy's habits were no secret: "Much too much talk about Jack's girls."

Kennedy had intended to change his ways if elected. He wrote notes during the campaign to save his strained voice and, in one, wrote, "I suppose if I win, my poon days are over." He told a friend, "I'm going to keep the White House white." But, as it turned out, attaining the White House didn't put a damper on his activities. The Duke of Devonshire said, "Kennedy is doing for sex what Eisenhower did for golf," and Clare Boothe Luce referred to Camelot as "came-a-lot." By apt chance, Kennedy's Secret Service name was *Lancer*. George Smathers recalled, "There's no question about the fact that Jack had the most active libido of any man I've ever known. He was really unbelievable—absolutely incredible in that regard, and he got more so the longer he was married."

Some observers have wondered why Kennedy wasn't able to stop his reckless activities—but there's no evidence Kennedy *tried* to stop. He seemed to have no fear of exposure or consequences. Lawyer Clark Clifford, called in to handle "delicate" incidents, said that Kennedy "was bold beyond human belief, *impossibly bold,* unbelievably bold and what the attitude of the family was, I do not know." (Would Kennedy's conduct be more or less deplorable if he'd tried, but failed, to resist, instead of proceeding without a qualm? In other words, is it worse to be a weak, guilty-minded cad or a bold, indifferent cad?)

Kennedy had seen his father and many prominent politicians

get away with this kind of behavior for decades, and he believed, rightly, that his opponents, his staff, his wife, and the press wouldn't interfere. Press secretary Pierre Salinger was confronted by only one reporter about Kennedy's affairs, and Salinger answered, "Listen, this man is the president of the United States. . . . If he does that all day long and still has time to have a mistress, what the hell difference does it make?" The reporter laughed and dropped the issue. This protective silence infuriated Kennedy's opposition. Pat Nixon said pointedly, "I knew Kennedy too well to think that the country would elect him."

Kennedy also openly indulged in sexually charged behavior. A stewardess on the Kennedy private plane, the *Caroline,* explained, "One of my functions as stewardess, which could not have pleased Jackie very much, were the neck and shoulder massages I gave JFK every day." Kennedy had a succession of secretaries trained to give him scalp massages, and McGeorge Bundy recalled walking into the office: "He was having one of his pretty girls rubbing some goo on his hair. . . . I said I didn't think this kind of thing was sufficiently dignified for the Oval Office."

Kennedy, obviously, never expected the public to learn about his sexual adventures;★ does the public, in fact, have any business

---

★29

KENNEDY'S EXPLOITS
Suppressed Facts Exposed

While Kennedy lived, custom protected his intimate secrets from exposure—but no longer. Many consider these raw details to be an illegitimate subject for discussion, and they argue that this aspect of Kennedy's life should not be examined at the same level as other aspects. Nevertheless, whether or not it is appropriate for people to pry into the private details of a prominent figure's life, they do eagerly search out these suppressed facts.

Kennedy trusted that his sexual exploits would remain hidden; certainly, he could never have imagined what intimate details would emerge. Now the public knows a great deal.

pressing for information? After all, Kennedy was a statesman. Should he be judged by his public acts alone?

Kennedy's defenders maintain that his sex life had no relevance to his ability to govern. Harris Wofford argues, "History shows no clear correlation between the private life of a leader and the ability to lead." Schlesinger agrees: "Martin Luther King, Jr., for example, had wayward sexual habits but was all the same a tremendous moral force. . . . Pol Pot of Cambodia was apparently a faithful family man." Elsewhere, Schlesinger made the point that "as one who worked at the White House throughout the Kennedy years, I can testify that if anything untoward happened at all, it did not interfere with Kennedy's conduct of the Presidency." Ben Bradlee acknowledges that Kennedy's promiscuity is "interesting," but, he adds, "it is hardly disqualifying."

Even Kennedy's defenders must admit, however, that Kennedy made the case that his character qualified him to be president. During the 1960 campaign, Kennedy emphasized that the next president "must set the moral tone, and I refer not to his language but to his actions in office. . . . For the Presidency . . . is preeminently a place of moral leadership, and I intend to restore that kind of leadership." In addition to emphasizing his heroism, intellect, and

---

People know, for example, about Kennedy's no-nonsense approach to sex. Inga Arvad told her son, "If he wanted to make love, you'd make love—now. They'd have fifteen minutes to get to a party and she'd say she didn't want to. He'd look at his watch and say we've got ten minutes, let's go." Marilyn Monroe told a reporter that Kennedy was too busy to indulge in foreplay. Secret Service logs for the March 8, 1963, White House dinner dance show that at 1:30 a.m., Kennedy spent eighteen minutes with a female guest in the pool area and, at 2:40 a.m., returned there with another female guest for twelve minutes.

The public has learned about Kennedy's preferences. One JFK girlfriend from 1940 reported, "Because of his back he preferred making love with the girl on top. He found it more stimulating to have the girl do all the work." Judith Exner came to resent this attitude. "Slowly I began to feel that he expected me to

disciplined temperament, Kennedy deluged the public with evidence of his idyllic home life.

Americans expect, perhaps unreasonably, that the president should be a moral leader. Kennedy's extraordinary popularity and his political power would have been destroyed had his lack of common moral scruples been known. Whether or not it's right that the public *should* judge him for his sexual behavior, they certainly *would,* as Kennedy understood very well. He was the one, after all, who tried to stop Jackie and Defense Secretary Robert McNamara from dancing the Twist at a White House party, for fear the image of Jackie gyrating in the White House would offend the public. The mere fact that he'd had adulterous sex would have had enormous political consequences—let alone that he'd had sex with a prostitute in a room off the Oval Office or in the Lincoln Bedroom with a young aide, or had group sex in the White House swimming pool, or brought an intern along on presidential travels for sex. Thus, his behavior put his career and reputation at extraordinary risk.

His activities were no secret. Jackie knew. "Jack kept assuring us that she didn't suspect," Jim Reed said, "when it was obvious that she knew exactly what was happening." While giving a jour-

---

come into bed and just perform," she recalled of his penchant for that position, and "the feeling that I was there to service him began to really trouble me."

The public has learned of Kennedy's taste for unconventional groupings. Joan Lundberg Hitchcock, a Kennedy mistress in the late 1950s, observed, "He loved threesomes—himself and two girls. He was also a voyeur." Kennedy and Torbert Macdonald sometimes caroused with the same woman in a ménage à trois. As senator, Kennedy and fellow senator George Smathers would meet women at a secret apartment on the Potomac. Smathers recalled, "Jack liked to go over there and meet a couple of young secretaries. He liked groups." Kennedy often used the White House swimming pool for skinny-dipping and group sex. Ellen Rometsch reported that at one party, the pool held five men and twelve girls.

nalist a White House tour, Jackie spotted two young female aides and explained, "Those two are my husband's lovers." Seeing one woman in a receiving line, Jackie said to Dave Powers and Kennedy's military aide, "Isn't it bad enough that you solicit this woman for my husband, but then you insult me by asking me to shake her hand!"

Secret Service agents, the White House staff, and many aides knew about Kennedy's escapades. Larry Newman, a Secret Service agent assigned to Kennedy's detail, explained, "You were on the most elite assignment in the Secret Service, and you were there watching an elevator or a door because the president was inside with two hookers." Kennedy didn't try very hard to hide his activities. One afternoon, Kennedy was in the Lincoln Bedroom when he answered a knock to find two top foreign affairs advisers with secret cables for him. Kennedy didn't bother to close the door, so the men could clearly see the woman on the bed as they waited for him to read the dispatches. High-priced New York prostitute Leslie Devereux recalled, "I visited him twice at the White House, the first time for only fifteen minutes in a small room off the Oval Office. His secretaries didn't so much as blink when they saw me."

People in Washington, Manhattan, Hollywood, and Europe

Kennedy added several sex partners to the government payroll. He insisted his twenty-three-year-old lover Pamela Turnure be made Jackie's press secretary, despite her youth and lack of experience. Kennedy placed another longtime lover, Diana de Vegh, on the staff of National Security Adviser McGeorge Bundy. That affair had begun in 1958, when she was a twenty-year-old Radcliffe junior. Kennedy put de Vegh at the National Security Council as a dig at Bundy, who, as a Harvard dean, had told Kennedy to end their relationship; placing her on Bundy's staff, explained NSC aide Mark Raskin, was "a way to get even." Other staffers were known to be sleeping with the president. Twenty-year-old White House secretaries Priscilla Wear, "Fiddle," and Jill Cowan, "Faddle," made frequent skinny-dipping trips to the swimming pool with Kennedy. When Fiddle told Kennedy she was considering taking stenography and typing, he laughed:

knew. After Bobby Baker came back from the Oval Office, Johnson asked, "Is ol' Jack gettin' much pussy?" French ambassador Hervé Alphand observed in his diary that the president's "desires are difficult to satisfy without raising fears of scandal and its use by his political enemies. This might happen one day, because he does not take sufficient precautions in this Puritan country." British prime minister Harold Macmillan, Douglas Dillon, McGeorge Bundy, Robert McNamara—they all knew.

And journalists knew. At Palm Beach in June 1961, Kennedy invited *Time*'s Hugh Sidey to join him for dinner. Aides "Fiddle" and "Faddle" were also there, and afterward, Sidey offered the two women a ride but then realized they weren't leaving: "It was reckless of [Kennedy], but he called it right. He knew I wasn't going to write about it." Reporter Maxine Cheshire recalled that at Hyannis Port after the election, she stood in the hallway talking to a well-known female journalist. Then, she recalled, "The President-elect suddenly appeared, took her by the hand, and, laughing, led her into a clothes closet and shut the door. . . . After a while they reemerged, all flushed and smirking."

Despite defenders' claims that Kennedy's adventures didn't influence his actions as president, they clearly did. Kennedy's decision to retain J. Edgar Hoover as FBI head astonished his supporters, as

---

"Why? Are you starting to get ambitious?" Marion "Mimi" Beardsley came to the White House as a nineteen-year-old intern and began an affair with Kennedy in June 1962. "She wasn't in the office very long before the press began to ask why she was there," recalled press aide Barbara Gamarekian. "Mimi had no skills."

Kennedy was sexually competitive: "Once I get a woman, I'm not interested in carrying on, for the most part. I like the conquest." Kenneth Tynan's diary records Marlene Dietrich's story of a White House tryst. Dietrich, then sixty-one, didn't have much time, so they skipped the preliminaries. Afterward, Kennedy asked, "Did you ever make it with my father?" When Dietrich said she hadn't, Kennedy responded, "Well, that's one place I'm in first." Not only did Kennedy have a longtime affair with Mary Meyer, his close friend Ben Bradlee's sister-in-law, he also made several unsuccessful passes at Tony Bradlee, Ben's wife and

did his appointment of Bobby as attorney general. But Hoover had too much evidence about Kennedy's womanizing to risk alienating him, and with Bobby as attorney general, the FBI would be firmly under Kennedy control. Hoover had information on Kennedy back to the wartime affair with suspected Nazi spy Inga Arvad, and he periodically sent memos to Bobby to remind him of the licentious secrets that crammed the FBI's ever-growing files—the first arrived just a few weeks after Kennedy's inauguration, and more would arrive every few months. In October 1963, the fact that Hoover had incriminating files on Kennedy likely helped pressure Bobby to authorize Hoover to use telephone wiretaps to investigate Martin Luther King Jr.—supposedly to determine whether King had communist ties but in reality to investigate his sex life. And Hoover wasn't the only danger. Kennedy's promiscuity could give any group—the radical Right, anti-Castro Cubans, the Soviets, the Republicans, the Mafia, or Marilyn Monroe—an explosive weapon.

The president's sexual activity affected government actions at important moments. Hugh Sidey sent a confidential memo to his editors about the administration's libertinism. Sidey noted that this atmosphere made his job difficult, because, at times, he couldn't reach government spokesmen, who were socially involved. Bobby

---

Mary's sister. "Jack was always so complimentary to me, putting his hands around my waist. I thought, 'Hmmmm, he likes me.' I think it surprised him I would not succumb." During the 1963 cruise to celebrate Kennedy's forty-sixth birthday, Tony Bradlee recalled, "He chased me all around the boat . . . and made a pass. It was a pretty strenuous attack, not as if he pushed me down, but his hands wandered."

Kennedy often boasted about his appetite. Bobby Baker recalled, "Kennedy seemed to relish sharing the details of his conquests; though he was not without charm or wit in relating the clinical complexities, he came off as something of the boyish braggart." One of his lovers observed, "Jack really wasn't comfortable unless Torby Macdonald or some other male friend was around to make macho jokes with. . . . He was nice. . . . But he gave off light instead of heat." He repeatedly

somehow got a copy of the memo and, shaking with rage, told Sidey, "We could sue you for slander." "I didn't make this up," Sidey responded, saying the situation was "disgusting" and "I don't think that this is the way the government should be run, or the way you people should encourage it to be run." (For all his criticism, Sidey served as an usher at the church service for Kennedy's funeral.) Newman recalled a military aide bringing a cable from the Situation Room for Kennedy's immediate attention. Kennedy was in the swimming pool area with the door shut. Newman told the aide, "Take your best shot if you want to go in," but despite the message's urgency, the aide decided to wait until Kennedy eventually appeared.

On the night of Monday, October 15, 1962, the CIA informed National Security Adviser McGeorge Bundy of a momentous discovery: photographs taken by U-2 flights had revealed Soviet ballistic missile launch sites in Cuba, which meant, Bundy knew, the terrifying possibility of nuclear war. Despite the enormity of the discovery, Bundy took it upon himself to keep the president in ignorance overnight. "I decided," he explained later, "that a quiet evening and a night of sleep were the best preparation." Kennedy did need sleep—in fact, he'd been so tired that that very morning, Monday, he'd arrived at the Oval Office three hours after

---

confided to people that he needed frequent sex: he told Clare Booth Luce, "I can't go to sleep without a lay," and told Harold Macmillan, "If I don't have a woman for three days I get a terrible headache."

There is no comprehensive list of Kennedy's sexual partners, but it includes grave security risks (Inga Arvad, Judith Campbell, Ellen Rometsch); actresses (Marilyn Monroe, Jayne Mansfield, Gene Tierney); socialites (Mary Meyer, Florence Pritchett, Marella Agnelli), and strippers (Blaze Starr, Tempest Storm).

Just as Kennedy's circle adopted his cool mannerisms and tough talk, they sought to ape his sexual habits. A mark of the chosen and superior is the ability to defy limits, and that Kennedy got the girls along with the devoted wife and shining reputation merely added an element of dangerous glamour to his image. "We're a bunch of virgins, married virgins," aide Fred Dutton said, "and he's like

2 GR2 GRETCHEN RUBIN

his usual time. He was tired partly from campaigning and partly because the night before, Sunday, October 14, he'd made an unexpected stop in New York City. There, he'd had a late night at the Kennedy penthouse in New York's Carlyle Hotel with one of his favorite playboy companions, Torbert Macdonald. Because he knew his boss was tired, Bundy waited until the morning of October 16 to tell Kennedy the vital news.

But even the pressures of the Cuban missile crisis didn't distract Kennedy from planning his next conquest. When an attractive secretary appeared in the Oval Office during that tense time, Kennedy asked Defense Secretary McNamara, "Who's that?" "She's filling in today," McNamara answered. "Bob," said Kennedy, "I want her name and her number. We may avoid war here tonight."

British prime minister Harold Macmillan was a great friend and admirer of Kennedy's, but he was very disappointed that they achieved only a *partial* test ban in 1963. Looking back during the 1980s, he accused Kennedy of missing the opportunity to achieve more, because he was "weakened by constantly having all those girls, every day. . . . I think this is a great opportunity that we missed, and I do blame Kennedy's weakness." He criticized the president for "spending half his time thinking about adultery, the other half about second-hand ideas passed on by his advisers."

Beyond the political risks, Kennedy placed himself at physical risk. The presidency is a unique role, and Kennedy had a duty to guard his safety. Kennedy's procurer-friends prevented the Secret Service from doing even a quick check of the women brought in

---

a God, fucking anybody he wants to anytime he feels like it." At a Hawaii campaign stop, Kennedy complained when some staffers didn't appear at a morning meeting. When an aide explained they'd met young women, Kennedy replied, "I brought them here to hunt delegates, not to hump hula girls!" Often, however, his aides' wives proved less tolerant of this behavior than Jackie, and many marriages broke up. Dutton, Jim Reed, Pierre Salinger, Arthur Schlesinger, Ted Sorensen, and Chuck Spalding split from their wives.

for sex: agents weren't allowed to look in their purses, which could have held listening devices, poison, weapons, or cameras, and their names weren't properly recorded. Women smuggled in to see Kennedy were often logged in as "David Powers Plus One Female" or "Kenny O'Donnell Plus One." Newman recalled, "We didn't know who these people were and we didn't know what they had on their person. You would just look up and see Dave Powers mincing down the hall and saying, 'Hi pal,' and we had no way to stop it."

Kennedy's Secret Service men admired him and were concerned by the threats to his safety. However, they traced the sloppiness to Kennedy himself. "You'd have to say it starts at the top and works its way down," explained Newman. "It caused a lot of morale problems. . . . We often joked . . . we couldn't even protect the president from getting a venereal disease."

Furthermore, not only did Kennedy's sexual adventures expose him to blackmail, injury, and death, they also embroiled him in potential scandals.

In February 1960, Frank Sinatra introduced his former girlfriend Judith Campbell to Kennedy. The two started an affair and, among other places, met for sex at Kennedy's Georgetown house, when a pregnant Jackie was out of town, and later, at the White House. They spoke dozens of times by phone.

This situation was lurid enough. What's more, Campbell was also sleeping with notorious Chicago mobster Sam Giancana as well as Giancana's associate John Roselli. (In fact, several times Campbell called the White House from Giancana's house.) Reporters might have laughed off Kennedy's womanizing, but they couldn't have ignored a story like that. And not only was Kennedy linked through Campbell to the Mob—at the very time that his Justice Department was zealously prosecuting organized crime—the CIA had recruited Giancana and Roselli in 1960 to join a secret plot to assassinate Castro.

Hoover learned about the relationship and, on March 22, 1962, informed Kennedy that the FBI knew about his affair with Campbell as well as hers with Giancana and Roselli. Kennedy and Campbell's last known phone call took place that afternoon. Hoover's warning, however, did nothing to discourage Kennedy's usual habits. Kennedy spent that weekend at Bing Crosby's Palm Springs house, where, in front of several witnesses, he carried on with Marilyn Monroe.

Although explosive, the Campbell story stayed hidden until 1975. During the last year of Kennedy's life, however, other secrets came closer to bursting into the open.

Scandal hit the British government when war minister John Profumo resigned because of his affair with Christine Keeler, a twenty-one-year-old prostitute who was also intimate with a Soviet military attaché.

The Profumo affair fascinated Kennedy, and he seemed to see no similarity to his own situation—even though he had been tied to its players. On June 29, 1963, the *New York Journal-American* reported, "One of the biggest names in American politics—a man who holds 'a very high' elective office—has been injected into Britain's vice-security scandal." Two days later, Bobby Kennedy summoned the reporters, James Horan and Dom Frasca, to his office; they told him that the story referred to JFK and that evidence showed he'd had affairs in 1960 and 1961 with "party girls" Maria Novotny and Suzy Chang, a friend of Christine Keeler. Bobby threatened to bring an antitrust suit against the *New York Journal-American* unless reporting on the scandal halted, and the paper let the matter drop. The day after he met with the reporters, Bobby asked Hoover about the allegations. The FBI had no convincing evidence that Kennedy had been involved with the two women, but the potential for scandal was huge. And where was Kennedy when Bobby was meeting with Horan and Frasca? At the Villa Serbelloni on Italy's Lake Como. He'd dismissed everyone except

Dave Powers and Kenny O'Donnell to have complete privacy with a guest—the beautiful Marella Agnelli, wife of Fiat chairman and playboy Gianni Agnelli.

At the same time, a third scandal was starting to break.

Only a few days after Bobby met with the *New York Journal-American* reporters, he received an alarming FBI memo about an alleged affair between Kennedy and Ellen Rometsch.

Rometsch was a twenty-seven-year-old German "party girl" associated with influence peddler Bobby Baker and his Quorum Club, a Capitol Hill retreat frequented by congressmen, lobbyists, and Hill staffers. Kennedy had asked Baker to introduce him to Rometsch, and she made at least ten visits to the White House. "She was very accommodating," Baker said of Rometsch. "I must have had fifty friends who went with her, and not one of them ever complained. She was a real joy to be with."

She was also a suspected spy. In July 1963, Hoover warned Bobby that, according to an FBI informant, JFK was involved with prostitute Ellen Rometsch, who was suspected of spying for the Soviets. In August, Bobby arranged to have Rometsch "rush deported" to West Germany, accompanied by his trusted friend and former aide LaVern Duffy, on a U.S. Air Force transport plane.

Unfortunately for the Kennedys, Rometsch's deportation didn't end the matter. The FBI and the Justice Department began investigating Baker after a lawsuit revealed suspicious activities; allegations included kickbacks of money and sexual favors for government contracts. In September and October, as the Senate Rules Committee began to investigate Baker, newspaper reports appeared on Rometsch's hasty deportation, her link to Baker's Quorum Club, and her alleged associations with very high government officials—including, reportedly, some in the White House.

While the Baker scandal was rocking Washington, and threatened Kennedy through his ties to Rometsch, JFK didn't change his ways. On November 15, 1963, he flew to Palm Beach with the ever-present Dave Powers and Torbert Macdonald (whom reporter Drew Pearson had linked to the Baker inquiry) as well as two regular White House pool-party girls. He'd also asked Dr. Max Jacobson, nicknamed "Dr. Feelgood," to fly to Florida separately, to treat him for back pain.

It was to be the last weekend of his life.

Kennedy was assassinated on Friday, November 22, 1963. That week, the subject of *Newsweek*'s cover—already printed but scrapped after Kennedy's death—was the Bobby Baker scandal.

30

KENNEDY'S COOL

A Secret of His Appeal

A saint or star has a constellation of virtues (or vices) that the public finds irresistible. Kennedy had a distinct cool that was at the root of many of his most attractive qualities. This attribute put a distance between him and others, and, as friendly as he was, he seemed somehow apart, not seeking outside approval, sufficient to himself. These were qualities people wanted to see in their leader.

One of Kennedy's most distinctive and winning characteristics was his extraordinary *cool*. His advisers and the public alike admired his calm, his self-confidence, his easy air of composure. Kennedy's cool also gave him his air of detachment and his irony—qualities that distinguished him from most politicians.

Unlike the Irish politicians of his heritage, for instance, Kennedy disdained baby-kissing, hat-wearing, arm-waving postures. He didn't like to mention Jackie or his children, and Pierre Salinger recalled that when Kennedy was advised to play up Jackie's pregnancy, he tried it only once. "Hell. If that's what it takes to be elected, I'll lose. I am not going to mention pregnancy again." But even Kennedy couldn't completely avoid the corniness of politics. He literally signed his name in his own blood in a Rotary Club register, after making a campaign speech to Rotarians dressed as pirates.

Kennedy's cool showed in the way he handled difficult situations. "Sometimes," Clark Clifford recalled, "watching him during a discussion on some contentious issue, I felt as if his mind had left his body and was observing the proceedings with a detached, almost amused air. . . . 'This may seem supremely, even transcendently important right now, but will it matter in fifty years?' " Even during times of greatest stress, Kennedy kept his sense of humor and calm. While serving in the Solomons, his response to his mother's news that nuns and priests were praying for him was to write, "I hope it won't be taken as a sign of lack of confidence in you all or the Church if I continue to duck." During the agonizing suspense of election night 1960, he was the most composed person in the crowd and even managed to sleep for several hours as returns trickled in. To maintain secrecy during the Cuban missile crisis, he stuck to his regular schedule and was able to concentrate on the other matters before him. While his newborn son lay dying in the hospital, Kennedy took a moment to ask about a burned child nearby and to write a comforting note to the child's mother.

Just as he dealt calmly with momentous events, Kennedy viewed himself with detachment. Reporter Laura Bergquist described him as "a watcher of everybody, especially a watcher of himself . . . looking at the whole picture, rather dispassionately." He was extremely conscious of the impression he created. Walking into a party, Kennedy would tell Inga Arvad, "OK, now it's time to turn on the BP—Big Personality." Kennedy evaluated his performance after his first televised debate with Nixon; " 'Party,' not 'pawty,' " he reminded himself. When guests at Hyannis Port watched a film of Kennedy's *Ich bin ein Berliner* speech, Kennedy applauded enthusiastically with the others, as if for someone else.

Kennedy's cool allowed him to perceive other people's unspoken criticisms and to deflate them with his deft use of self-deprecating humor. For example, in his first campaign, knowing he might seem a spoiled rich boy among opponents who each described their childhood struggles, Kennedy admitted, "I do seem to be the only one here who did not come up the hard way." Of elected office, Kennedy said, "If you don't want to work for a living, this is as good a job as any." In a nod to criticism of his efforts to manage the news, Kennedy opened his 1963 Gridiron Club dinner speech by addressing his "fellow managing editors."

By joking about criticism, Kennedy drew its sting. During the presidential race, reporters questioned a campaign estimate that a rally had attracted thirty-five thousand people. Asked how they'd arrived at the number, Kennedy joked that his press secretary "counts the nuns, and then multiplies by 100." Bradlee observed that by "making a joke about a subject that was sensitive, to say the least, Kennedy made the reporters laugh, and probably avoided a story about inflated crowd counts by his staff. Questioning of a crowd count . . . [by] the Nixon team usually brought a lecture about bias."

Kennedy made jokes about his father's controversial reputation. When asked in the early 1940s about book sales for *Why England Slept,* he said, "Going like hotcakes. Dad's seeing to that." At the 1958 Gridiron dinner, Kennedy pretended to read a telegram from his father. "Dear Jack—don't buy a single vote more than is necessary. I'll be damned if I'm going to pay for a landslide." At a dinner in 1960, Kennedy said, "I had announced earlier this year that if successful I would not consider campaign contributions as a substitute for experience in appointing ambassadors. Ever since I made that statement I have not received one single cent from my father."

He used wit to point out uncomfortable truths. Not long after becoming president, Kennedy said to a group of businessmen, "It would be premature to seek your support in the next election, and inaccurate to express thanks for having had it in the last one." At the birthday party for Kennedy at Madison Square Garden, where Marilyn Monroe sang her supersexy "Happy Birthday, Mr. President," Kennedy defused the moment by saying, "I can retire from politics after having had 'Happy Birthday' sung to me in such a sweet, wholesome way." Kennedy may even have discreetly mocked his sexual escapades, when he said, pointing to the pits in the Oval Office floor made by Eisenhower's golf shoes, "Well, I guess we all have our way of relaxing from the burdens of office; at least I won't leave any marks on the floor."

His humor was proof of his self-assurance, which is one of a leader's most important characteristics. He wasn't defensive, he didn't try to puff himself up. When asked how he became a war hero, he replied, "It was involuntary. They sank my boat." When Arthur Schlesinger Jr. said he wasn't sure what he'd do as special assistant, Kennedy told him, "Well, I am not sure what I will be doing as President either, but I am sure there will be enough at the White House to keep us both busy." When a reporter asked him at a 1962 press conference to comment on his media coverage, he drew a laugh: "Well, I am reading more and enjoying it less." Of Jackie's tremendous popularity: "I am the man who accompanied Jacqueline Kennedy to Paris." Of his job as president: "The pay is good and I can walk to work."

Kennedy didn't spare himself. In his comments on John Hersey's draft of the flattering "Survival" piece about the *PT-109* adventure, Kennedy described his current military assignment: "Once you get your feet upon [*sic*] the desk in the morning the heavy work of the day is done." When Jackie gave him a painting of himself wearing a three-cornered hat and standing like Napoleon,

Kennedy joked, "I wonder where she ever got the idea I had a commander-in-chief complex." Kennedy poked fun at his habit of cultivating intellectuals. When Alfred Kazin published a caustic piece in *The American Scholar,* Kennedy said, "We wined him and dined him, and talked about Hemingway and Dreiser with him, and I later told Jackie what a good time she missed, and then he went away and wrote that piece!"

Kennedy recognized his strengths, but he was not dazzled by them, as many of his colleagues were. His self-deprecatory humor saved him from being a fool for flattery—a risk for Kennedy, who was surrounded by adoring advisers and crowds. "He observes the tributes paid to him," Manchester noted, "almost as though they were meant for someone else . . . He does convey a third-person air." When he was introduced as potentially the greatest president in American history, he said, "George Washington wasn't a bad president and I do want to say a word for Thomas Jefferson." Of his phone call to Mrs. King, deemed a brilliant stroke because it won him a huge boost in black votes, Kennedy admitted, "The finest strategies are usually the result of accidents." Of his American University speech proposing a new relationship with the Soviet Union, considered one of his greatest, Kennedy pointed out that he'd received 896 letters about the speech, and 28,232 letters about a freight-rate bill.

He didn't get caught up in the image he worked so hard to create. Two weeks after the Bay of Pigs debacle, a Gallup poll showed that a remarkable 83 percent of the American people supported him. "It's just like Ike," said Kennedy. "The worse you do, the better they like you." When a friend reminded Kennedy that Theodore White's *Making of the President, 1960* had described aide Richard Donahue as "coruscatingly brilliant," Kennedy laughed, then observed, "Sometimes these guys forget that fifty thousand votes the other way and they'd all be coruscatingly stupid." He could take the same attitude toward Jackie. During the Kennedys' triumphant trip to France, Kennedy watched her in conversation with de Gaulle. "God, she's really laying it on, isn't she?"

Backing Kennedy's cool was the fact that he had a counterpart in his brother. While Jack was cool, Bobby was hot.

Jack Kennedy would watch, calm and detached, while Bobby raged and threatened. Reliable, fiercely loyal, spoiling for a fight, Bobby was an ideal protector and enforcer for his brother. He said during the 1952 Senate campaign, "I don't care if anyone around here likes me, as long as they like Jack." When the Kennedy brothers wanted to throw their weight around, it was Bobby who made the call. When Twentieth Century Fox refused to allow Marilyn Monroe to attend the Kennedy birthday gala at Madison Square Garden, because her absences had delayed production of *Something's Got to Give,* Bobby took up the fight. He told Fox's Milton Gould that Monroe's appearance was "of critical importance to the current administration" and that "the President wants it, and I want it." When Gould refused, Bobby threatened him, telling him that he would be "sorry for this" and that he was "dealing with the First Family in America."

So that Jack Kennedy could maintain his air of amused detachment, Bobby took on the job of hectoring Kennedy critics into silence. Undersecretary of State Chester Bowles told reporters that he'd opposed the Bay of Pigs invasion. When Bobby saw him, he prodded Bowles in the chest and snarled, "So you advised against this operation. Well, as of now, you were all for it."

Although Schlesinger repeatedly praises Kennedy's "cool," he admits that "some thought him detached or indifferent. But," he explains, "only the unwary could really conclude that his 'coolness' was because he felt too little. It was because he felt too much and had to compose himself for an existence filled with disorder and suffering."

But Kennedy's cool was real—even chilly. He viewed himself

with detachment and calculation, and he judged others likewise. Clark Clifford observed, "Between him and the large number of men and women who were devoted to him and considered themselves to be his special friend, I believe there was a deeply impersonal factor at work."

Kennedy's cool kept him from becoming emotionally committed to issues, and he was uncomfortable with passionate talk of morals or idealism. In 1956, when asked about "the somewhat emotionless quality of his liberalism," he explained, "in my family we were interested not so much in the ideas of politics as in the mechanics of the whole process." In his public addresses, he spoke of exalted ideals, but these were his set speeches; off-the-cuff or in conversation, he never took that tone. In fact, he was sheepish if he couldn't avoid it: "It may sound corny," he told an aide, "but I am thinking not so much of our world but the world that Caroline will live in."

And if Kennedy was cool, he wanted the people around him to be cool, too, and his closest advisers were ironic, pragmatic, and skeptical. He didn't like being around people—even his brother—when they couldn't hide their earnestness, as when he scoffed, "Don't worry about Bobby. He's probably all choked up about Martin Luther King and his Negroes today."

Perhaps Kennedy's cool partly stemmed from his treatment by his father, Joe Kennedy. Jack had a rich, well-connected father who was determined to make him president—and Jack had become president. But he hadn't been his father's first choice.

First, Joe himself had hoped to be president. Then, after his defeatism during World War II shattered his own political career, Joe decided that Joe Jr. must win the prize. Firstborn son Joe was in better health than Jack, a far more successful athlete and student, better-looking, more outgoing. He was the star of the family; in fact, when testing showed that Jack's IQ was higher than Joe's, his mother protested the "error" to their school.

Maybe Jack's cool irony came from the realization that, if events had been a bit different, he wouldn't have become President John F. Kennedy. He had his father's absolute commitment, but only because Joe and then Joe Jr.—whom Joe described as "the best of the lot"—had been forced aside. It was only by quirks of fortune that Jack Kennedy had gotten his chance. This realization may have given him the quality of detached cool that was one of his greatest assets.

31

KENNEDY'S HEALTH
A Condition of His Existence

A full chronological account of a subject's life can be misleading, because the crush of facts obscures their import. Consider Kennedy's health—surely one of the significant aspects of his existence. A detailed biography that notes a hospital visit by Kennedy here, an episode of back pain there, is factually accurate, but its very comprehensiveness mutes the actual significance of the facts. Only an unblinking examination of Kennedy's health record can convey the gravity of his infirmities, the depth of his deception of the public, and the triumph of his fulfillment of great responsibilities with grace and energy, despite tremendous pain.

What Was the Condition of Kennedy's Health?

Kennedy's health was far worse than was known during his lifetime. Although he radiated vigor, Kennedy suffered throughout his life from various ailments and chronic pain.

What Was the Nature of Kennedy's Ill Health?

Kennedy was an unusually sickly child, who, as a two-year-old, contracted a life-threatening case of scarlet fever and was hospitalized for two months, and also came down with bronchitis, chicken pox, ear infections, German measles, measles, mumps, and whooping cough. Kennedy also suffered from sinusitis, asthma, and severe allergies, especially to dog hair. Kennedy's principal health problems, however, fell into four categories.

GASTROINTESTINAL PROBLEMS

For most of his life, Kennedy suffered from serious gastrointestinal ailments, including colitis, ulcers, gastroenteritis, and diarrhea.

Beginning in 1934, at age seventeen, or perhaps earlier, he began to suffer from colitis, which plagued him throughout his life. According to Robert Dallek, the biographer who has made the most comprehensive study of Kennedy's health, Kennedy may have begun to take corticosteroids—compounds derived from adrenal extracts—for his colitis as early as 1937. Doctors didn't then understand their negative long-term effects; if he did take steroids, this treatment may have actually caused or exacerbated other major health problems that would soon flare up—his Addison's disease, ulcers, and bad back.

In November 1943, at age twenty-six, he was diagnosed with duodenal ulcers.

Throughout his life, he frequently suffered abdominal pain, and he spent a great deal of time consulting doctors, staying in hospitals, and attempting various cures. For example, just in his first term as senator, he was hospitalized nine times—totaling more than six weeks—for various gastrointestinal ills.

At various periods of his life, diarrhea from intestinal difficulties made him lose weight. Because of his weak stomach, he ate a great deal of bland food, and in particular, soup. He couldn't tolerate much alcohol and seldom had more than one drink at a time.

BACK PAIN

If Kennedy did start taking steroids in the 1930s for his colitis, the medication may have caused his osteoporosis and degeneration of his lumbar spine. In any event, Kennedy began to have significant back pain beginning in 1938, which worsened in 1940. College football injuries and his *PT-109* adventure may have exacerbated his problems.

Kennedy's chronic back pain was so debilitating by 1954 that he underwent a very risky operation on his spine and, when that one wasn't successful, endured a second one four months later.

The operations, however, didn't relieve his agony. Kennedy tried to manage the pain by using specially designed chairs and beds, soaking in hot baths, and wearing a stiff corset under his clothes. He received frequent procaine injections, and when doctors determined that these were being overused, began an exercise regime to strengthen his muscles. He also secretly relied on Dr. Max Jacobson's "vitamin" injections to control pain.

ADDISON'S DISEASE

In 1947, Kennedy was diagnosed with Addison's disease, a life-threatening condition in which the adrenal glands fail to produce the hormones that regulate the immune system, maintain blood pressure, and control the response to stress.

His Addison's disease may have been caused by the steroids he'd taken to treat his colitis, although the fact that his sister Eunice also had Addison's suggests genetic factors.

If untreated, Addison's is almost always fatal, but by 1947, treatment with pellets of corticosteroid implants had extended life expectancy, and later advances made it possible for an Addisonian to live an almost normal existence. For the rest of Kennedy's life, he depended on daily cortisone in various forms—pellets, injections, and pills. Joe Kennedy put supplies of cortisone around the world in safe-deposit boxes, to make sure that Jack would never risk missing his medication.

Those who suffer from Addison's disease are more prone to infection, especially during surgery. It was the Addison's that made Kennedy's back operations so risky.

The cortisone taken for Addison's accounts for the fact that Kennedy's face often looked bloated and jowly.

UROLOGICAL SYMPTOMS RELATED TO PERSISTENT OR RECURRENT INFECTION

For much of his life, Kennedy endured urinary tract infections, nonspecific and nongonococcal urethritis, and persistent prostatitis. He suffered recurrent symptoms of excruciating pain when urinating, prostate pain, inflammations of the genital area, and discharge of pus. These symptoms were treated, mostly with massive doses of antibiotics, but couldn't be cured.

In addition to the pain he suffered, Kennedy worried about the effects on his fertility. During the first year of his marriage, he had his sperm count tested to make sure that he was able to father children.

Was Kennedy Dependent on Medication While President?

Yes. Because of his Addison's disease, Kennedy depended on cortisone to live. Also, although his back pain wasn't life-threatening, at times it would have been completely disabling if untreated.

Who Knew about Kennedy's True Condition?

Kennedy's health was a closely guarded secret. Apparently, only Jackie, Bobby, Joe, and some of Kennedy's several doctors knew the full extent of his ailments.

Could Kennedy's Ailments or His Medications Have Had Any Effect on His Personality or Performance?

Yes. Addisonians taking cortisone have noted side effects, including an increased sense of well-being and confidence, unusually high social functioning, energy, concentrating power, muscular endurance, and heightened libido—all of which seem applicable to Kennedy. Cortisone made Kennedy restless and gave him insomnia. At the same time, Kennedy also secretly consulted Dr. Max Jacobson, "Dr. Feelgood," who injected his patients with "vitamin shots" that contained amphetamines. Amphetamines are potentially addictive and can cause nervousness, impaired judgment, overconfidence, and depression—side effects that could have had serious repercussions.

In December 1962, Kennedy was in unusually poor spirits. For a few days, he took an antipsychotic drug, Stelazine, which relieved his mood.

Is There Any Evidence That Kennedy's Ailments or His Medications Hurt His Performance as President?

Kennedy biographer Robert Dallek, an authority on Kennedy's health, maintains that his research showed that Kennedy was at all times lucid and highly competent, despite his pain and medication.

How Did Kennedy Manage to Look and Act So Healthy?

Whenever possible, Kennedy ignored his health problems. During his school days and later, although his ailments, bad back, and frail frame made sports difficult, he pushed himself to participate. During the war, he sought to be assigned to PT boats, despite the back-punishing pounding of the small vessels across the water's surface. He had astounding stamina and kept to a grueling schedule—especially during campaigns—that would have exhausted men in perfect health.

Kennedy radiated vigor and grace, despite the fact that he wore a heavy steel-rodded and canvas back brace under his clothes and that his back pain at times was so severe that he had trouble climbing stairs, couldn't bend his body, and could rise from a chair only with much effort. In 1953, at a time when his back pain was crippling, the *Saturday Evening Post* described him as "a walking fountain of youth," "with a lean, straight, hard physique." To keep himself looking healthy, Kennedy maintained a constant tan, either by visiting Florida or by using a sunlamp, and kept his weight down. He often had to use crutches but hid them before any appearance. He would stand on receiving lines for hours, or greet the public outdoors in bad weather, while in severe pain. His physical condition was at its worst point in years during the summer of 1961, which was the very period when he made his important trip to meet de Gaulle in Paris, Macmillan in London, and—most crucially—Khrushchev in Vienna, and also the time of the Berlin crisis.

He once told a friend that he'd give his political success and his money "just to be out of pain." He never complained, and his friends learned not to mention the subject.

How Often Did Kennedy's Illness Interfere with His Planned Activities?

As described below, Kennedy's career as a student, in the navy, and in Congress was interrupted frequently, often for months at a time, by infirmity.

CHILDHOOD

In his early childhood, Kennedy suffered from a wide range of illnesses. Most serious was his bout with scarlet fever at age two, when he spent more than two months in a hospital and sanatorium.

At age thirteen, Kennedy collapsed with abdominal pains and had his appendix removed. The operation didn't cure his symptoms but did cause him to miss part of the school semester.

In 1934, at age sixteen, during his junior year at Choate, he became very ill and was rushed to a hospital. Doctors suspected leukemia, but his symptoms lifted without diagnosis.

Later that year, ill again, he spent a month at the Mayo Clinic and a nearby hospital. Tests showed he had "spastic colitis" and digestive difficulties.

After graduating from Choate in June 1935, he was hospitalized for two months for either colitis or a combination of colitis and ulcers. He'd intended to spend a year studying under Professor Harold Laski at the London School of Economics, but illness forced him to withdraw and come home before he started.

COLLEGE

Upon returning to the United States, Kennedy enrolled at Princeton in late October 1935, after school had begun. Because of ill health, he was forced to drop out after just six weeks and lost the full year of college. He spent two months at a Boston hospital and two months at a ranch in Arizona trying to recover his health. He returned to college—this time, to Harvard—in fall 1936.

In the summer of 1937, he developed a severe case of hives.

Beginning in 1938 and continuing until 1940, Kennedy had severe intestinal problems. He also began to suffer occasional back pain.

In February 1938, he returned to the Mayo Clinic for more tests.

In June 1938, he spent two weeks in the hospital, plagued by weight loss and continuing stomach and colon problems.

In February 1939, he again returned to the Mayo Clinic.

In November 1939, he received injections of liver extracts, but they didn't alleviate his symptoms of low weight, abdominal pain, and spastic colon.

In 1940, he contracted "non-specific urethritis," possibly from a sexual encounter, which later became chronic prostatitis.

In late 1940, at age twenty-two, while playing tennis, he experienced sudden back pain and was hospitalized for ten days. From then on, he had periodic attacks of severe pain.

He considered entering Yale Law School in the fall of 1940 but decided against it because of health problems.

At the end of 1940, he returned to the hospital for extended periods.

NAVY

In 1941, he initially failed the physical exams for the army's and navy's officer candidate schools but passed the navy test on the second try. At this time, he was suffering severe attacks of back pain as well as stomach pain.

In April 1942, after a mere six months of active duty, he requested six months' inactive duty to have an operation for a preexisting back problem. He spent the next several months under evaluation and treatment, but doctors disagreed about the advisability of surgery. He returned to duty in June 1942 and arrived in the Solomons in March 1943.

In August 1943, a Japanese destroyer split Kennedy's PT boat in half, and he and his crew spent a week in difficult conditions before being rescued. This ordeal taxed his already weak system.

In November 1943—just nine months after Kennedy had arrived in the South Pacific—a doctor ordered him relieved of his command due to back problems. He was diagnosed with an early duodenal ulcer. In December, Kennedy left for home. One of his first stops was the Mayo Clinic, for more tests.

He spent much of 1944, his last year in the navy, in and out of hospitals and had back surgery in mid-June 1944, with a difficult recovery, marked by severe and almost constant abdominal pain.

On December 27, 1944, a navy retirement board recommended his discharge, and he was transferred to the retired list "for reasons of physical disability" in March 1945.

In 1945, he went to Arizona for four months to try to regain his health. He had almost constant back pain as well as digestive problems.

In April, he returned to the Mayo Clinic.

In August 1945, in London as a special correspondent for the Hearst newspapers, he collapsed with a high fever and vomiting.

CONGRESS

In 1946, during his first campaign for the House, he collapsed at a parade. He suffered from fatigue, back pain, abdominal pain, vomiting, and pain when urinating. He limped, appeared jaundiced and weak, and was extremely thin.

In the fall of 1947, Kennedy collapsed in London and was diagnosed with Addison's disease. Returning home on the *Queen Mary,* Kennedy was so ill that a priest came aboard to give him last rites.

By 1950, Kennedy's back pain was almost constant, and in 1951, he often needed crutches.

In October 1951, in Japan, he had a life-threatening Addison's crisis and was rushed to a military hospital, where he was given last rites.

In 1952, during his Senate campaign, Kennedy suffered various maladies, including headaches, stomachaches, and bladder and prostate discomfort. His chronic back pain was agonizing, and because of his prostatitis, he urinated pus and had to be hospitalized.

By spring 1954, his back pain had become so severe that he couldn't put on his own socks. Doctors warned he might lose the ability to walk.

In October 1954, at age thirty-seven, his back pain was so intense that he risked a spine operation; he "couldn't take any more pain." The operation was very dangerous, especially for someone suffering from Addison's, which increases the risk of infection.

After the surgery, he nearly died from a urinary tract infection and went into a coma. A priest administered last rites.

In December 1954, he had recovered enough to go to Palm Beach to recuperate, but the site of the operation became infected.

In February 1955, he required another back operation and again received last rites.

In May 1955, Kennedy, aged thirty-eight, returned to Washington after an absence from the Senate of seven months.

It was at this time that Kennedy began to see pain-management specialist Dr. Janet Travell, who treated his back pain with the anesthetic procaine, which gave him great, though temporary, relief.

In July 1955, he was hospitalized twice, once for a week and once for five days.

In January 1956, he spent three days in the hospital and received antibiotics for respiratory and urinary tract infections.

In January 1957, he was in the hospital for two days for nausea, vomiting, and urinary discomfort.

In July 1957, he spent two days in the hospital for abdominal pains.

In September and October 1957, he spent twenty-two days in the hospital for fever, abdominal pain, weight loss, throat and urinary tract infections, and back pain.

Throughout the presidential campaign, Kennedy suffered from continuing back pain and spasm.

PRESIDENT

In the spring of 1961, Kennedy's back pain was extreme, and he received procaine injections two or three times a day.

When Kennedy met de Gaulle and Khrushchev, he had terrible back pain. Doctors recommended using crutches, but he refused. However, "Dr. Feelgood," Max Jacobson, flew to France (not on *Air Force One* but on a chartered jet, to hide his presence) to administer his signature injections to help Kennedy withstand the strain of long consultations.

Between mid-May and mid-October, not including the European trip, Dr. Jacobson spent thirty-six days with Kennedy, in Palm Beach, Washington, New York City, and Hyannis Port. Jacobson would visit the White House more than thirty times, according to gate logs. His medical license was later revoked.

In the fall of 1961, on the advice of doctors who believed he was depending too heavily on procaine, Kennedy began an exercise regime to relieve back spasms and increase mobility.

Kennedy continued to take his wide array of medication—for his colitis, urinary tract problems, back pain, Addison's, as well as other ailments—until his last day.

32

KENNEDY'S LIES
What He Concealed

Kennedy's extraordinary appeal was as much a product of what he concealed as of what he revealed. In a way, Kennedy's lies are more telling than his disclosures, because they show us exactly how he wanted to differ from the way he truly was. He hid information that would have undercut his image of health, vigor, and exceptional intellect. He was fortunate to live in a time when his claims—which could have been investigated—went unchallenged.

Kennedy and his advisers carefully edited the facts to support the idea of John F. Kennedy. In retrospect, Kennedy's most successful public deception was his image as a loyal family man, when in fact he was flagrantly promiscuous. This deception didn't require outright public lies on Kennedy's part, however, because no one openly challenged him on the subject. By contrast, Kennedy's protection of an image of health and intellectual achievement called for actual falsehoods. Some lies were told by Kennedy himself; some, by others—with Kennedy's tacit approval.

Kennedy projected an image of glowing health, but he couldn't keep his numerous medical problems entirely hidden. For this reason, his navy stint proved invaluable, because his wartime heroics could be used to explain—and glorify—his infirmities. Whenever he was in pain or needed crutches, it was attributed to the *PT-109* ordeal or else tied to old football injuries. For example, after he seriously aggravated his back trouble in 1961 at a tree planting in Canada, the *New York Times* reported, "Mr. Kennedy's back problems began with a football injury at Harvard. . . . A severe recurrence of this trouble came when his PT boat was cut in half by a Japanese destroyer. . . . Until this new injury, he had been without back trouble for years." It wasn't true that Kennedy's back problems were largely due to football or the *PT-109* incident, and it wasn't true that he'd been without back pain for years. Similarly, when Kennedy became sick, it was often blamed on malaria. After he collapsed in London and was diagnosed with Addison's disease, his office issued a press release explaining, "Congressman John F. Kennedy announced today that he was 'much better' after a month's bout with malaria."

Kennedy's back operations in 1954 and 1955 attracted attention, but not close examination. A front-page *New York Times* story explained that the surgery was required by war wounds, which wasn't true, and the article didn't disclose the severity of the complications. After *seven months* of convalescence following the surgeries, Kennedy made a triumphant return to the Senate; newspapers described him looking "brown and strong" and walking without crutches, but in fact, Kennedy was still in terrible pain and spent the next several days in New York City receiving further treatment.

Kennedy himself worried whether his health would permit a run for the presidency in 1960. Dr. Janet Travell recalled that from 1956 onward, "he discussed freely with me the potential of his health in relation to the stringent responsibilities of the Presidency."

In 1957, after more back trouble, Joe Kennedy called Dr. Travell: "Maybe Jack should stop torturing himself and he should call the whole thing off. Do you think he can make it?" Once Kennedy decided to run, however, he publicly denied any health problems. In 1959, he claimed, "I have had no special medical care, no special checkup, no particular difficulty on this [medical] score at all." Around the same time, his doctor said that "his back is entirely well." Sometimes Kennedy told half-truths; he mentioned a "partial adrenal insufficiency" and the fact that "until recently, at least," he "occasionally" wore a back corset.

CRUEL

But Kennedy did more than answer questions with falsehoods. In a dig at Johnson, who had a bad heart, he argued that the White House demanded "strength and health and vigor" and noted that "during my lifetime alone four out of our seven Presidents have suffered major heart attacks . . . Voters deserve to know that [the president's] strength and vigor will remain at the helm." Striking back during the 1960 convention fight, the Johnson camp claimed that Kennedy had the life-threatening Addison's disease and was kept alive by cortisone. Quite true. The Kennedy campaign, decrying these "despicable tactics," denied the charge. Bobby said that Kennedy "does not now [have] nor has he ever had an ailment described classically as Addison's Disease" and released a medical report describing Kennedy's health as "excellent." Asked about his health in his first postelection press conference, Kennedy answered, "I never had Addison's disease. . . . My health is excellent."

FLAGRANT LIE

He lied to his own advisers as well as the public. He told Schlesinger, "No one who has the real Addison's disease should run for the presidency, but I do not have it." When his press secretary, Pierre Salinger, reported that opponents were saying he took cortisone, Kennedy—who took cortisone daily—answered, "Well, I used to take cortisone, but I don't take it anymore."

SHAMELESS

The public knew about Kennedy's back pain but not about its crippling severity. At one point—after his consultation with

Khrushchev—his back was so bad he couldn't climb the steps to board an airplane, and a cherry picker had to lift him aboard. To manage the pain, Kennedy relied on exercises, soaking in hot water, and a variety of medications. Dr. Max Jacobson supplied secret injections of painkillers and amphetamines that helped Kennedy appear in top form. Secret Service agent Joseph Paolella observed that Kennedy "wasn't a real healthy guy. On the other hand, I used to be amazed because . . . he seemed almost inexhaustible. . . . The Secret Service guys would be dragging. He just had unlimited energy." Kennedy didn't know, or care, what was in the injections— "I don't care if it's horse piss," he declared—as long as it was effective. He also installed customized chairs in the Executive Office, the Cabinet Room, the three boats he often used, his helicopters, *Air Force One,* the presidential limousine, and at home, and he had a special mattress in the White House and on board *Air Force One.*

Kennedy also lied about his academic credentials. These untruths both hid the severity of Kennedy's illnesses—he might have been thought unfit for office had he disclosed his long periods of ill health—and reinforced Kennedy's intellectual image.

Much of the Kennedy literature asserts that, after Choate, Kennedy spent a year studying at the London School of Economics under the famous Harold Laski. Even as president, Kennedy was telling visitors "that he himself had studied for a term under Laski." Not true. Kennedy did register, but he fell ill almost immediately and returned home before starting. He enrolled in Princeton (weeks after classes had begun), left Princeton after just weeks because of ill health, spent two months in a Boston hospital, and then went to Arizona for several months to try to recover his health. By creating the impression that he'd studied under Laski, Kennedy both enhanced his academic credentials and hid the fact that he'd twice had to drop out of school.

Kennedy entered Harvard the next fall. In his senior year, he wrote a thesis that his father managed to have edited and published as *Why England Slept*. Kennedy later suggested he sold about eighty thousand copies, a number that was widely accepted; however, when Kennedy wrote the publisher during the campaign in November 1959 to ask for the final sales figure, he was corrected: total sales were about twelve thousand.

Kennedy also exaggerated his Stanford record. Despite various assertions that, after Harvard, he entered Stanford Business School and spent six months or a year there, in fact, Kennedy enrolled in fall 1940 merely to audit two courses without credit and left after only ninety days.

These misconstructions of Kennedy's record are prominent and widespread enough to hold the Kennedy team responsible. For example, a major 1958 *New York Times Magazine* piece about Kennedy asserted that he had "a year each at Stanford and the London School of Economics" and that "a back injury incurred in that [*PT-109*] exploit continued to plague him up to a couple of years ago."

Kennedy's desire to be taken seriously as an intellectual also underlies one of the most controversial questions of his career: whether he himself wrote the Pulitzer Prize–winning *Profiles in Courage*.

His winning of the Pulitzer Prize was itself questionable. *Profiles in Courage* hadn't been ranked among the judges' five recommendations for biography to the Pulitzer advisory board, but, in an extraordinary move, the board awarded Kennedy the prize for biography. Arthur Krock, the influential journalist and Joe Kennedy crony (who at least once took a five-thousand-dollar retainer), lobbied for Jack's book: "I worked as hard as I could to get him that prize." Rose Kennedy acknowledged that it was the "careful spadework on their father's part as to who was on the committee and how to reach such and such a person through such and such a friend" that secured the Pulitzer for *Profiles in Courage.* Joe often said, Rose recalled, "Things don't happen, they are made to happen."

But the chief controversy wasn't about improper influence in the award process but about authorship. In December 1957, columnist Drew Pearson claimed in a TV interview that *Profiles in Courage* had been ghostwritten. Kennedy—and his father—took swift action to force the network to apologize.

Did Kennedy write *Profiles in Courage*? It's clear he had the idea for the book, edited it, and took responsibility for its final form. Others, however, did the actual work of gathering information and putting ideas on paper. Of course, politicians often "write" books and speeches in this way; in Kennedy's case, however, *he* won the Pulitzer Prize.

Kennedy always insisted that he had written the book in the conventional sense. However, according to biographer Herbert Parmet's extensive review of handwritten material, typescripts, and tapes, Kennedy made no drafts related to most of the book's material, and little of what he did draft appeared in the final version. His dictated notes were disorganized, with chance thoughts mixed with bits from secondary sources. Kennedy's perfunctory efforts may have convinced him he was in fact the book's author, but the evidence doesn't support this claim.

Also, while the book was being written, Kennedy was either very ill (he was recovering from two major operations and was also hospitalized additional times), traveling in Europe, or making national appearances to raise his visibility in preparation for a presidential run. Ted Sorensen, by contrast, worked on the book full-time for six months, often for twelve-hour days. James MacGregor Burns said that when the controversy broke, Kennedy believed Sorensen wasn't forceful enough in denying authorship of *Profiles in Courage,* and their relationship became "temporarily strained." Sorensen later explained, "I still feel some inhibitions in talking about this matter frankly even today. . . . I'll tell you that I did have a substantial role in all of the output, and his role was that of being the final responsible person who signed it."

In a telling exception, Kennedy—who easily laughed at himself—couldn't be teased about whether he'd actually written *Profiles in Courage*.

33

KENNEDY AS MUSE

What He Inspired

In his 1940 book Why England Slept, *Kennedy observed, "Personalities have always been more interesting to us than facts." Kennedy's charismatic personality—in its setting of dramatic encounters and glamorous surroundings—has stirred artists of all kinds to recount and reimagine the circumstances of his life.*

The biography and character of John Kennedy have inspired hundreds of historical accounts: memoirs, documentaries, histories, and oral histories. Not only that, but Kennedy acted as a muse for artists, musicians, novelists, poets, and filmmakers roused by the facts of his life and, even more, by its unanswered questions; imagination flourishes where precise facts are hidden. That Kennedy's time in the White House became known as "Camelot" illustrates the mythic grandeur that his era came to possess, and the Camelot legend has proved irresistible to those exploring the myths of America. Optimism, possibility, fame, beauty, consumerism, money, martyrdom, sex—Kennedy could be used as a symbol for all these, and more.

It's not typical for a U.S. president to be a popular subject for art, music, and literature—at least, not a positively portrayed subject—but Kennedy generated an outpouring. Many of these works center on his assassination, but it was the exceptional resonance of JFK's life that made his death so enthralling.

Many artists have used Kennedy's image—or associated images—in their work. One of pop artist James Rosenquist's most important paintings is *President Elect* (1960–1961/1964), in which Kennedy's looming face—an image taken from a 1960 campaign poster—is juxtaposed with a woman's hand offering a slice of frosted cake and the side of a yellow Chevrolet. Robert Rauschenberg incorporated JFK's image in his famous silk-screen paintings *Retroactive I* and *Retroactive II* (1964), which show Kennedy pointing his finger in a distinctive pose. Around the same period, Andy Warhol drew on Kennedy imagery in a series of silk-screen prints. Instead of JFK, however, Warhol uses Jackie's image at the time of the assassination in renowned works such as *Jackie (The Week That Was)* (1963) and *16 Jackies* (1964). Warhol would return to Kennedy iconography, as in his assassination-related series *Flash—November 22, 1963* (1968). And even during his presidency, Kennedy inspired works such as Larry Rivers's *Friendship of America and France (Kennedy and de Gaulle)* (1961–1962), commemorating Kennedy's meeting with de Gaulle in Paris, and Pablo Picasso's *Rape of the Sabines* (1963), protesting the threat of nuclear war posed by the Cuban missile crisis. Artists' fascination with Kennedy continues; Maurizio Cattelan's sculpture *Now* (2004) depicts the dead JFK lying barefoot in an open casket.

Among musicians, Kennedy's most dedicated follower was Frank Sinatra. Sinatra was an enthusiastic Kennedy campaigner and even recorded a campaign jingle based on his hit "High Hopes."

> K-E-double-N-E-D-Y
> Jack's the nation's favorite guy.

After Kennedy's victory, Sinatra staged the lavish preinaugural gala, where he sang a special version of "That Old Black Magic": "That old Jack magic has me in its spell." But Sinatra wasn't the only musician drawn to Kennedy. In 1962, Jimmy Dean had a hit song, "PT 109," that celebrated Kennedy's wartime exploits.

> In '43 they put to sea thirteen men and Kennedy
> Aboard the *PT 109* to fight the brazen enemy.

Kennedy's assassination, too, became a subject for songwriters. In 1965, the Byrds remade a folk standard as a Kennedy tribute: "He Was a Friend of Mine."

> Though I never met him, I knew him just the same
> Oh he was a friend of mine.

In 1968, Dick Holler wrote a hit song, "Abraham, Martin, and John," about the liberators of black Americans.

> Anybody here seen my old friend John?
> Can you tell me where he's gone?

"Abraham, Martin, and John" enjoys enduring appeal and has continued to be covered by musicians, including Ray Charles, Kenny Rogers, Marvin Gaye, Smokey Robinson, Mahalia Jackson, Whitney Houston, Emmylou Harris, and Bob Dylan.

Many novelists have used Kennedy's life and assassination as a basis for their work. A partial survey includes George Bernau's *Promises to Keep,* Don DeLillo's *Libra,* Philip Kerr's *The Shot,*

Michael Korda's *The Immortals,* Robert Mayer's *I, JFK,* Charles McCarry's *Tears of Autumn,* Stanley Shapiro's *A Time to Remember,* and D. M. Thomas's *Flying in to Love.* In dozens of other novels, Kennedy appears as a character. Norman Mailer, with his resentful, competitive admiration for JFK, couldn't resist opening his 1964 novel *An American Dream* by assuming the voice of a character who was a friend and an equal to JFK. "I met Jack Kennedy in November, 1946. We were both war heroes, and both of us had just been elected to Congress. We went out on a double date . . . I seduced a girl who would have been bored by a diamond as big as the Ritz." Ward Just incorporates Kennedy as a character, as JFK himself or lightly disguised, in novels such as *Echo House, Jack Gance,* and *A Family Trust*—to explore the JFK phenomenon.

Surprisingly—because poets rarely find a muse in a president—poets, too, were inspired by Kennedy. Kennedy invited renowned poet Robert Frost to contribute a poem to the inauguration. When Frost was blinded by snow glare at the podium, he instead recited an older poem from memory, but the new poem he was unable to read prophesied that the Kennedy administration would be:

> A golden age of poetry and power
> Of which this noonday's the beginning hour.

Norman Mailer wrote several "open poems" addressed to Kennedy. *Of Poetry and Power,* a book of poems inspired by Kennedy's life and presidency, includes contributions by such prominent poets as Frost, W. H. Auden, John Berryman, Gwendolyn Brooks, and Allen Ginsberg.

Filmmakers, too, have drawn on Kennedy material. Even while he lived, Kennedy's adventures became fodder for Hollywood when Robert Donovan's book *PT 109: John F. Kennedy in World*

War II was made into a 1963 movie. Later, the Kennedy story became the basis or inspiration for movies such as *Thirteen Days, Executive Action, Parallax View, Ruby,* and most notoriously, Oliver Stone's enormously popular and historically inaccurate *JFK.*

Kennedy may have acted as a muse, but with his usual ironic detachment, he didn't seem particularly interested in the works he inspired. When asked his view of Mailer's adulatory *Esquire* piece "Superman Comes to the Supermarket," which described him as an existential hero as "handsome as a prince in the unstated aristocracy of the American dream," Kennedy observed, "It really runs on, doesn't it?" When the movie *PT 109* was shown for the first time, in the White House's East Wing, Kennedy left before it was over.

Although historians do a good job of recording political achievements and diplomatic successes, Kennedy's inspiration of artists may do more to win him an enduring place in memory. Artists, with their peculiar gifts, often capture Kennedy and his time more vividly than do memoirists who were actual participants, or scholars with all their facts. Novelist Ward Just describes the dawn of Camelot: "A regnant culture was assembled, part clubhouse, part Park Avenue, with the dizzier aspects of Mayfair and Harvard Yard thrown in. In the winter of 1961 Washington was a kind of Forbidden City suddenly liberated, the Dowager Empress exiled to Gettysburg and the eunuchs to their corporate board rooms. Suddenly Marco Polo was in the Oval Office."

Nevertheless, although Kennedy as muse inspired an outpouring, no great genius memorialized him. Like Alexander the Great, who traveled with a poet but wept because he had no Homer to record his deeds, Kennedy's elusive qualities have been much described but never quite captured.

Artists may paint, and writers may grope for words to describe Kennedy's haunting power, but they fail; they lack the gifts that could preserve Kennedy's charisma forever. After Kennedy died, Bobby realized that no one was able to illuminate his brother's rare quality. When a friend tried to comfort him by reminding him that Julius Caesar is immortal, even though he was emperor of Rome for only three years, Bobby replied, "Yes, but it helps if you have Shakespeare to write about you."

34

KENNEDY—QUESTIONS HE RAISED

Something to Talk About

Part of the enduring fascination with JFK comes from the compelling questions raised by his life. The mysteries, controversies, and unresolved issues about Kennedy spur debate, and such topics, by giving people subjects to consider and discuss, keep him vivid in the public mind.

Kennedy went to great lengths to hide his poor health and history of long periods of pain, hospitalization, and invalidism. His brother Bobby explained, "At least one half of the days that he spent on this earth were days of intense physical pain."

Was Kennedy's endurance of such pain with humor and courage admirable, or was his concealment of his condition from the public deplorable?

Was it courageous for Kennedy to have misrepresented his condition in order to join the navy, when he need not have served, or was his action, which could have put other men at risk due to his physical problems, irresponsible?

Off the air, television interviewer Larry King asked Robert McNamara, "You all knew about the women, didn't you?" McNamara answered, "Yeah, but it was a different era." How has the change in American values since the 1960s altered the way the public judges Kennedy's sexual behavior?

In 1962, Edward McCormack planned to run against Ted Kennedy for the U.S. Senate. The Kennedys offered McCormack a deal: if he dropped out, they'd find him lucrative legal work as well as a high government position. Meanwhile, aides at the Justice Department searched for material to use against McCormack, and Pentagon aides examined his service records for fodder to use against him. Were these actions acceptable or unacceptable?

One of Kennedy's oldest and closest friends, Lem Billings, was widely believed to be gay, and Kennedy's circle included several other secretly gay men. What, if anything, does this tell us about Kennedy? The era?

Richard Nixon often justified his actions with the claim that other presidents had behaved similarly. Does the knowledge that both Kennedy and Nixon performed the following actions change your view of either or both men? Both Kennedy and Nixon . . .

- ran a presidential campaign that included "dirty tricks";
- canceled the White House subscription to a newspaper perceived to be unfair;
- attempted to cut off access to reporters critical of the administration;
- conducted secret taping in the Oval Office and Cabinet Room;

- cultivated a cadre of men who performed unsavory work in secret;
- threatened to use the IRS against opponents;
- had a firing "massacre" of top administration officials;
- used extremely vulgar language in the Oval Office.

Kennedy inspired such veneration that people believe practically anything about him and his family. Some purportedly true, but possibly apocryphal, stories include:

- That in November 1949, after watching a squad of high school kids practicing football, Representative Kennedy borrowed a uniform and joined the practice, which prompted one student to say, "He needs a lot of work, coach. What year's he in?"
- That, as Manchester claims, "Kennedy could have spent the rest of his life in Congress with every reason to believe that eventually he would become Speaker of the House."
- That Jackie translated and summarized ten French books on Southeast Asian politics for Kennedy in the early days of their relationship.
- That Jack and Jackie Kennedy spent a foggy day at Hyannis Port reading Shakespeare's *Coriolanus* aloud to each other.
- That Jackie asked actress Grace Kelly to dress up as a nurse to surprise Jack while he was in the hospital recuperating from back surgery.
- That for almost twenty years after the *PT-109* incident, the Solomon Islanders sang a folk song about "Captain" Kennedy's bravery. "The singers were gratified to learn that the captain had been picked headman of his tribe back home."
- That Jackie memorized Jack's favorite poem, Alan Seeger's "I Have a Rendezvous with Death," and he often asked her to recite it.

> But I've had a rendezvous with Death. . . .
> I shall not fail that rendezvous.

• That just two hours before his assassination, JFK told Jackie, "Jackie, if somebody wants to shoot me from a window with a rifle, nobody can stop it, so why worry about it?"

Although Kennedy himself drank little, one striking feature of his time was the enormous rate—by today's standards—of alcohol consumption. People drank and danced at White House parties until 4:00 a.m. Secretary of State Dean Rusk served scotch at State Department backgrounders. Until Jackie ordered that only two wines accompany official White House lunches, guests had been served cocktails and three wines. How did this drinking affect the Washington atmosphere? How is it different today?

A notable feature of Kennedy's administration was its youth; most remarkably, Kennedy became president at age forty-three, and his brother Bobby was named attorney general at age thirty-four. How receptive do you believe the public, today, would be to such a young president and attorney general? Consider that in 1960, 65 percent of thirty-year-old American men were married, had children, and were fully self-supporting; by 2000, that number had dropped to 31 percent.

For many people, Kennedy symbolizes intellect, achievement, and the positive role of government. Did Kennedy, then, raise political standards? Or did he in fact lower political standards, because his supremely winning appearance and performance taught the public to favor these superficial qualities at the expense of more substantive qualifications?

Some argue that Kennedy should have used his public popularity to press more aggressively for civil rights advances. Others maintain that Kennedy acted most effectively by preparing the country for change but not pushing reform too far in advance of public opinion. Which was the better course for Kennedy to have followed?

According to Samuel Butler, "He is greatest who is most often in men's good thoughts." Discuss.

35

KENNEDY ALCHEMY
The Secret of His Legend

> *Historians may protest, critics may attack, but nevertheless, Kennedy stands as one of the most compelling actors in American history. So many people have tried to probe and copy the secrets of his extraordinary appeal, but without his success.*
>
> *Kennedy evades definitive analysis; his influence lies outside straight rational thought. His stature rests on something elusive, something more profound than statutes or treaties, words or photographs.*
>
> *It is this quality that is most important about Kennedy, and most difficult to describe.*

Journalist Tom Wicker described Kennedy "as one of those sure-sell heroes out of whose face or words or monuments a souvenir dealer can turn a steady buck." Certainly, booksellers, television executives, magazine editors, and memorabilia peddlers have spared no efforts to push Kennedy, but they're feeding, not creating, a demand in the public.

Kennedy fulfilled many versions of the hero: he was the patriot who fought for his country and saved his men; the moral leader who provided a sense of uplift and possibility; the cool performer who dazzled his audience; the rich, elegant style-setter who set the tone for his generation; the loving husband and tender father; and in the end, the martyr. And yet . . . and yet, there was something more.

There was some radiance that Jack Kennedy possessed, some touch of genius that everyone recognized but no one could define. He reigned over those who knew him; they felt themselves in the presence of someone utterly exceptional. Dean Rusk reflected, "He was an extraordinary man; we all felt it; we knew it. I suppose in one sense his thousand days were a special moment in the life of the country." Those who worked with him were certain that history would judge him high. Ted Sorensen argued, "Without demeaning any of the great men who have held the Presidency in this century, I do not see how John Kennedy could be ranked below any one of them." Journalist Hugh Sidey praised Kennedy: "It is my belief that when he is viewed from that distance which scholars deem appropriate, John F. Kennedy will be high on the horizon of history."

Not only to those who knew him, but to the public, Kennedy's reserves of force and intellect seemed beyond measure. Extraordinarily winning, exceptionally memorable, he somehow penetrated very deeply into people's minds. Joe Kennedy couldn't define his son's special quality, but he recognized and gloated over it. He boasted in late 1959 that his son had become "the greatest attraction in the country today. . . . Why is it that when his picture is on the cover of *Life* or *Redbook* that they sell a record number of copies? You advertise that he will be at a dinner and you will break all records for attendance. . . . Why is that? He has the greatest universal appeal. I can't explain that. There is no answer to Jack's appeal. He is the biggest attraction in the country today." And Joe was right.

Kennedy's most loyal admirers argue that his presidential accomplishments account for his appeal. Theodore White maintained that Kennedy was "an enormously large figure" because he so enhanced opportunities for Catholics, blacks, Jews, women, and youth. Arthur Schlesinger Jr. listed Kennedy's accomplishments: "the new hope for peace on earth, the elimination of nuclear testing in the atmosphere and the abolition of nuclear diplomacy, the new policies toward Latin America and the third world, the reordering of American defense, the emancipation of the American Negro, the revolution in national economic policy, the concern for poverty, the stimulus to the arts, the fight for reason against extremism and mythology."

Some admirers protest when Kennedy's appeal is not credited to his high purposes but to his "style" or some other trifling attribute. Sorensen, for example, insisted that the significance of Kennedy's speeches "lay not in the splendor of their rhetoric but in the principles and policies they conveyed."

But was that it? Few disinterested observers would argue that the actual policies or achievements of Kennedy's abbreviated presidency can account for the tremendous popular enthusiasm for him. Nevertheless, today he's recalled far more clearly, and with much greater affection, than his successors.

Other admirers, admitting that Kennedy's assassination prevented him from accomplishing much, find Kennedy's greatness in the sense of "promise," "hope," and "spirit" he roused. Pierre Salinger wrote, "I believe that future generations will rank him as one of our greatest Presidents—not because of his specific accomplishments, and there were many, but because he brought to a world, cynical after almost two decades of cold war, the hope that a better life was possible." Ben Bradlee acknowledged, "His brief time in power seems to me now to have been filled more with hope and promise than performance. But the hope and the promise that he held for America were real." Chester Bowles: "No newly elected American President aroused greater expectations not only in his own country but throughout the world." Helen Thomas: "If spirit can be assessed, as I think it can, Kennedy was an outstanding President. He led the people with a sense of hope and direction, a feeling that there was more to fulfill in their own lives and for future generations." John Kenneth Galbraith: "I would put JFK up with the majors. We should measure presidents in accordance with the sense of the country, and esteem the country felt: the spirit of change that emanated from Washington." Harold Macmillan: "Perhaps his biggest achievement was to take the disillusioned and saddened youth of all the world and make them think there was some purpose to life." This, Macmillan added, was a "spiritual achievement, not political."

But was that it? Critics argue that Kennedy's eulogists invoke this vague and unverifiable claim—that Kennedy brought "promise" or "hope"—to justify their sweeping assertions of Kennedy's greatness, in the absence of solid accomplishments.

Other observers of Kennedy's unique power remain unconvinced by these arguments. Instead, they dissect Kennedy in search of the concrete element that explains his uncanny ability to charm: his family, his money, his glamour, his favorable press, his flair for the dramatic.

In particular, many point to Kennedy's physical beauty, and it's true that such remarkable personal appeal is often linked with good looks. Kennedy was gorgeous to look at, but in terms of sheer appearance, he wasn't unusually handsome. His eyes were close together, and one was off-center, one leg was shorter than the other, and he had heavy jowls puffed up by cortisone. His hair was often distractingly bushy. He moved with awkward carriage and tensed shoulders. Even in the Kennedy family, Jack wasn't considered handsomest—Teddy was. The same was true for Jackie; Joan, not Jackie, was the prettiest of the Kennedy ladies, and Jackie's sister, Lee, was the more classically beautiful of the two Bouvier sisters.

Both Jack and Jackie often appear to have oddly oversize heads. Yet somehow, Kennedy gave the impression of beauty and vigor.

Those who argue that Kennedy had *grace* are closer to the mark—he had some grace that gave him an exceptionally pleasing appearance. As Norman Mailer described, "His appearance changed with his mood . . . and this made him always more interesting than what he was saying. . . . Kennedy had a dozen faces." Men and women alike wanted to gaze at him. Joe Kennedy understood this, and he urged that the back jacket of *Profiles in Courage* carry a large author photograph instead of a description of the author.

But was that it? Others argue that Kennedy's attraction comes from the associations he invoked, which somehow grabbed the public imagination. It's tempting to assume that these possessed an independent energy that they lent to Kennedy—yet, in truth, they had no particular magic apart from him. Who would have predicted that the country would go mad for a Catholic preppy, a war hero who enjoyed poetry and biography, a young, rich politician who enjoyed black-tie dinner parties and yacht cruises? Kennedy, who barely won the election, wasn't embraced by the public until he became president. Then, after only a few months, a Harris poll put Kennedy's ratings at 92 percent. That last element of high office allowed him to arouse a string of associations that mysteriously interacted to fascinate. His glamour and wit, Jackie's beauty, their young family—these were not incidental details but the tools necessary to ignite the American imagination.

But was that it? There was also the shock and grief of his assassination, of course. But William McKinley was assassinated, too, and he was largely forgotten by the public after his death in 1901.

Somehow, Kennedy seemed to embody the excellent and the well intentioned. Schlesinger recalled Kennedy's effect as president: "Washington seemed engaged in a collective effort to make itself brighter, gayer, more intellectual, more resolute. It was a golden interlude." As ambassador to France Chip Bohlen observed, Kennedy convinced people that "we can do better": "There was an unknown quality about Kennedy, despite all his realism, that gave you infinite hope that somehow or other he was going to change the course of history."

That the reverence for Kennedy is so great, and so enduring, and so far in excess of what seems appropriately generated by his words, actions, and appearance, shows that he possessed some . . . *indefinable quality* . . . some attribute beyond the normal run of human gifts. For all his glittering surface, he suggested great depths. Sorensen wrote, "I think it will be difficult to measure John Kennedy by any ordinary historical yardstick. For he was an extraordinary man, an extraordinary politician and an extraordinary President."

Some mysterious alchemy transmuted Kennedy into a golden, mythic leader—one able to command the spirits of men and women to an extraordinary degree. This power is a power beside which everything else pales. Lincoln wrote, "Public sentiment is everything. With public sentiment, nothing can fail; without it, nothing can succeed. Consequently he who molds public sentiment goes deeper than he who enacts statutes or pronounces decisions. He makes statutes and decisions possible or impossible to be executed."

The consequence of this alchemy was perceived by both Democrats and Republicans, by those close to Kennedy and those who saw him only through media reports, by Americans and people abroad. Kennedy's critics fumed at the respect and attention Kennedy received, which they believed far exceeded his desserts. One politician scoffed that Kennedy's popularity was "like that of a movie actor—it's not related to legislation." Nixon groused to his chief of staff H. R. Haldeman that "JFK did nothing but appeared great." However, although detractors may believe his appeal is illegitimate, they can't deny it; it was apparent to everyone.

Dave Powers recalled the reaction to Kennedy in his first campaign: "He's no great orator and he doesn't say much, but they certainly go crazy over him." He told Kennedy, "I've never seen such a reaction from a crowd of people in my whole life." When lawyer Newton Minow met Kennedy in 1956, he recalled, he "fell in love with Jack Kennedy immediately . . . I was taken with his whole attitude, his whole appearance, his whole—He really sent me." Norman Mailer suggested that Kennedy was a candidate who could be the hero America needed, "a hero central to his time, a man whose personality might suggest contradictions and mysteries . . . because only a hero can capture the secret imagination of a people."

People all over the world reacted to the JFK alchemy. When Kennedy visited cities across West Germany in June 1963, where people shouted, "Ken-ne-dy! Ken-ne-dy!" the State Department's William Tyler observed that Kennedy's popularity "went far beyond anything that could be accounted for by any act. . . . Something about him . . . just seemed to echo in the hearts and voices of all the people when they greeted him." Secretary of State Dean Rusk said that Kennedy's reception there was "the most remarkable spectacle he ever saw." Master politician Lyndon Johnson admitted his puzzlement over Kennedy's success.

> Here was a young whippersnapper, malaria-ridden and yellah, sickly, sickly. He never said a word of importance in the Senate and he never did a thing. But somehow with his books and his Pulitzer Prizes he managed to create the image of himself as a shining intellectual, a youthful leader who would change the face of the country. Now, I will admit that he had a good sense of humor and that he looked awfully good on the goddam television screen and through it all he was a pretty decent fellow, but his growing hold on the American people was simply a mystery to me.

But although Johnson wasn't able to identify what alchemy changed Kennedy into *Kennedy,* he recognized its effect.

> I used to think that old Joe Kennedy had a lot to do with it, pouring his money in strategic places all over the country and getting the press out front on his son's behalf, but I've finally come to realize there was something in John Kennedy himself, some sort of dignity that people just liked when they saw it, for without that his incredible rise to power simply makes no sense at all.

Kennedy developed his astonishing appeal over the course of his life. One friend observed, "Jack Kennedy evolved from a shy, bashful, nonambitious, nice, always nice, nice man . . . into a very, very motivated, well-spoken, good-looking determined fellow. I never in my life have ever seen a transformation like that. Exactly why—I couldn't tell you why."

Groping for a way to explain Kennedy's charisma, his admirers often adopt the metaphor of *light.* Of the 1960 campaign, Theodore White wrote, "Whoever traveled with the Democratic candidate became dazzled, then blinded, with the radiance of approaching victory"; Larry Newman, Kennedy's Secret Service agent, said, "You could see so many qualities he had that just glowed"; Ben Bradlee recalled "this remarkable man who lit the skies of this land bright with hope and promise"; Dean Rusk: "He was an incendiary man who set most of the people around him on fire"; State Department official Pedro Sanjuan: "When he came into the room, he was like the sun: he radiated confidence and glory." Charley Bartlett reflected, "Jack was selfish too, and he was spoiled and he had a lot wrong with him. But there was something that was very luminous about Jack." After Kennedy died, journalist James Reston wrote, "He never reached his meridian: we saw him only as a rising sun." Ted Sorensen wrote, "The world had suddenly changed and the brightest light of our time had suddenly been snuffed out." Red Fay recalled, "We did not know then that the extraordinary man . . . would die in the blazing summer of his youth." Cambodia's Prince Sihanouk said, "A light was put out which may not be re-lit for many years to come." When it fell to nanny Maud Shaw to tell Caroline and John of their father's death, she said, "[Baby] Patrick was so lonely in heaven. . . . Now he has the best friend anyone could have. . . . God is making your father a guardian angel over you and your mother, and his light will shine down on you always." Jackie, so gifted at building a metaphor, seized the light imagery after Kennedy's death. She insisted on the inclusion of an eternal flame at his gravesite. Her composed TV address to the nation, made a few weeks after the assassination, includes one striking fragment of a sentence: "All his bright light gone from the world." Concluding her remarks at a reception at the Democratic National Convention in 1964, she said in benediction, "May his light always shine in all parts of the world."

Now, why does Fortune have favorites? Why did Kennedy possess a marvelous gift of pleasing, while others (think of Nixon) arouse such dislike? No one can say what alchemy transformed Kennedy—but Kennedy, with his cool detachment, recognized the power he'd gained.

Of course, not everyone felt this power during his life or feels it now. As president, he earned widespread opposition. Newspapers were full of criticism. He aroused hostility because of his background, his wealth, his party, his assumed hostility to business interests, his policies on civil rights, and his goal of outreach to the Soviets. Some believed him opportunistic, without fixed principles, and too preoccupied with his image. And while the glamour of the Kennedy White House charmed many, others complained: "Too many parties, swimming pool dunkings, running around too much."

Nevertheless, Kennedy's appeal in office was striking. Early in his term, he had a higher approval rating than either Roosevelt or Eisenhower had enjoyed at the same point—a success particularly surprising given that he'd barely defeated Nixon. Gallup polls showed that Kennedy hit an 83 percent approval rating just after the Bay of Pigs disaster in April 1961, and he remained within the sixtieth and seventieth percentiles until the fall of 1963. After the Cuban missile crisis in November 1962, Kennedy had a 76 percent overall approval rating. (Furthermore, in the spring of 1962, national campus polls showed that college girls thought Kennedy had more sex appeal than anyone else.) In the 1962 off-year election, the Democrats led by Kennedy achieved the best midterm showing of an incumbent party since 1934.

Americans felt his death with a unique intensity. Joseph Alsop asked "whether or when I have *ever* felt anything at all before this; for nothing has been quite like this." Reporter Laura Bergquist said her mother "cried as much when he was assassinated as she had cried at my father's death. And my mother was never a real Kennedy fan." Poet Kathleen Raine recalled, "I am as a rule utterly unmoved by public events, and cynical about politicians, but this was altogether different. . . . He raised the United States to a great height; and I feel, as many do, that the grandeur of the national mourning was upon the level to which he had tried to raise his nation; even in spite of the fearful depths the assassination revealed. But they are always there, the heights perhaps not."

About 175 million Americans watched Kennedy's funeral on television, and millions more watched internationally. The funeral was even shown on Soviet state television, and a Moscow reporter observed, "It was absolutely fantastic the impact that this assassination had made in the Soviet Union, the loss of Kennedy." In France, Charles de Gaulle said, "I am stunned. They are crying all over France. It is as though he were a Frenchman, a member of their own family." The American ambassador in Britain, David

Bruce, sent a confidential report to Dean Rusk: "Great Britain has never before mourned a foreigner as it has President Kennedy. . . . Many demonstrations of effectionate [*sic*] respect spring from the hearts of those who believe he might have become the creator of a new world order. Like other symbols, this is not subject to analysis, and is mystically interpreted." When an American made a purchase in a remote Sudanese village, the shopkeeper drew a dark border on the bill. Asked why, he said, "Haven't you heard? The greatest man in the world is dead today." Embassies in Africa, Asia, South America, and elsewhere reported an astonishing response to the news.

The alchemy's magic might have been reversed—gold returned to base metal—had Kennedy remained in office. But in death, Kennedy never fell short of his goals, he never grew old or idle, he never hurt his proud family with scandal. He continued to represent a glowing future, *one that now could never be.* His death didn't mean the end of his power, but its fulfillment. His violent end and stately funeral earned him glory and tribute he never could have won in life and so intensified his appeal that, to this day, it extends to everyone who carries the Kennedy name.

Even though the public devours every salacious detail about Kennedy, he's nevertheless remembered in legendary terms—his faults and failures accepted, his ambitions outshining the reality. In the romanticized history of Camelot, and in Kennedy's highly constructed personality, the public finds its political ideal, and the sublime passion Kennedy can arouse is as noteworthy as the legislative records of politicians who did "more."

36

KENNEDY'S DEATH
The Facts

Few choose when or how they die, yet death, however it comes, always seems somehow characteristic; its dramatic flourish influences our interpretation of a life. A different death would have utterly changed Kennedy's legacy.

On the morning of November 22, 1963, President Kennedy and Mrs. Kennedy arrived in Dallas, Texas. At 12:30 p.m., as the presidential motorcade traveled through downtown Dallas along a route lined by enthusiastic crowds, President Kennedy was shot by a sniper and received a fatal head injury.

John Fitzgerald Kennedy, aged forty-six, died on Friday, November 22, 1963, at approximately 1:00 p.m.

37

WHO KILLED JOHN F. KENNEDY?

The Mystery of His Assassination

Part of what makes Kennedy such an enduring figure—and keeps his memory fresh—is the abiding fascination with his assassination. Beside the reverential and revisionist biographies, the presidential histories, the lavish photography books, and the Camelot reminiscences stand an enormous number of accounts that purport to find a new solution to the question: who killed John F. Kennedy?

In fact, this mystery was solved long ago; that such debates continue to grip the public shows Kennedy's extraordinary hold on the public imagination.

Debate about Kennedy's assassination feeds the enduring fascination with Camelot. However, despite the confusion created by the flawed inquiries of congressional committees, evidence overlooked or deliberately hidden by government officials, mistakes made during investigation, and elaborate theories put forward by enthusiasts, the truth is, in fact, well established: Lee Harvey Oswald, acting alone, shot Kennedy. A prodigious number of books, movies, and articles claim to make the case that other forces were at work, but all the most recent, authoritative, exhaustive examinations have found nothing to challenge the original conclusion that Oswald alone was responsible. Certainly, various groups and individuals were motivated to want Kennedy dead, but that isn't proof of action.

Lee Harvey Oswald's past shows that it was quite in character for him to plan the assassination. Born in 1939, he was early identified as withdrawn, demanding, with the potential for explosive and aggressive behavior. He often hit his mother. He moved constantly throughout his childhood, went to many different schools, and he was for a time placed in a home for disturbed boys and given psychiatric care. At age fifteen, he began to expound communist doctrine and say he wanted to join a communist cell. Despite this professed interest in communism, he joined the marines at age seventeen. There, he trained in rifle use and exceeded the score needed to qualify as a "sharpshooter."

Throughout his life, Oswald believed he was smarter and better than other people and was frustrated that he didn't receive proper recognition. In 1959, aged twenty, after saving his money and studying the Russian language, he defected to the Soviet Union, out of a belief that there he'd have stature and respect. Fellow marine Kerry Thornley recalled, "He wanted to be looked back upon with honor by future generations. He was concerned with his image in history. . . . He expected the Russians to accept him on a much higher capacity."

The Soviets, however, didn't give Oswald the special treatment he wanted. He came home in May 1962, disappointed, with his Russian wife, Marina, and their baby. Upon his return, Oswald was again crushed by the lack of attention; he'd expected to be met by reporters and photographers. Life was no better back in the United

States than it had been in the Soviet Union; Oswald was unable to keep a job, regularly beat his wife, and was chronically frustrated.

By the spring of 1963, he was ready to try assassination, and his first target was right-wing major general Edwin A. Walker. Oswald photographed the Dallas alley near Walker's house and mail-ordered a twenty-dollar rifle with a four-power (4x) scope. It arrived on March 25. On April 10, after weeks of planning, Oswald fired one shot at Walker as the general sat behind a window. The window's wooden frame deflected the bullet, and Oswald failed to hit his target.

Soon after, the unemployed Oswald decided to look for work in New Orleans, where he had family. Marina and their daughter remained in Dallas for a time with family friend Ruth Paine, then joined Oswald in New Orleans in May. By this time, Oswald had turned his attention to Cuba and Fidel Castro. In New Orleans, he started a chapter of the Fair Play for Cuba Committee.

On September 23, 1963, Marina returned to Dallas to have her second baby. On September 25, Oswald left New Orleans for Mexico City, which had the nearest Cuban consulate from which he could get a visa to travel to Cuba. He had expected to obtain a visa to Cuba in a few days and was shocked to be turned down. He also tried to get a visa to the Soviet Union but failed there as well. Short of money, Oswald returned to Dallas on October 3.

Back in Dallas, Oswald continued to live separately from Marina, who was staying with Ruth Paine until he found a job and an apartment. On October 14, 1963, Paine heard that the Texas School Book Depository was hiring, and on October 16, Oswald began work there. On November 19–20, Dallas newspapers published the presidential motorcade route, which would run right past the Book Depository.

Oswald—aggravated by his marriage, unable to keep a job, rejected by both Cuba and the Soviet Union—now saw his chance.

He had told a fellow Marine "that one day he would do something which would make him famous." Like an American Herostratus, Oswald knew that he would blaze his name in history if he could destroy so enormous a figure as John F. Kennedy.

On November 22, 1963, Oswald brought his rifle to work in a brown paper parcel. At lunchtime, he used book cartons to make a sniper's nest on the sixth floor, where windows overlooked Dealey Plaza.

At 12:30, over the space of eight seconds, as the open car carrying President Kennedy, Governor John Connally, and their wives passed, Oswald fired three shots. The third shot was fatal. John Kennedy was pronounced dead at 1:00 p.m.

In even greater measure than he could have expected, Oswald caught some of Kennedy's fame. Not only did he kill Kennedy, but he himself was dramatically gunned down by nightclub owner Jack Ruby—an act carried live on television. Long decades in prison would have diminished Oswald in the public mind, but dead and silent, he's gained the notoriety for which he always longed. The conspiracy theorists constantly study and reinvent Oswald, and today his signature is more valuable than Kennedy's.

Studies of the footage taken by Abraham Zapruder on his home movie camera, sophisticated computer analysis, expert consultants, advanced ballistics studies, and extensive investigations confirm that Oswald alone shot Kennedy.

First, marksmanship specialists confirmed that Oswald was easily capable of making the shots that hit Kennedy. Enhancements of the Zapruder film and firsthand accounts show that the three shots took place over a period of eight seconds—ample time for Oswald to aim and fire three times. The trajectories of the bullets establish that they were fired from the Texas School Book Depository; no shots came from the grassy knoll to the right of the motorcade or from anywhere else.

Oswald's first shot missed; a branch probably blocked it from its target.

The second shot hit both Kennedy and Connally. This bullet has been mocked as a "magic bullet" by those who argue that no single bullet could have caused the injuries attributed to it. In fact, analysis shows that the bullet entered Kennedy's back and exited his throat. Tumbling as it traveled, the bullet hit Connally's shoulder, then exited Connally's chest and continued through to pierce Connally's right wrist (held in front of his body), exited, and stopped on Connally's left thigh. The bullet didn't make any odd changes in direction; it moved in a straight line until deflected by Connally's rib.

The bullet has also been derided as the "pristine bullet," because it was allegedly too pristine to have inflicted the injuries attributed to it. In fact, the bullet was a fully jacketed military bullet—that is, one encased in metal to stop it from fragmenting within its target—and it was damaged in a way quite consistent with its design and the wounds it caused. And although the fact that the bullet was retrieved from Connally's hospital stretcher aroused suspicions that it had been planted, analysis shows that the bullet found on the stretcher was indeed the same one that hit Connally.

The third, final, and fatal shot ripped off the right side of Kennedy's head.

Rifle and ballistics evidence shows that the rifle that shot Kennedy was the same rifle that Oswald ordered by mail and owned. Oswald's fingerprints and palm prints were at the crime scene at the Texas School Book Depository's sixth-floor window, and three empty cartridge cases were found on the floor.

After firing the three shots, Oswald managed to leave the Book Depository amid the chaos to return to his apartment. There he picked up the pistol he would use, minutes later, to shoot police officer J. D. Tippit. (Oswald had ordered both the pistol and the rifle through the mail, using the same alias.) Oswald tried to hide in the Texas Theatre but was captured there just ninety minutes after he shot Kennedy. He told a police captain, "Everybody will know who I am now."

Evidence shows that not only was Oswald the lone shooter, but he acted alone. There is no proof he was part a conspiracy.

A week after Kennedy's death, President Johnson appointed Chief Justice Earl Warren to lead a blue-ribbon panel to investigate the assassination. The Warren Commission concluded in September 1964 that a single assassin, Lee Harvey Oswald, was responsible.

However, the Warren Commission's conclusions were tainted by its inadequate investigation. The commission felt pressure to reach its conclusion quickly and to dispel various rumors. Because of its haste, the commission didn't grapple with conflicting testimony, ambiguous photographs, or contradictory evidence.

Also, both the CIA and the FBI withheld information. The CIA failed to disclose that the CIA and the Mafia had joined in an operation to assassinate Castro, and although both Bobby Kennedy and commission member Allen Dulles, former head of the CIA, knew about these efforts, they remained silent. FBI Chief J. Edgar Hoover worked to downplay the FBI's contacts with Oswald and to hide the agency's mistakes.

The commission's rushed and incomplete job bred suspicion that the panel was attempting to mislead the public, as did its decision to close its hearings to the public, its failure to provide an index to allow readers to cross-reference evidence, its misstatement of some evidence, and its classification of a large number of documents. What's more, four of the seven commission members themselves later expressed skepticism about their conclusion.

Because of continued widespread questions about the shooting not only of John Kennedy but also of Martin Luther King Jr., in 1976, the House Select Committee on Assassinations formed to reinvestigate these cases. The committee issued a final report in 1979, after an investigation that accomplished some important work but, in the end, was almost as faulty as the Warren Commission's.

Investigators confirmed that Kennedy had been hit only twice and that both shots came from Oswald's rifle, fired from the Texas School Book Depository. But not long before the committee was ready to issue its report, it changed it to conclude that circumstantial evidence pointed to a conspiracy to kill Kennedy. The committee based this conclusion on a tape recording, made when a Dallas police officer's radio jammed "on," that seemed to reveal the sounds of four shots, giving "a high probability that two gunmen fired." Although the report suggested that members of the Mob, the CIA, or other conspirators were likely involved, the commission had no evidence to identify a second gunman.

Before long, this acoustical evidence was disproved. Subsequent expert review determined that the tape had been made after the assassination and at a considerable distance—which explained the whistling, instead of pandemonium, that could be heard on the tape.

Because of a continuing sense among Americans that the truth about Kennedy's assassination had been covered up, and as a result of public pressure following the release of the Oliver Stone movie *JFK,* in 1992 Congress created the Assassination Records Review Board to gather and open records related to Kennedy's assassination. The Assassination Records Review Board put more than 4 million pages of secret records into the public domain.

None of these efforts by the government, however, have quieted the clamor swirling around Kennedy's death. From the first minute the shots were fired, rumors have multiplied about the assassination.

No brief account of JFK's assassination can possibly catalogue the countless shifting scenarios proposed by conspiracy theorists. They have accused the CIA, Castro, anti-Castro Cubans, the FBI, the Mafia, right-wingers, the Teamsters, Texas oil millionaires, the Secret Service, Lyndon Johnson—even government agents who shot Kennedy because he threatened to reveal secret dealings with extraterrestrials—of responsibility for the assassination. The limitations of government investigations meant that the conspiracy theorists have had much to work with, but while they've shed doubt on aspects of the government findings, none has built a credible alternative case.

In large part, they've built their theories on highly questionable evidence. For example, they often rely on testimony from people who changed their stories after their initial reports or on witnesses who disagree with the overwhelming majority of other witnesses. For example, 88 percent of witnesses heard only three shots. The credibility of Jean Hill, a famous eyewitness for the grassy-knoll theory, isn't considered undermined by her failure to mention that shot during a November 22, 1963, TV interview—but she did, however, recall seeing Kennedy looking at a "little dog" riding between him and Jackie. (There was no dog.) Conspiracy theorists invoke witnesses' claims to have seen a flash of light and puff of smoke on the grassy knoll—even though modern weapons don't create light or smoke. They find hidden figures in the dark blurs of photographs.

Conspiracy-theory buffs spin stories that would require cooperation and silence among dozens or hundreds of conspirators, who accomplished unlikely feats such as swapping corpses, injecting Ruby with cancer cells, replacing Oswald with a look-alike, or subjecting Oswald to a CIA mind-control program.

Conspiracy theorists ignore facts that refute their claims. Oswald fired three bullets in 8 seconds—not 4.8 seconds, as previously believed—which gave him plenty of time to aim and shoot. Although many blame organized crime, despite years of extensive bugging of the Mafia, catching conversations about every possible crime, there was no hint of Mob involvement. Witnesses, instead of "dying like flies" as some claim, died from natural causes and at a predictable rate. When Oswald's grave was opened in 1981, it held the remains of Oswald, not a Russian agent, as one theorist had insisted. For the unconvinced, any evidence that undermines a particular conspiracy theory is explained away by expanding the conspiracy. For instance, those who insist on the existence of the grassy-knoll shooter argue that the final autopsy findings—which show that bullets struck Kennedy from behind, not from the front—only demonstrate that Kennedy's wounds were altered with a swap of his body, or that the autopsy photographs were doctored.

In fact, by far the great preponderance of eyewitness testimony, physical evidence, and the most advanced analysis of photographs, footage, and recordings prove that Lee Harvey Oswald, acting alone, killed John F. Kennedy.

If overwhelming evidence shows that Oswald, acting alone, was the killer, why is the belief in conspiracy so deep and persistent?

Partly, the faith in conspiracy grows out of a desire to make Kennedy's death more meaningful. The event of his death was so enormous that people refuse to accept that such a shabby person as Oswald could have accomplished it. So, instead of having been murdered by a sociopathic loser, Kennedy gains the dignity of having been the subject of elaborate plots by determined, important people.

Also, it's disquieting to consider the power of a single evildoer. It's more comforting to believe that Kennedy's murder required high-level planning and effort rather than to confront the fact that a twenty-four-year-old man ordered a rifle through the mail, took it to work, aimed it out the window, and gunned down the president.

The conspiracy theories, too, tap into the belief that politicians lie; that the CIA, the FBI, and the military carry on their own nefarious plots; and that powerful organizations control the U.S. government.

But there's something else at work—something that accounts for the diligent, painstaking, imaginative work of these self-appointed investigators. Like Oswald himself, the conspiracy theorists seek to share Kennedy's fame. Through their efforts to solve his murder—by examining the evidence with their own eyes, by seeing new clues, by offering new solutions—ordinary people can make themselves part of the Kennedy legacy.

The first to try to earn fame by inserting himself into the drama of the assassination was Oswald's killer, Jack Ruby. Ruby had always tried to attract recognition, and he was a constant nuisance at the newspaper offices and police station. "He really wanted to be somebody, but didn't have it in him," recalled one of his employees. Reporter Tony Zoppi agreed: "He had to be where the action was. . . . That's why the President's assassination and all the follow-up activity at the jail with Oswald and the press attracted Jack like a magnet." Ruby killed Oswald believing it would make him a famous hero. In 1966, flamboyant, headline-seeking Jim Garrison, a New Orleans district attorney, launched an investigation into Kennedy's assassination. He abused the powers of his office to try to prove his conspiracy theories and to thrust himself into the national spotlight, but his charges were completely discredited. Since Garrison, scores of others have added their theories to the mix.

Even if few completely accept their conjectures, the conspiracy theorists do succeed in winning for themselves a measure of renown. Their books are published, they're interviewed for newspapers and for TV documentaries; they've made themselves part of the Kennedy story. For, despite the contrary facts, an eager audience awaits any new, provocative theory. Preferring the complications of a spy novel to the dull simplicity of the truth, the public welcomes the heady mix of real and imagined details of the assassination and the improbable accounts of Oswald body doubles, corpse tampering, and widespread government cover-ups. Therefore, no investigation, no evidence, no authoritative report will ever be able to put to rest the cherished mystery of Kennedy's death.

38

FORTUNE'S FAVORITE
His Extraordinary Destiny

To an uncanny degree, Kennedy seemed singled out by Fortune to achieve a rare destiny. Every turn of events worked to his advantage; everything supported his efforts. People understood that he somehow stood outside the common range of human experience— but instead of feeling resentful or angry, they felt invigorated by his distinction.

"When . . . fortune's favorites sail close by us," wrote Herman Melville, "we, though all adroop before, catch somewhat of the rushing breeze, and joyfully feel our bagging sails fill out." Kennedy, with his brilliant personality and life, had this effect on the entire country.

Four elements made Kennedy what he was. First, there were the circumstances into which he was born: American, Catholic, Irish, good-looking, in bad health, the second son of a rich, ambitious, and devoted father. Second, there was the character he developed, as shaped by nature and experience: charismatic, witty, well-read, politically minded, promiscuous. Third, there were the decisions he made, whether or not he fully realized the consequences: to run for office, to marry Jackie, to hire Ted Sorensen, to write a book, to make Bobby his attorney general. Fourth, there were the mishaps that befell him, within the course he tried to set: the Japanese destroyer that split his PT boat, the failure to win the vice presidential nomination. In each of these aspects, Kennedy was favored by Fortune.

Even moments of disaster or possible failure turned to Kennedy's advantage. For instance, newspapers lifted the PT boat incident—which could have humiliated him—into a triumph that made him a highly electable hero. Later, Kennedy was dejected when his former girlfriend married celebrated journalist John Hersey, but when Hersey met Kennedy at the Stork Club, the writer was so intrigued by JFK's *PT-109* adventure that he wrote the 1944 *New Yorker* piece "Survival," which became a key campaign tool. In 1956, Kennedy's failed bid to be Adlai Stevenson's VP running mate propelled him into stardom while preserving him from the taint of defeat when Eisenhower triumphed at the polls.

Fortune threw unexpected favors in Kennedy's path. As he campaigned for the presidency, he appeared with his sisters Eunice, Pat, and Jean in their husbands' vote-critical home states of Illinois, California, and New York. Kennedy explained, "In preparation for this campaign, I had sisters living in all the key states." Kennedy's wife, advisers feared, was too glamorous to be popular with the public; instead, her passion for couture clothing and interior decoration gave an unexpected boost to the administration's popularity. During the 1962 Cuban missile crisis, by chance the ship to make the first stop and search of a Soviet vessel, the *Marucla,* was the USS *Joseph P. Kennedy, Jr.,* which had been named for the eldest Kennedy son and on which Bobby had served in 1946. Kennedy observed, "The press will never believe we didn't stick the *Kennedy* in the way of the *Marucla* just to give the family publicity." Things happened so conveniently for Kennedy. After Marilyn Monroe sang her famous "Happy Birthday, Mr. President" to JFK at Madison Square Garden, their dangerous affair threatened to spin out of control. When rumors began to spread, and Kennedy cut off all contact, Monroe began calling Bobby. Unstable, demanding, and hooked on alcohol and pills, Monroe posed a real danger—but eleven weeks after the birthday gala, Monroe was found dead. Even Kennedy's illnesses helped him: the Addison's disease that threatened his life also kept his hair brown and thick; the consequent cortisone treatment gave him an increased sense of well-being, confidence, and energy; his weak stomach protected him from the alcohol problems suffered later by some of his siblings.

Kennedy was Fortune's favorite even to the end, with a death that secured his place in history. He seemed to sense the destiny that would befall him. Repeatedly, he'd promised voters "one thousand days of exacting presidential leadership," and he died soon after he passed his one thousandth day as president.

And so, just when Kennedy appeared at the height of his powers, but before any of several threatening scandals could explode, Providence snatched him away—in a spectacular manner that strengthened and protected his legacy.

The fall of 1963 was a dangerous time for Kennedy. The Senate Rules Committee was investigating Bobby Baker on influence-peddling charges. Kennedy was tied to Baker, because Baker had procured women for him—bad enough. Worse, one of Baker's women was Ellen Rometsch, who, FBI head Hoover told Bobby in July, was suspected of being an East German spy and to be sleeping with the president. Not long after that meeting, in August 1963, the Kennedys arranged to have Rometsch rush-deported to Germany. But Rometsch's expulsion didn't put an end to the matter. In late October and November 1963, questions began to circulate about Rometsch's ties to government officials and the unusual circumstances of her deportation. Kennedy's actions suggest that

1963.
John Kennedy Jr.
plays while his father works
in the Oval Office.

he sensed danger. For a year and a half, *Look* photographer Stanley Tretick had been trying to do a story about Kennedy and his son. Just at the time Baker resigned, Kennedy invited Tretick to the White House to take pictures for what would become the delightful photo essay "The President and His Son." The pictures would hit the newsstands the week Kennedy died.

It seems no accident that Kennedy decided to highlight his role as loving father at a time when the Rometsch scandal threatened to burst into view. At his November 14, 1963, press conference—his last press conference—a reporter asked Kennedy about Bobby Baker. He answered, "I think we will know a good deal more about Mr. Baker before we get through. Other people will be investigated as time goes on." *Other people*—including, in all likelihood, Kennedy himself.

And Kennedy had another potential scandal on his hands—a financial scandal involving his key adviser and friend Kenny

O'Donnell. In the summer of 1963, Paul Corbin—a trusted aide of Bobby's, considered abrasive and meddlesome by many, including JFK—accused O'Donnell of skimming campaign contributions. Kennedy didn't seem concerned about the situation, perhaps because Corbin hated O'Donnell and had a reputation as a liar, or perhaps because instead of taking cash for personal gain, O'Donnell was using the money to address top secret problems—such as Kennedy's Rometsch difficulty. Corbin continued to gather evidence against O'Donnell and, in November, took it to Bobby; Bobby called JFK, who was in Texas; Bobby promised Corbin that they would all meet Monday morning, November 25, to address the issue. Instead, this was the day of Kennedy's funeral.

Apart from these specific scandals, there lurked the danger that political opponents would exploit his sexual hijinks. Foy Kohler, ambassador to the Soviet Union, wondered whether the Republicans might use such information to defeat Kennedy in the 1964 election. Hoover, too, might have leaked scandalous information. "Hoover hated Kennedy," observed Edwin Guthman, Bobby's Justice Department press secretary. "Hoover was not bashful about using the raw files on people and leaking stuff out on people. There's no question in my mind absolutely that if Jack Kennedy had lived . . . the Judith [Campbell] Exner thing would have been a factor. . . . It would have been an issue in the campaign. I have no question in my mind." Mark Raskin, a National Security Council aide, agreed. "The White House was a bawdy house . . . I think Kennedy thought that he was keeping all of this stuff separate . . . The reality was that one piece of this was collapsing in on the other. . . . The FBI is keeping tabs on him."

Kennedy probably exaggerated his ability to control his secrets. In the past, his father's money, his brother's authority, reporters' customary respect for politicians' privacy, and his own charm had allowed him to escape numerous possible scandals. But information was building to a point where it might have been irrepressible.

These possible scandals put all of Kennedy's efforts under threat. Several people noticed that in the last weeks of his life, Kennedy was in a somber, distracted mood.

And then, as if in circumstances artfully composed to blaze his name in history, Kennedy was struck down by an assassin's bullet.

Outwardly, Kennedy was at a triumphant moment. He had greater mastery of the presidency and the executive branch. In his 1963 State of the Union address, he announced that the United States had "the tides of human freedom in our favor. . . . We have every reason to believe that our tide is running strong." In a sixteen-day period in June 1963, he gave three of his greatest speeches: his American University speech, in which he called for a reexamination of Soviet-American relations; the very next day, his great TV address on civil rights, in which he explained, "We are confronted primarily with a moral issue. It is as old as the scriptures and is as clear as the American Constitution"; and his famous "*Ich bin ein Berliner*" speech, to an adoring, frenzied mass in West Berlin. As he left the city, he told Sorensen, "We'll never have another day like this one as long as we live." After Berlin, he traveled to Ireland, where he was met with ecstatic crowds. He told a friend, "These were the three happiest days I've ever spent in my life." That summer, he'd signed the Nuclear Test Ban Treaty, which he considered his greatest achievement. He was talking about pulling the United States out of Vietnam. Polls taken abroad showed U.S. prestige to be very high. At home, he'd awakened to the challenge of civil rights and introduced an ambitious civil rights bill.

In mid-November, Kennedy had held his first strategy meeting for the 1964 presidential race and said he expected to beat Barry Goldwater in a historic landslide. To many observers, his marriage with Jackie seemed at its strongest point ever. His physical condition was good; Dr. Travell reported that his health was the best it had been since she'd known him. Kennedy had even said good-bye to his father. On his last visit, on October 20, just a few weeks before the assassination, he gave his father his usual good-bye kiss and headed to leave—then returned to give his father one more kiss. "It almost seemed," wrote O'Donnell and Powers, "as if the President had a feeling that he was seeing his father for the last time."

The blow, when it came on November 22, 1963, was just as Fortune designed. John F. Kennedy had a rendezvous with death. Matters were so neatly arranged, in fact, that many would later see proof of conspiracy.

The fatal shot took him looking his most presidential, waving to cheering crowds, flanked by dignitaries, smiling in the bright sunshine. "We can say only that he died as he would have wanted to die," Sorensen wrote, "at the center of action."

Jackie hadn't traveled with her husband on a political domestic trip since 1960, she hadn't been scheduled to resume her activities as first lady until early 1964, and she wavered several times about making the trip. But that day in Dallas, she sat beside him in the convertible. "To think that I very nearly didn't go! . . . Thank God I went with him!" She held not yellow roses, symbol of Texas, but red roses, symbol of martyrdom and love.

Providence had cleared the way for its agent, Lee Harvey Oswald, by placing him just five weeks earlier as an employee of a building on the motorcade route. Oswald fired three shots from the sixth floor, and the third killed Kennedy.

A curious, formal perfection marks the assassination, in the way Kennedy's fateful tendencies played their roles in the inevitable end.

Kennedy's long history of back pain was important, because that day he was, as usual, wearing the stiff back brace, which held his torso in ramrod posture. Oswald's fatal shot might not have hit its target had the brace not continued to hold Kennedy erect after he was struck the first time.

Kennedy's eagerness to engage crowds and his disregard of security played a part. Even Jackie realized this; after saying the Secret

Service should have done more to protect him, she added, "Oh, well, I guess Jack would only have gotten more reckless as time went on, anyway." Efforts to shield him from crowds annoyed Kennedy, who believed that "politics and protection don't mix." During his June 1963 trip to Ireland, for example, Kennedy had left his car and allowed himself to be mobbed by enthusiastic crowds. In Manhattan just days before the assassination, Kennedy ordered the presidential limousine to leave behind its motorcycle escort and drive through a crowded downtown area. Kennedy rode in an open car, whatever the weather, when more than a few people gathered. On November 22, 1963, Kennedy preferred not to use the bubble top, to have greater contact with the public. (The bubble top wasn't bulletproof, but it might have deflected the bullets or obscured Oswald's view.) And because Kennedy wanted to see a big turnout, newspapers were allowed to publish the motorcade route.

The timing and manner of Kennedy's death sealed his legacy in history. In studying the elements of presidential stature, Kennedy had considered the advantages of dying in office. "Would Lincoln have been judged so great a President," he asked, "if he had lived long enough to face the almost insoluble problem of Reconstruction?" At a White House seminar on the presidency, Kennedy asked who the great presidents were, and why. He observed, "I think maybe to be a great president, you have to die in office." And so it was arranged by Fortune.

His early death lifted Kennedy into triumph and assured that he'll be remembered as beautiful, young, and full of promise. He was vouchsafed the destiny of his particular hero and model Raymond Asquith: "Sometimes . . . the promise of youth dulls into a dreary middle age of success. . . . But for the chosen few, like Raymond, there is no disillusionment. They march on into life with a boyish grace, and their high noon keeps all the freshness of the morning."

With his great charisma, Kennedy raised expectations very high; because he died when he did, his administration's brevity excused the promises he didn't keep. In office, Kennedy would surely have been embroiled in compromises and decisions that would have disillusioned the public. Instead, Kennedy's admirers can imagine that, had he lived, he would have pursued the course *they* would have preferred: pulling out of Vietnam or staying the course without disaster; following a more aggressive approach to civil rights but a less divisive one; achieving a new understanding with the Soviet Union or standing up to the Soviets more strenuously. Jackie, too, could imagine that after years in a difficult marriage, her life with Jack was about to change. Not long after he died, she recalled, "It took a very long time for us to work everything out, but we did, and we were about to have a real life together." After Jack died, Jackie could replace her unfaithful husband with the gallant hero of Camelot.

The shock and grief aroused by the assassination helped Kennedy further his ideals in death, perhaps more than in life. Alive, Kennedy had been frustrated by Congress, but President Johnson was able to use Kennedy's memory to help score legislative victories for the Kennedy agenda. At the same time that Kennedy's death molded public sentiment to further his goals, it protected Kennedy from their consequences. He is associated with the ringing words of his speeches but not the consequent horrors of Vietnam and the escalating arms race; with the goals of equality and freedom but not with busing or race riots; with the promise to "get America moving" but not the unsettling social changes of the 1960s. His death allows admirers to suppose that, had he lived, he could have realized his aims without rousing antagonism, resentment, or turmoil.

Kennedy's death and solemn funeral lifted his stature far above what he could have achieved himself; he would never have been the subject of such ceremonial adoration in life. Also, the circumstances of his assassination ensure the enduring fascination of the public. Dramatic, simple, captured on film, with a cast of colorful characters, and an unsolved mystery—these few seconds are among the most intriguing of Kennedy's life. And the mysteries about the assassination, *if mysteries there are,* keep the public riveted.

It's all just as Kennedy would have wanted. In a notebook of quotations he kept, he copied a passage describing his hero Raymond Asquith—a passage that came to describe Kennedy himself: "He loved his youth, and his youth has become eternal. Debonair and brilliant and brave, he . . . knows not age or weariness or defeat."

39

My Kennedy

Judgment

Every biography raises questions of judgment, because without judgment, the life lacks significance.

Now you must decide how to balance faults against virtues and successes against failures, what to pardon because of changing standards, how to weigh the evidence, old and new.

You must judge whether Kennedy was an idealist or an opportunist, whether he was a great statesman or a talented but shallow charmer, whether his success was due to his own merits or his lucky circumstances, whether he could be both an unfaithful husband and a fine man. Does he deserve to be so often in men's good thoughts?

Here is my Kennedy. Others look at this history and see a different "Kennedy," but this is mine.

A constellation of fortunate elements came together in Kennedy. He was the all-American hero—splendid, graceful, with a confident ease in himself. He grew up in a remarkable household of wealth, politics, and competition. He had a winning personal style, a rapport with reporters, and a rare aptitude for television. He died a terrible death. He inspired extraordinary veneration. But do we judge him to be truly great?

Although good looks, an interesting life, and a witty style don't seem appropriately substantial to account for the enormous regard for Kennedy, nevertheless, it's such superficial qualities that interest the public in more serious matters. *Law alone cannot make men see right.* Without a war or crisis, how does a leader engage the public, except by winning their attention?

Kennedy's glamour, heroism, and eloquence were the tools by which he roused the country. But none of these elements—or even their combination—was enough to create a Kennedy. It was he who transformed them. He worked hard to create an image of John Kennedy—but images take their power from ideas, and the idea that lay behind Kennedy was excellence. Perhaps others helped write the words Kennedy spoke and the books he published, but they wrote those words *for him;* only he made those expressions possible and persuasive. He held out a strenuous vision of dedication to the public good, of commitment to American ideals, of appreciation for culture and intellect, even of physical fitness. His striking personality summed up the American dream, with all its responsibilities and pleasures—for Americans themselves and for people across the world.

Despite the passage of time, despite the exposure of many of his secrets, despite the litany of things he did and didn't do, the public's reverence for Camelot has continued. People want to be lifted up, to be dazzled by an ideal—and they don't mind a little sizzle, too. They won't allow the legend they admire to be supplanted by a disappointing truth.

And, after all, did Kennedy disappoint the public? His image wasn't wholly true, but a man's actions can be greater than himself.

Was the hidden Kennedy, now revealed, more true than the hero the public sees in him?

Although many argue that Kennedy should have used his power more assertively, he did try to be a force for the country's good. And if he did not achieve all the good he might have, consider the harm he might have inflicted, with the tremendous power of his charisma, if he'd wished. Despite his slowness to act, he ushered in a period of great expectations, and those expectations laid the groundwork for progress. And before deciding whether his success was merely based on "image," we must acknowledge that we have nothing else. Although we strive to go beyond image, although we say we distrust appearances, we know nothing except what we see and hear, or what we learn from reports from those who have seen and heard. Furthermore, the gift of image making—although sometimes derided as mere public relations—is what permits great leaders to inspire trust, rally support, and sway public sentiment. When Kennedy said, "*Ask not what your country can do for you—ask what you can do for your country,*" the world rose up to answer.

He is greatest who is most often in men's good thoughts. This, Kennedy achieves. Through words, photographs, symbols, and actions, Kennedy projected himself into the public mind, and, far more difficult, he inspired people with a sense of hope and possibility, with a sense of the positive achievements of government, and with a standard of excellence. "This country is moving and it must not stop," he'd intended to say on November 22, 1963. "It cannot stop. For this is a time for courage and a time for challenge."

It's hard to make people want to do good—harder, even, than to do good oneself. To achieve this, Kennedy created the idea of John F. Kennedy, a man magnificent enough to capture the imagination of a people who wouldn't have attended to a more realistically portrayed leader. Bored with abstract ideals and concepts, the public needs a personality to dramatize them, and although this dependence seems primitive, it is necessary. The principles Kennedy espoused may have been vague, but had he been more specific, he couldn't have aroused such support. The idealized portrait of John Kennedy is what people saw and believed; it is the reason that "Camelot" seems a fitting description; it fulfilled a longing that still exists.

The intense interest in Kennedy allowed him to accomplish something extraordinarily difficult: he influenced the atmosphere of the country. As Lincoln said, public sentiment is everything. *This* is Kennedy's great and important accomplishment—whatever his personal merit. He fixed the public's imagination on great matters and challenged them to right action, and somehow, although people and the press are usually eager to criticize, he was large enough that people enthusiastically admired him, in his superiority. And because people thought so highly of him, he lifted the stature of the presidency and, with it, the prestige of the country.

If Kennedy manipulated our perceptions by staging the unguarded moments, if he hid the facts that would have shaken our trust—well, we chose to pursue the constant spying, waiting to catch any glimpse we could, like a lover watching through a window, or an investigator gathering evidence.

The fact that Kennedy was *Kennedy* can't simply have been the result of manipulation, because so many have tried to copy him and failed. They've struggled to duplicate the visible elements of his appeal—the high-toned rhetoric, the casual athleticism, the happy family, the cultural interests. They've memorized quips and upgraded their wardrobes. But without the peculiar Kennedy alchemy, these methods don't work. The life of his own son shows that wealth, good looks, a political dynasty, and a beautiful wife aren't enough to make even a Kennedy, *Kennedy*.

And there he is, my Kennedy, caught on an endless Zapruder loop, smiling and waving to adoring crowds. Jackie sits beside him,

September 1960. During the presidential campaign, Senator John Kennedy works composedly; he seems unaware of the people behind him, spying through the window, or the photographer in front of him, taking his picture.

red roses in her lap. Hopeful, young, full of promise; what happened then has never stopped happening.

Fortune provided Kennedy with great advantages, and he lived up to these gifts and made something extraordinary from them. True, he showed us an image that was, in many ways, false. We know that now. But for Kennedy, Fortune's favorite as always, it is the good that he did that lives after him. He embodies to people all over the world the qualities desired in a leader and in a government. It's true: law alone cannot make men see right.

There was something golden about Kennedy, and, although all adroop, we still feel the dazzling light and rushing breeze of excellence and possibility.

Yes, yes, John F. Kennedy was truly great. How do I know? *I can see it with my own eyes.*

40

REMEMBER JOHN F. KENNEDY

Epitaph

Not seldom in this life, when, on the right side, fortune's favorites sail close by us, we, though all adroop before, catch somewhat of the rushing breeze, and joyfully feel our bagging sails fill out.

—HERMAN MELVILLE

JOHN FITZGERALD KENNEDY
1917–1963

Notes

Works listed in the select bibliography are cited in shortened form throughout the notes. Works not listed in the select bibliography are cited in full upon first mention in the notes for each chapter and thereafter cited in shortened form.

INTRODUCTION

Page

5 *a 1970 Harris poll* . . .   Brown, *JFK: History of an Image,* 65.

5 *as did a 1983 Gallup poll,*   Ibid., 100.

5 *in New York Times* . . .   Marjorie Connelly, "Americans Are Still Voting for J.F.K.," *New York Times,* August 18, 1996, E4.

5 *Of all presidents* . . .   Frank Newport, "Examining Presidential Job Approval," July 25, 2001, Gallup Organization.

5 *A 1988 American Heritage* . . .   As cited in Arthur Schlesinger Jr., "JFK Revisited," *Cigar Aficionado,* November–December 1998.

5 *A 1997 survey* . . .   Ibid.

6 *I was struck* . . .   Virginia Woolf, *A Writer's Diary* (New York: Harcourt, Brace and Company, 1953), 136.

1. KENNEDY AS IDEAL LEADER

11 *Jack's father, Joseph* . . .   Lasky, *J.F.K.: Man and Myth,* 39.

13 *The book won* . . .   S. T. Williamson, "Why Britain Slept While Hitler Prepared for War," *New York Times,* August 11, 1940, 70.

13 *Jack's heroic actions . . .* "Kennedy's Son Is Hero in Pacific as Destroyer Splits His PT Boat," *New York Times,* August 20, 1943, 1.

14 *Even his father . . .* Goodwin, *Fitzgeralds and Kennedys,* 714.

15 *"the Senate's gay young bachelor"* Paul F. Healy, "The Senate's Gay Young Bachelor," *Saturday Evening Post,* June 13, 1953, 127.

15 *(Jack donated the prize . . .* Burns, *John Kennedy,* 158.

16 *In 1958, he said . . .* Graham, *Personal History,* 259.

16 *In a compelling . . .* Address to the Greater Houston Ministerial Association, Houston, Texas, September 12, 1960. From the website of the John F. Kennedy Library and Museum (http://www.jfklibrary.org/speeches.htm).

17 *Back in Washington . . .* Goodwin, *Remembering America,* 86.

17 *Kennedy later explained, . . .* Galbraith, *Name-Dropping,* 112.

17 *In his ringing . . .* Address accepting the Democratic Party nomination for the presidency, Los Angeles, July 15, 1960. From the website of the John F. Kennedy Library and Museum (http://www.jfklibrary.org/speeches.htm).

18 *After "eight years . . .* Ibid.

18 *Also, the elderly . . .* West with Kotz, *Upstairs at the White House,* 175, 184.

18 *As Kennedy himself . . .* Louis Menand, "Masters of the Matrix: Kennedy, Nixon, and the Culture of the Image," *New Yorker,* January 5, 2004, 83.

18 *An old friend . . .* Blair and Blair, *The Search for JFK,* 522.

18 *By the end of the . . .* White, *Making of the President, 1960,* 326.

19 *"Ask not what . . .* Inaugural address, Washington, D.C., January 20, 1961. From the website of the John F. Kennedy Library and Museum (http://www.jfklibrary.org/speeches.htm).

19 *The Kennedys, one . . .* Maxine Cheshire with John Greenya, *Maxine Cheshire, Reporter* (Boston: Houghton Mifflin, 1978), 40.

20 *He worried that . . .* Beschloss, *Crisis Years,* 105.

21 *"All free men, . . .* Address, West Berlin, June 26, 1963. From the website of the John F. Kennedy Library and Museum (http://www.jfklibrary.org/speeches.htm).

21 *ExComm's first instinct . . .*   Doyle, *Oval Office*, 128.

21 *ExComm member Treasury . . .*   Ibid., 134.

22 *On October 22, 1962, . . .*   From the website of the John F. Kennedy Library and Museum (http://www.jfklibrary.org/speeches.htm).

22 *Undersecretary of State . . .*   Giglio, *Presidency of Kennedy*, 211.

22 *Secretary of State . . .*   Reeves, *President Kennedy*, 401.

24 *When someone asked . . .*   Strober and Strober, *"Let Us Begin Anew,"* 273.

25 *After watching a replay . . .*   Thomas, *Robert Kennedy*, 248.

25 *He spoke for eighteen . . .*   Smith, *Grace and Power*, 371.

25 *In this speech, . . .*   Radio and television report to the American people on civil rights, White House, June 11, 1963. From the website of the John F. Kennedy Library and Museum (http://www.jfklibrary.org/speeches.htm).

25 *He'd initially been . . .*   Parmet, *JFK*, 76.

26 *Many advised Kennedy . . .*   Martin, *Hero for Our Time*, 539.

26 *Within thirty minutes . . .*   William Manchester, "Then: 1963," *New York Times*, November 4, 1973, 321.

26 *Bobby was dressing . . .*   Kenney, *Kennedy: Presidential Portfolio*, 224.

27 *A few days later, . . .*   Barnouw, *Tube of Plenty*, 332.

27 *In Washington, Johnson . . .*   Ibid., 334.

27 *In the United States, . . .*   Ibid., 332.

2. KENNEDY AS SHOWY OPPORTUNIST

31 *She took frequent . . .*   Mulvaney, *Diana & Jackie*, 82.

32 *In high school, . . .*   Kenney, *Kennedy: Presidential Portfolio*, 13.

32 *He ran for a . . .*   Hamilton, *JFK: Reckless Youth*, 227.

32 *She'd spent time . . .*   Beschloss, *Crisis Years*, 613.

32 *When rumors of . . .*   Goodwin, *Fitzgeralds and Kennedys*, 633.

33 *He used the combined . . .*   Dallek, *Unfinished Life*, 89.

34 *Jack's brother Joe . . .*   Ibid., 106.

34 *Jack later admitted . . .*   Reeves, *Question of Character*, 68.

34 *Joe had once . . .*   Martin, *Hero for Our Time*, 42.

34 *Each dispatch was . . .*   Parmet, *Jack*, 132.

34 *Jack produced a . . .*   Blair and Blair, *The Search for JFK,* 377, 586.

36 *Fellow Massachusetts congressman . . .*   O'Neill with Novak, *Man of the House,* 87.

37 *At the 1956 Democratic . . .*   "Party's Film Aids Kennedy's Drive," *New York Times,* August 1, 1956, 3.

38 *according to aide . . .*   Heymann, *Jackie,* 242.

38 *In fact, journalist . . .*   White, *Making of the President, 1960,* 332.

38 *The 1952 and 1956 . . .*   Kutler, *Wars of Watergate,* 50.

39 *During the campaign, . . .*   Lasky, *J.F.K.: Man and Myth,* 538.

39 *In that office, . . .*   Reeves, *Question of Character,* 225.

39 *He'd earned mostly . . .*   Thomas, *Robert Kennedy,* 55.

39 *Bobby also used . . .*   Wills, *Kennedy Imprisonment,* 154; Lasky, *J.F.K.: Man and Myth,* ix.

40 *During the campaign, . . .*   Parmet, *JFK,* 8.

40 *Even the worshipful . . .*   Manchester, *Portrait of a President,* 212.

40 *columnist Walter Lippmann . . .*   Beschloss, *Crisis Years,* 529.

40 *Bobby explained that . . .*   Leaming, *Mrs. Kennedy,* 70.

41 *Khrushchev's belligerence visibly . . .*   Dallek, *Unfinished Life,* 407.

41 *Far from being . . .*   Beschloss, *Crisis Years,* 283.

41 *After the failure . . .*   Thomas, *Robert Kennedy,* 149.

42 *Under Bobby's goading, . . .*   Ibid., 151.

42 *The undermining of . . .*   Beschloss, *Crisis Years,* 351, 410, 564.

42 *Later, when the administration . . .*   Hersh, *Dark Side of Camelot,* 373.

43 *The administration approved . . .*   Reeves, *Question of Character,* 416.

43 *although he initially . . .*   Collier and Horowitz, *The Kennedys,* 306.

43 *as General Maxwell Taylor . . .*   Matthews, *Kennedy and Nixon,* 232.

43 *The Peace Corps was . . .*   Smith, *Grace and Power,* 177.

44 *As Saul Bellow put it, . . .*   Saul Bellow, "White House and Artists," in *It All Adds Up* (New York: Viking, 1962), 70.

44 *Not only that . . .*   Beschloss, *Crisis Years,* 135.

3. KENNEDY'S EXCELLENCE

47 *He believed the . . .*   Sorensen, *Kennedy,* 182.

47 *In the first televised . . .*   From the website of the John F. Kennedy Library and Museum (http://www.jfklibrary.org/speeches.htm).

47 *as a freshman* . . .   Leamer, *Kennedy Men,* 249.

47 *in 1952, the Capitol* . . .   Latham and Sakol, *Encyclopedia,* 250.

47 *John Kenneth Galbraith* . . .   Halberstam, *Best and Brightest,* 98.

48 *Kennedy remained true* . . .   Lowe, *Remembering Jack,* 107.

48 *Looking over a speech* . . .   Parmet, *Jack,* 512.

48 *Not many politicians* . . .   Sorensen, *Kennedy,* 64.

49 *In an address made* . . .   Address to the National Press Club, Washington, D.C., January 14, 1960. From the website of the John F. Kennedy Library and Museum
(http://www.jfklibrary.org/speeches.htm).

49 *In a speech in October* . . .   Adler, *Kennedy Wit,* 14.

49 *In the last press* . . .   Press conference, Washington, D.C., November 14, 1963. Kennedy quoted from Arthur Hugh Clough's "Say Not the Struggle Naught Availeth." From the website of the John F. Kennedy Library and Museum
(http://www.jfklibrary.org/speeches.htm).

49 *A friend recalled,* . . .   Exner with Demaris, *My Story,* 104.

49 *Kennedy reflected, "Nixon* . . .   Galbraith, *Name-Dropping,* 102.

49 *When asked if* . . .   Third televised Nixon-Kennedy presidential debate, October 13, 1960. From the website of the John F. Kennedy Library and Museum (http://www.jfklibrary.org/speeches.htm).

49 *Kennedy's self-assurance extended* . . .   Anthony, *As We Remember Her,* 128.

50 *"I never saw* . . .   O'Neill with Novak, *Man of the House,* 86.

50 *"Kennedy amazed his* . . .   Sidey, *Kennedy, President,* 352.

50 *One aide admitted,* . . .   Galbraith, *Journal,* 632.

50 *Kennedy's ambassador to* . . .   Beschloss, *Crisis Years,* 674.

51 *After one freewheeling,* . . .   Ibid., 70.

51 *British prime minister* . . .   Horne, *Macmillan,* 575.

51 *Kennedy displayed his* . . .   Schlesinger, *A Thousand Days,* 105.

51 *Theodore White described* . . .   White, *In Search of History,* 510.

51 *He once reminded* . . .   Dallek, *Unfinished Life,* 209.

51 *When the microphone* . . .   Sorensen, *Kennedy,* 180.

51 *His brother-in-law Sargent* . . .   Strober and Strober, *"Let Us Begin Anew,"* 53.

51 *For example, Kennedy* . . .   Matthews, *Kennedy and Nixon,* 124.

52 *When Theodore White* . . .   Reeves, *President Kennedy,* 465.

52 *Columnist Rowland Evans* . . .   Reeves, *Question of Character,* 89.

52 *Longtime friend Lem* . . .   Goodwin, *Fitzgeralds and Kennedys,* 464.

52 *Columnist Joseph Alsop* . . .   Alsop and Platt, "*I've Seen the Best of It,*" 464.

52 *Charley Bartlett recalled,* . . .   Lieberson, *John Fitzgerald Kennedy,* 73.

52 *When special counsel* . . .   Sorensen, *Kennedy,* 262.

52 *When Schlesinger asked* . . .   Reeves, *President Kennedy,* 234.

52 *Bobby Baker, who* . . .   Baker with King, *Wheeling and Dealing,* 45.

53 *"I loved him—more* . . .   Strober and Strober, "*Let Us Begin Anew,*" 55.

53 *For example, Kennedy* . . .   Leaming, *Mrs. Kennedy,* 196.

53 *Jackie agreed: "People* . . .   Anthony, *As We Remember Her,* 129.

54 *at the same time,* . . .   Wofford, *Of Kennedys and Kings,* 147.

5. KENNEDY AND MONEY

60 *Although Joe Kennedy* . . .   Burns, *John Kennedy,* 37.

60 *Anxious on the* . . .   White, *Making of the President, 1960,* 114.

60 *Racing to complete* . . .   Reeves, *Question of Character,* 49.

60 *In his first House race,* . . .   Lasky, *J.F.K.: Man and Myth,* 64.

61 *Even when Kennedy* . . .   O'Donnell and Powers with McCarthy, "*Johnny, We Hardly Knew Ye,*" 243.

61 *(Twenty years later,* . . .   West with Kotz, *Upstairs at the White House,* 205.

61 *He never carried* . . .   Collier and Horowitz, *The Kennedys,* 158.

61 *While Jackie racked up* . . .   Bradlee, *Conversations with Kennedy,* 119.

61 *Jack imposed modest* . . .   West with Kotz, *Upstairs at the White House,* 211–212.

61 *In one Kennedy* . . .   Collier and Horowitz, *The Kennedys,* 196.

61 *in another, she redecorated* . . .   Bradford, *America's Queen,* 115.

62 *As Congressman Roman* . . .   Strober and Strober, "*Let Us Begin Anew,*" 52.

62 *When Jackie gave* . . .   Sorensen, *Kennedy,* 20.

62 *He didn't allow* . . .   Thomas, *Robert Kennedy,* 191.

62 *When word got out* . . .   Lasky, *J.F.K.: Man and Myth,* 505.

6. KENNEDY FACT SHEET

64 *IQ: 119.*   Dallek, *Unfinished Life,* 33.

65 *Age at which . . .*   Collier and Horowitz, *The Kennedys,* 65.

65 *First year he . . .*   Hamilton, *JFK: Reckless Youth,* 786.

65 *Usual breakfast: freshly . . .*   Martin, *Hero for Our Time,* 171.

65 *How many children . . .*   Ibid., 126.

65 *Actor whom he . . .*   Wills, *Kennedy Imprisonment,* 134.

66 *His first executive . . .*   Sorensen, *Kennedy,* 248.

66 *His golf score: . . .*   Salinger, *With Kennedy,* 93.

66 *His ideas for . . .*   Parmet, *JFK,* 308.

66 *Magazines he read . . .*   Hugh Sidey, "The President's Voracious Reading Habits," *Life,* March 17, 1961, 57.

66 *Most unhappy periods . . .*   Leamer, *Kennedy Women,* 527.

66 *What he believed . . .*   Reeves, *President Kennedy,* 311.

66 *The honor that . . .*   Reeves, *Question of Character,* 142.

67 *The quality he . . .*   Schlesinger, *A Thousand Days,* 672.

67 *What he said was . . .*   Martin, *Hero for Our Time,* 84. Jackie asked him these questions a week before their marriage.

67 *Kennedy's greatest fear: . . .*   Salinger, *With Kennedy,* 255.

67 *Things at which he . . .*   Hamilton, *JFK: Reckless Youth,* 629.

67 *Essence of the . . .*   Martin, *Hero for Our Time,* 570.

67 *What Kennedy wanted . . .*   O'Donnell and Powers with McCarthy, "*Johnny, We Hardly Knew Ye,*" 343.

67 *Some favorite books as a child: . . .*   Kennedy, *Times to Remember,* 111–112.

68 *Books he'd take to . . .*   Lincoln, *Twelve Years,* 85.

68 *A favorite quote . . .*   White, *Making of the President, 1960,* 340.

69 *Favorite story about . . .*   Reeves, *President Kennedy,* 286.

69 *Favorite New York . . .*   Leaming, *Mrs. Kennedy,* 260.

69 *A favorite aphorism: . . .*   Goodwin, *Remembering America,* 92.

70 *Favorite musicals: My . . .*   Manchester, *Death of a President,* 29.

7. KENNEDY AND HIS FATHER

71 *"He's the one . . .*   O'Donnell and Powers with McCarthy, "*Johnny, We Hardly Knew Ye,*" 39.

72 *he wasn't present* . . .   Burns, *John Kennedy,* 37.

72 *More than anything,* . . .   Kennedy, *Times to Remember,* 143.

72 *"All my ducks* . . .   Collier and Horowitz, *The Kennedys,* 69.

73 *He also hired* . . .   Hamilton, *JFK: Reckless Youth,* 470.

73 *Later, when asked* . . .   Manchester, *Portrait of a President,* 177.

73 *Joe wrote his son* . . .   Burns, *John Kennedy,* 57.

73 *Influential New York* . . .   Blair and Blair, *The Search for JFK,* 81, 84.

73 *After its publication,* . . .   Reeves, *Question of Character,* 50.

73 *Joe believed these* . . .   Blair and Blair, *The Search for JFK,* 85.

74 *Joe wrote a friend,* . . .   Hamilton, *JFK: Reckless Youth,* 665.

74 *Jack explained, "My* . . .   Reeves, *Question of Character,* 73.

74 *After discovering that* . . .   Hamilton, *JFK: Reckless Youth,* 674.

75 *The Kennedys offered* . . .   Matthews, *Kennedy and Nixon,* 31.

75 *Another candidate was* . . .   Blair and Blair, *The Search for JFK,* 464.

75 *It was Joe who* . . .   Goodwin, *Fitzgeralds and Kennedys,* 714.

75 *This check, and many* . . .   Matthews, *Kennedy and Nixon,* 29.

75 *He used a press* . . .   Blair and Blair, *The Search for JFK,* 514.

76 *(In 1954, Bobby* . . .   Thomas, *Robert Kennedy,* 67.

76 *He bought the Boston* . . .   Goodwin, *Fitzgeralds and Kennedys,* 765.

76 *Jack admitted to* . . .   Reeves, *Question of Character,* 101.

76 *When Jack ran* . . .   Goodwin, *Fitzgeralds and Kennedys,* 793.

76 *Joe was so confident* . . .   Dallek, *Unfinished Life,* 226.

76 *After Jack began* . . .   Kennedy, *Times to Remember,* 373.

76 *He'd been featured* . . .   Parmet, *Jack,* 85.

76 *As Theodore White* . . .   White, *Making of the President, 1960,* 33.

77 *Joe also began* . . .   Leuchtenburg, *Shadow of FDR,* 87.

77 *Kennedy called his* . . .   Beschloss, *Crisis Years,* 108.

77 *Joe told her* . . .   Cassini, *In My Own Fashion,* 308.

78 *"Dad," Jack once* . . .   Martin, *Hero for Our Time,* 54.

78 *Inga Arvad recalled* . . .   Blair and Blair, *The Search for JFK,* 143.

78 *Jack warned female* . . .   Collier and Horowitz, *The Kennedys,* 174.

78 *Eunice toasted her* . . .   Latham and Sakol, *Encyclopedia,* 259.

78 *One of Jack's* . . .   Hersh, *Dark Side of Camelot,* 20.

78 *During the inaugural* . . .   Goodwin, *Fitzgeralds and Kennedys,* 816.

78 *"What nobody should* . . .   Martin, *Hero for Our Time,* 322.

8. KENNEDY AND HIS WIFE

79 *Kennedy friend Chuck* . . .   Martin, *Hero for Our Time,* 376.

80 *she didn't vote* . . .   Anthony, *As We Remember Her,* 220.

80 *She told one friend,* . . .   Heymann, *Jackie,* 341.

80 *She ignored many* . . .   Ibid., 268.

80 *When asked what* . . .   Reeves, *President Kennedy,* 154.

80 *She considered herself* . . .   Anthony, *As We Remember Her,* 155.

80 *Bobby said, "She's* . . .   Bradford, *America's Queen,* 129.

80 *Dismayed by the* . . .   Thomas, *Dateline: White House,* 4.

81 *As White House Chief* . . .   West with Kotz, *Upstairs at the White House,* 254.

81 *Also, to identify* . . .   Kenney, *Kennedy: Presidential Portfolio,* 131.

81 *Jackie hit the* . . .   "Life and Leisure," *Newsweek,* January 1, 1962, 31.

81 *Jackie said, "All* . . .   Gallagher, *My Life,* 52.

81 *She soon topped* . . .   Anthony, *As We Remember Her,* 231.

81 *She was even* . . .   Shulman, *"Jackie"!,* 80.

82 *Lawyer and adviser* . . .   Clifford with Holbrooke, *Counsel to the President,* 361.

82 *(one even had its* . . .   Koestenbaum, *Jackie under My Skin,* 9.

82 *Communist students at* . . .   Anthony, *As We Remember Her,* 152.

82 *In Colombia, a sign* . . .   Ibid., 153.

82 *When a front-page* . . .   Nan Robertson, "Mrs. Kennedy Defends Clothes; Is 'Sure' Mrs. Nixon Pays More," *New York Times,* September 15, 1960, 1.

83 *In fact, according* . . .   Gallagher, *My Life,* 57. The 2004 dollar equivalent was determined using the American Institute for Economic Research's Cost-of-Living Calculator (www.aier.org/cgi-aier/colcalculator.cgi).

83 *In 1962, she spent* . . .   Bradford, *America's Queen,* 209. The 2004 dollar equivalent was determined using the American Institute for Economic Research's Cost-of-Living Calculator (www.aier.org/cgi-aier/colcalculator.cgi).

83 *She claimed that* . . .   Marton, *Hidden Power,* 123.

83 *She used her pregnancy* . . .   Smith, *Grace and Power,* 373.

83 *"The boss can't* . . .   Thomas, *Dateline: White House,* 10.

83 *Longtime friend Lem* . . .   Goodwin, *Fitzgeralds and Kennedys,* 774.

83 *Noting that when* . . .   West with Kotz, *Upstairs at the White House,* 268.

9. KENNEDY AS HUSBAND

84 *Mutual friends brought* . . .   Burns, *John Kennedy,* 128.

84 *Nevertheless, Jack's brother* . . .   Bradford, *America's Queen,* 58.

84 *He tried to shield* . . .   Travell, *Office Hours,* 312. In 1955.

85 *"This book would* . . .   Kennedy, *Profiles in Courage,* xx.

85 *"I was so proud* . . .   Martin, *Hero for Our Time,* 12.

85 *On their way* . . .   Schlesinger, *A Thousand Days,* 1.

85 *Arthur Schlesinger Jr.* . . .   Ibid., 671.

86 *away from the* . . .   Leamer, *Kennedy Men,* 701, citing letter of October 5, 1963.

86 *In the summer* . . .   Fay, *Pleasure of His Company,* 183.

86 *"I only got* . . .   Bradford, *America's Queen,* 100.

86 *Lem Billings recalled* . . .   Heymann, *Jackie,* 117.

86 *Even Kennedy's doting* . . .   Leamer, *Kennedy Women,* 429.

87 *He never wrote* . . .   Manchester, *One Brief Shining Moment,* 63.

87 *he proposed by telegram* . . .   Collier and Horowitz, *The Kennedys,* 194.

87 *and he left the selection* . . .   Klein, *All Too Human,* 145.

87 *Jackie's wedding band* . . .   Manchester, *Death of a President,* 334.

87 *After losing his* . . .   Bradford, *America's Queen,* 108.

87 *Just weeks after* . . .   Smith, *Grace and Power,* 185.

87 *Reporter Helen Thomas* . . .   Thomas, *Dateline: White House,* 1.

87 *Even Jack admitted,* . . .   O'Donnell and Powers with McCarthy, *"Johnny, We Hardly Knew Ye,"* 233.

87 *When a journalist* . . .   Marton, *Hidden Power,* 109.

88 *Publisher Dorothy Schiff* . . .   Jeffrey Potter, *Men, Money and Magic: The Story of Dorothy Schiff* (New York: Coward, McCann and Geoghegan, 1976), 261.

88 *As presidential aide* . . .   Strober and Strober, *"Let Us Begin Anew,"* 470.

88 *Many echoed deputy* . . .   Martin, *Hero for Our Time,* 534.

89 *Although together in . . .*   Smith, *Grace and Power*, 427 and 563, note accompanying p. 427 ("In the two weeks before").

10. KENNEDY THE FOX

90 *hedgehogs are those . . .*   Berlin, *Hedgehog and Fox*, 3.

90 *while foxes are . . .*   Ibid.

92 *"I'd be very happy . . .*   Paul F. Healy, "The Senate's Gay Young Bachelor," *Saturday Evening Post*, June 13, 1953, 127.

92 *"The fear of . . .*   Burns, *John Kennedy*, 245.

93 *Recalling the campaign, . . .*   White, *Making of the President 1960*, 55.

93 *During the presidential . . .*   O'Donnell and Powers with McCarthy, *"Johnny, We Hardly Knew Ye,"* 216.

93 *During the Cuban . . .*   Ibid., 316.

93 *According to O'Donnell . . .*   Ibid.

93 *Their conversations included . . .*   Bradlee, *Conversations with Kennedy*, 146.

93 *discussion of someone's . . .*   Ibid., 201.

93 *In one cable, . . .*   Galbraith, *Journal*, 90–91. Cable of April 27, 1961.

93 *Kennedy said, "Ken's . . .*   Hugh Sidey, "The President's Voracious Reading Habits," *Life*, March 17, 1961, 61.

94 *Although Jackie in . . .*   Bradlee, *Conversations with Kennedy*, 208.

94 *Bradlee insists he . . .*   Bradlee, *A Good Life*, 217.

94 *so does Galbraith.*   Galbraith, *Name-Dropping*, 116.

94 *Similarly, after reading . . .*   Barry Bearak, "Book Portrays J.F.K. as Reckless and Immoral," *New York Times*, November 9, 1997, 1.

94 *On the other hand, . . .*   Baker with King, *Wheeling and Dealing*, 76.

94 *Schlesinger dismissed the . . .*   John Kifner, "Kennedy Aides Unaware That Talks Were Taped," *New York Times*, July 19, 1973, 20.

94 *Dave Powers said . . .*   Bob Woodward and Patrick Tyler, "JFK Secretly Taped White House Talks," *Washington Post*, February 4, 1982, A1.

94 *After their public . . .*   Ibid.

94 *Then, in 1982, . . .*   Edward A. Gargan, "Kennedy Secretly Taped Sessions in White House," *New York Times*, February 4, 1982, A16;

Woodward and Tyler, "JFK Secretly Taped White House Talks," A1.

95 *His aides struggled* . . .   Ibid.

95 *Just days before* . . .   From the website of the John F. Kennedy Library and Museum (http://www.jfklibrary.org/speeches.htm).

96 *Harris Wofford noted* . . .   Wofford, *Of Kennedys and Kings,* 129.

96 *nevertheless, Wofford concluded,* . . .   Ibid., 176.

96 *Dr. Janet Travell* . . .   Travell, *Office Hours,* 315.

11. KENNEDY REVISED

98 *In the 1959* . . .   Burns, *John Kennedy,* 42.

98 *According to Choate* . . .   Blair and Blair, *The Search for JFK,* 37.

99 *Rose Kennedy wrote* . . .   Kennedy, *Times to Remember,* 261.

99 *The Harvard professors* . . .   Parmet, *Jack,* 75.

100 *According to John* . . .   John Hersey, "Survival," *The New Yorker,* June 17, 1944, 38.

100 *After the wreck* . . .   Reeves, *Question of Character,* 66.

101 *According to Ted* . . .   Sorensen, *Kennedy,* 49.

101 *In 1977, Sorensen* . . .   Parmet, *Jack,* 310, citing an April 27, 1977, interview with Sorensen.

102 *From Theodore White's* . . .   White, *Making of the President, 1960,* 330.

102 *From Jerry Bruno* . . .   Bruno and Greenfield, *Advance Man,* 47.

103 *According to Norman* . . .   Mailer, *Presidential Papers,* 46–47.

103 *According to magazine* . . .   Manso, *Mailer,* 302.

104 *According to Theodore* . . .   White, *Making of the President, 1960,* 114.

104 *According to William* . . .   Manchester, *One Brief Shining Moment,* 106.

105 *According to Kennedy* . . .   Wofford, *Of Kennedys and Kings,* 65.

105 *Wofford continues his* . . .   Ibid., 65–66.

106 *A conversation, according to Ted* . . .   Sorensen, *Kennedy,* 756.

106 *A conversation, according to William* . . .   Manchester, *One Brief Shining Moment,* 246. Throughout this book, Manchester uses *you* to stand for any close Kennedy associate.

107 *According to Arthur* . . .   Schlesinger, *Robert Kennedy and His Times,* 519–520.

107 *According to Ben . . .*   Bradlee, *Conversations with Kennedy,* 166.

107 *According to Ralph . . .*   Strober and Strober, *"Let Us Begin Anew,"* 38.

107 *Henry James, a Kennedy . . .*   Hamilton, *JFK: Reckless Youth,* 354.

107 *Jackie said to . . .*   Martin, *Hero for Our Time,* 217.

108 *According to Hugh . . .*   Hugh Sidey, "The President's Voracious Reading Habits," *Life,* March 17, 1961, 59.

108 *According to Sidey's 1963 . . .*   Sidey, *Kennedy, President,* 54.

108 *According to Red . . .*   Fay, *Pleasure of His Company,* 194.

108 *In his oral . . .*   Hersh, *Dark Side of Camelot,* 223n★.

110 *Of Kennedy's statement . . .*   Sorensen, *Kennedy,* 450.

110 *According to Ben . . .*   Bradlee, *Conversations with Kennedy,* 76–77.

111 *According to Pierre . . .*   Salinger, *With Kennedy,* 312.

111 *Pamela Turnure and . . .*   Leaming, *Mrs. Kennedy,* 41.

112 *According to Kenny . . .*   O'Donnell and Powers with McCarthy, *"Johnny, We Hardly Knew Ye,"* 264.

112 *According to presidential . . .*   Bryant with Leighton, *Dog Days at the White House,* 22–23.

12. KENNEDY'S MYSTIQUE

115 *Chuck Spalding recalled . . .*   Blair and Blair, *The Search for JFK,* 483.

115 *While campaigning in . . .*   Schlesinger, *A Thousand Days,* 758.

115 *Kennedy knew, as . . .*   Ibid., 722.

115 *Civil rights leader . . .*   Kenney, *Kennedy: Presidential Portfolio,* 97.

116 *When he visited . . .*   Parmet, *JFK,* 223.

116 *Few believed he . . .*   Leamer, *Kennedy Men,* 305.

117 *The election was . . .*   Spada, *Peter Lawford,* 262.

117 *Throughout Kennedy's presidency, . . .*   James Reston, "What Was Killed Was Not Only the President but the Promise," *New York Times,* November 15, 1964, 24.

117 *Reporter Maxine Cheshire . . .*   Maxine Cheshire with John Greenya, *Maxine Cheshire, Reporter* (Boston: Houghton Mifflin, 1978), 40.

117 *one reporter inquired . . .*   Donaldson, *Hold On, Mr. President!,* 17.

117 *Dwight Eisenhower commented, . . .*   Heymann, *Jackie,* 646.

117 *the escape of the . . .* "Caroline's 2 Hamsters Hunted in White House," *New York Times,* March 5, 1961, 95.

118 *a reporter once . . .* Thomas, *Dateline:White House,* 20; Salinger, *With Kennedy,* 315 (the hamster had crawled into the president's bathtub and drowned).

118 *their activities inspired . . .* Elizabeth McCracken, "The Temporary Kennedy," *New York Times Magazine,* January 2, 2004, 26.

118 *One of his first . . .* Hamilton, *JFK: Reckless Youth,* 765–766.

118 *(so far apart . . .* Kenney, *Kennedy: Presidential Portfolio,* 124.

119 *One concerned citizen . . .* Klapp, *Symbolic Leaders,* 131.

13. KENNEDY IN HIS OWN WORDS

121 *Kennedy wrote his . . .* Blair and Blair, *The Search for JFK,* 282–283.

122 *In a letter . . .* Thomas, *Robert Kennedy,* 41.

122 *Kennedy wrote to . . .* Hamilton, *JFK: Reckless Youth,* 683. Letter of February 20, 1945.

122 *In 1958, when . . .* Alsop and Platt, *"I've Seen the Best of It,"* 406.

122 *As he discussed . . .* O'Donnell and Powers with McCarthy, *"Johnny, We Hardly Knew Ye,"* 193.

122 *Kennedy remarked that . . .* Wofford, *Of Kennedys and Kings,* 62.

123 *"Sam Rayburn may . . .* Sorensen, *Kennedy,* 152.

123 *When Nixon said . . .* Ibid., 185.

123 *In his powerful . . .* Address to the Greater Houston Ministerial Association, Houston, Texas, September 12, 1960. From the website of the John F. Kennedy Library and Museum (http://www.jfklibrary.org/speeches.htm).

123 *After he was . . .* Bradlee, *Conversations with Kennedy,* 32.

123 *Let the word . . .* Inaugural address, Washington, D.C., January 20, 1961. From the website of the John F. Kennedy Library and Museum (http://www.jfklibrary.org/speeches.htm).

124 *Of his invitation . . .* Glikes and Schwaber, *Of Poetry and Power,* 4.

125 *"There is an old . . .* Press conference, Washington, D.C., April 21, 1961. From the website of the John F. Kennedy Library and Museum (http://www.jfklibrary.org/speeches.htm).

125 *At the April 29, . . .* Thomas, *Dateline:White House,* 15.

125 *In his speech . . .*   From the website of the John F. Kennedy Library and Museum (http://www.jfklibrary.org/speeches.htm).

125 *When Jackie appeared . . .*   Sorensen, *Kennedy Legacy,* 171.

125 *During the Cuban . . .*   Dallek, *Unfinished Life,* 555.

126 *During a White House . . .*   Baldridge, *Kennedy Style,* 119.

126 *In a December . . .*   Fairlie, *Kennedy Promise,* 219.

126 *"In politics nobody . . .*   Goodwin, *Remembering America,* 454.

126 *Our problems are . . .*   From the website of the John F. Kennedy Library and Museum (http://www.jfklibrary.org/speeches.htm).

127 *I hope that every . . .*   Ibid.

128 *In West Berlin, . . .*   Smith, *Grace and Power,* 381.

128 *There are many . . .*   Address, West Berlin, June 26, 1963. From the website of the John F. Kennedy Library and Museum (http://www.jfklibrary.org/speeches.htm).

128 *At the dedication . . .*   Remarks at the dedication of the Robert Frost Library, Amherst College, October 26, 1963. Ibid.

128 *Kennedy explained, "This . . .*   Ibid.

129 *We, in this country, . . .*   Remarks prepared for delivery at the Trade Mart in Dallas. Ibid.

14. KENNEDY'S USE OF THE MEDIA

130 *As Norman Mailer . . .*   Mailer, "Superman Comes to the Super-market," in *Presidential Papers,* 44.

131 *During the 1956 . . .*   Reeves, *Question of Character,* 279.

132 *Life called Kennedy . . .*   Kenney, *Kennedy: Presidential Portfolio,* 115.

132 *Within a month . . .*   "A Day with John F. Kennedy," *New York Times,* February 19, 1961, 204.

132 *When he spotted . . .*   Salinger, *With Kennedy,* 53.

132 *Reporter Helen Thomas . . .*   Thomas, *Dateline: White House,* 3.

132 *Even his unprintable . . .*   Bradlee, *A Good Life,* 209.

132 *He called Gore Vidal . . .*   Robert Stanton and Gore Vidal, eds., *Views from a Window: Conversations with Gore Vidal* (Secaucus, N.J.: Lyle Stuart, 1980), 271.

132 *Kennedy's friend Washington . . .*   Felsenthal, *Power, Privilege, and the "Post,"* 187.

132 *When rumors of* . . .   Reeves, *President Kennedy*, 316.

133 *Writers frequently submitted* . . .   Bradlee, *Conversations with Kennedy*, 224.

133 *In general, the press* . . .   Smith, *Grace and Power*, 391.

133 *Bradlee checked with* . . .   Wills, *Kennedy Imprisonment*, 87–88.

133 *Bradlee noted, "The* . . .   Bradlee, *Conversations with Kennedy*, 11.

133 *Kennedy himself said,* . . .   Martin, *Hero for Our Time*, 305.

133 *An August 1962* . . .   Fletcher Knebel, "Kennedy vs. the Press," *Look*, August 28, 1962, 17.

134 *The article quoted* . . .   Ibid.

134 *"I'll wind up owning* . . .   Parmet, *JFK*, 113.

134 *On the evening* . . .   Bradlee, *Conversations with Kennedy*, 228.

135 *Kennedy soon steered* . . .   Ibid.

135 *As if he'd never* . . .   Ibid.

135 *Kennedy and Bradlee* . . .   Ibid., 230.

135 *"Kennedy has box* . . .   Lasky, *J.F.K.: Man and Myth*, 174.

135 *In 1950, 11 percent* . . .   Farber and Bailey, *Columbia Guide to America in the 1960s*, 396.

136 *Kennedy grasped the* . . .   Barnouw, *Tube of Plenty*, 277.

136 *Theodore White observed* . . .   White, *Making of the President, 1960*, 276.

136 *Norman Mailer described* . . .   Mailer, *Presidential Papers*, 47.

137 *Writing about television's* . . .   Hellman, *Obsession*, 92, quoting John F. Kennedy, "A Force That Has Changed the Political Scene," *TV Guide*, November 14, 1959, 7.

137 *To prepare for* . . .   Spada, *Peter Lawford*, 260.

137 *After Kennedy's appearance* . . .   Leamer, *Kennedy Men*, 364.

138 *The press conferences* . . .   Salinger, *With Kennedy*, 56.

138 *Her Emmy Award–winning* . . .   Kenney, *Kennedy: Presidential Portfolio*, 131.

138 *Before one appearance,* . . .   Sidey, *Kennedy, President*, 334.

138 *He watched reruns* . . .   Salinger, *With Kennedy*, 140.

138 *Aide Burke Marshall* . . .   Strober and Strober, *"Let Us Begin Anew,"* 484.

139 *In a then-unusual* . . .   Lowe, *Remembering Jack*, 10.

140 *"He knew damn well* . . .   Thomas, *Robert Kennedy*, 191.

140 *Look's Stanley Tretick* . . .   Collier and Horowitz, *The Kennedys*, 245n★.

140 *On November 22,* . . .   Wicker, *Kennedy without Tears*, 46.

141 *Kennedy understood the* . . .   Lubin, *Shooting Kennedy*, 203; "Day with Kennedy," 204.

141 *Watching the dog* . . .   Bryant with Leighton, *Dog Days at the White House*, 45.

141 *He held up a picture* . . .   Sidey, *Kennedy, President*, 188.

142 *Somehow, seeing the* . . .   "Senator Kennedy Goes A-Courting," *Life*, July 20, 1953.

143 *When a friend* . . .   Lasky, *J.F.K.: Man and Myth*, 160.

145 *Photographer Slim Aarons* . . .   Heymann, *Jackie*, 141.

145 *Kennedy would never* . . .   Horne, *Macmillan*, 441.

145 *He didn't want* . . .   Don Van Natta Jr., *First Off the Tee* (New York: Public Affairs, 2003), 35.

145 *In the ten weeks* . . .   Ibid., 41.

145 *Jackie was never* . . .   West with Kotz, *Upstairs at the White House*, 203.

146 *Photographers did manage* . . .   Taraborrelli, *Jackie Ethel Joan*, 181n.

147 *Joe Kennedy had* . . .   Collier and Horowitz, *The Kennedys*, 150.

147 *Johnson berated his* . . .   Halberstam, *Best and Brightest*, 585.

15. KENNEDY'S CIRCLE

149 *"Kennedy had an* . . .   Alsop and Platt, *"I've Seen the Best of It,"* 463.

150 *By the middle* . . .   Strober and Strober, *"Let Us Begin Anew,"* 99.

150 *Choate roommate Lem* . . .   Leamer, *Kennedy Men*, 532.

150 *"I was at* . . .   Blair and Blair, *The Search for JFK*, 31.

150 *Of these longtime* . . .   Hamilton, *JFK: Reckless Youth*, 205.

151 *Schlesinger described Billings* . . .   Smith, *Grace and Power*, 30.

151 *Press aide Barbara* . . .   Ibid., 82.

151 *(Sorensen, by contrast,* . . .   Salinger, *With Kennedy*, 72.

151 *Kennedy friend Henry* . . .   Hamilton, *JFK: Reckless Youth*, 780.

151 *Outside this tight* . . .   Sidey, *Kennedy, President*, 83.

151 *Bartlett acknowledged that* . . .   Smith, *Grace and Power*, 125.

151 *He later acknowledged* . . .   Alsop and Platt, *"I've Seen the Best of It,"* 449.

151 *When someone said Sorensen* . . .   Manchester, *Portrait of a President,* 115–116.

152 *Sorensen himself described* . . .   Sorensen, *Kennedy,* 263.

152 *Traphes Bryant recorded* . . .   Bryant with Leighton, *Dog Days at the White House,* 37.

152 *Dean Martin's ex-wife* . . .   Reeves, *Question of Character,* 202.

152 *Washington Post publisher* . . .   Heymann, *Jackie,* 330.

152 *Graham friend Jean* . . .   Felsenthal, *Power, Privilege, and the "Post,"* 197.

152 *Bobby Baker also* . . .   Hersh, *Dark Side of Camelot,* 301.

152 *Journalist Gloria Emerson* . . .   Ibid., 24.

152 *A Kennedy observer* . . .   Ibid., 30.

153 *Old friend Jewel* . . .   Leaming, *Mrs. Kennedy,* 250.

153 *"Either you informed* . . .   Giglio, *Presidency of Kennedy,* 259.

153 *Bartlett recalled, "He* . . .   Lieberson, *John Fitzgerald Kennedy,* 73.

153 *As aide Harris* . . .   Wofford, *Of Kennedys and Kings,* 360–361.

153 *Despite many close* . . .   Goodwin, *Remembering America,* 142.

153 *A cabinet member* . . .   Manchester, *Death of a President,* 411.

154 *Their grief was* . . .   Alsop and Platt, *"I've Seen the Best of It,"* 464.

154 *"It was a shattering* . . .   Ibid., 463–464.

154 *McGeorge Bundy also* . . .   Ibid., 464.

154 *Roswell Gilpatrick said* . . .   Ibid.

154 *Bobby Kennedy Jr. recalled* . . .   Michaelis, *Best of Friends,* 182.

16. THE IDEA OF JOHN F. KENNEDY

156 *Walking through the* . . .   Bryant with Leighton, *Dog Days at the White House,* 102.

156 *His aides asked* . . .   Leuchtenburg, *Shadow of FDR,* 91.

156 *as soon as he was* . . .   Beale, *Power at Play,* 71.

157 *Appointments secretary and* . . .   O'Donnell and Powers with McCarthy, *"Johnny, We Hardly Knew Ye,"* 112.

157 *During the transition* . . .   Salinger, *With Kennedy,* 57.

157 *Kennedy was horrified* . . .   Bradlee, *Conversations with Kennedy,* 29.

157 *Because he often* . . .   Leamer, *Kennedy Men,* 523.

157 *Secretary Mary Gallagher* . . .   Gallagher, *My Life,* 271, 297.

157 *His writing two* . . .   Matthews, *Kennedy and Nixon,* 199.

158 *Cigar-smoking Kennedy* . . .   Lieberson, *John Fitzgerald Kennedy,* 178.

159 *Joe's film-industry* . . .   Blair and Blair, *The Search for JFK,* 483.

159 *Hubert Humphrey warned* . . .   Kenney, *Kennedy: Presidential Portfolio,* 39.

159 *Joe boasted about* . . .   Hamilton, *JFK: Reckless Youth,* 753.

159 *The New York Times* . . .   "Kennedys Excel at Sailing," *New York Times,* September 4, 1940, 39.

159 *She put it simply:* . . .   Mailer, *Presidential Papers,* 90.

160 *She sent people* . . .   Hamilton, *JFK: Reckless Youth,* 812.

160 *Jackie, however, decided* . . .   Ibid., xx.

161 *Brother-in-law Sargent Shriver* . . .   Manchester, *Death of a President,* 636.

17. KENNEDY REMEMBERED

163 *Jane Suydam first* . . .   Blair and Blair, *The Search for JFK,* 68.

163 *Johnny Iles, Kennedy's* . . .   Hamilton, *JFK: Reckless Youth,* 543.

164 *A close friend* . . .   Ibid., 544.

164 *Ted Sorensen wrote,* . . .   Sorensen, *Kennedy,* 23.

164 *In 1956, Eleanor* . . .   Wofford, *Of Kennedys and Kings,* 31.

164 *But in an August* . . .   Parmet, *JFK,* 36.

164 *Jewel Reed, later* . . .   Blair and Blair, *The Search for JFK,* 348.

164 *Kennedy's doctor Janet* . . .   Travell, *Office Hours,* 339.

164 *Jackie Kennedy described* . . .   Donald Wilson, "John Kennedy's Lovely Lady," *Life,* August 24, 1959, 80.

165 *To Tip O'Neill,* . . .   O'Neill with Novak, *Man of the House,* 83.

165 *Jackie Kennedy wrote* . . .   Sorensen, *Kennedy,* 120.

165 *Gore Vidal wrote,* . . .   Gore Vidal, "The Holy Family," in *United States: Essays, 1952–1992* (New York: Random House, 1993), 810.

165 *Betty Spalding, wife* . . .   Blair and Blair, *The Search for JFK,* 484.

165 *Aides Kenny O'Donnell* . . .   O'Donnell and Powers with McCarthy, "*Johnny, We Hardly Knew Ye,*" 407.

165 *After Kennedy's inaugural* . . .   Martin, *Hero for Our Time,* 12.

165 *Just a few days* . . .   Beschloss, *Crisis Years,* 57.

166 *Time editorial director* . . .   Hedley Donovan, *Roosevelt to Reagan: A Reporter's Encounters with Nine Presidents* (New York: Harper and Row, 1985), 74.

166 *Joseph Alsop recalled,* . . .   Hamilton, *JFK: Reckless Youth,* 186.

166 *Close friend Lem* . . .   Goodwin, *Fitzgeralds and Kennedys,* 786.

166 *When a former* . . .   Strober and Strober, "*Let Us Begin Anew,*" 336.

166 *Around the time* . . .   Reeves, *Question of Character,* 273.

167 *Press secretary Pierre* . . .   Salinger, *With Kennedy,* 63.

167 *Critic Alfred Kazin* . . .   Alfred Kazin, "President Kennedy and Other Intellectuals," in *Alfred Kazin's America* (New York: HarperCollins, 2003), 240.

167 *British ambassador David* . . .   Bradford, *America's Queen,* 240.

167 *Norman Podhoretz observed* . . .   Strober and Strober, "*Let Us Begin Anew,*" 492.

167 *Joseph Kennedy's nurse* . . .   Dallas with Ratcliffe, *Kennedy Case,* 229.

168 *Budget Director David* . . .   Doyle, *Oval Office,* 101.

168 *James MacGregor Burns* . . .   Ibid., 136.

168 *Norman Mailer observed,* . . .   Norman Mailer, "The Leading Man: A Review of *J.F.K.: The Man and the Myth,*" in *Cannibals and Christians* (New York: Dial Press, 1966), 169.

168 *Roger Hilsman said,* . . .   Strober and Strober, "*Let Us Begin Anew,*" 466.

168 *"That poor President* . . .   André Malraux, *Felled Oaks: Conversations with de Gaulle* (New York: Holt, Rinehart and Winston, 1971), 78.

18. KENNEDY'S HIGH IDEALS

169 *The 1950s had* . . .   White, *Making of the President, 1960,* 334.

170 *Aide Edward McDermott* . . .   Strober and Strober, "*Let Us Begin Anew,*" 468.

170 *Harris Wofford admitted* . . .   Wofford, *Of Kennedys and Kings,* 76.

171 *Sometime after Kennedy* . . .   Lincoln, *Twelve Years,* 86.

171 *Cellist Pablo Casals* . . .   Leaming, *Mrs. Kennedy,* 166.

171 *So many people* . . .   Fairlie, *Kennedy Promise,* 184.

171 *It's a sign of* . . .   Wofford, *Of Kennedys and Kings,* 250.

172 *Although one of . . .*   Burns, *John Kennedy,* 247.
172 *Civil rights leader . . .*   Strober and Strober, *"Let Us Begin Anew,"* 452.
172 *When Louis Martin, . . .*   Reeves, *President Kennedy,* 357.
172 *Nancy Dickerson, a . . .*   Dickerson, *Among Those Present,* 63.
172 *Ben Bradlee explained, . . .*   Marton, *Hidden Power,* 113.
172 *In a 1963 interview, . . .*   Smith, *Grace and Power,* 390.
172 *But his inspiring . . .*   Giglio, *Presidency of Kennedy,* 143.
173 *When he spoke . . .*   Manchester, *One Brief Shining Moment,* 210.
173 *German chancellor Konrad . . .*   Dallek, *Unfinished Life,* 624.
173 *Texas senator Ralph . . .*   Strober and Strober, *"Let Us Begin Anew,"* 468.

19. KENNEDY AS CIVIL RIGHTS LEADER
174 *Civil rights leader . . .*   Strober and Strober, *"Let Us Begin Anew,"* 273.
175 *Several times during . . .*   Reeves, *President Kennedy,* 491.
175 *During the campaign, . . .*   Ibid., 62.
175 *In 1961, his . . .*   Giglio, *Presidency of Kennedy,* 163.
176 *Schlesinger explained Kennedy's . . .*   Schlesinger, *A Thousand Days,* 965–966.
176 *Afterward, civil rights . . .*   Reeves, *President Kennedy,* 585.
176 *Kennedy was willing . . .*   Manchester, *One Brief Shining Moment,* 241.
176 *Referring to a list . . .*   Wofford, *Of Kennedys and Kings,* 125.
176 *"Unhappily," Wofford writes, . . .*   Ibid., 176.
177 *When asked whether . . .*   Kenney, *Kennedy: Presidential Portfolio,* 205.
177 *Jackie, with her . . .*   Corry, *Manchester Affair,* 39.
177 *As journalist Tom . . .*   Strober and Strober, *"Let Us Begin Anew,"* 321.
177 *After Kennedy's death, . . .*   Thomas, *Dateline: White House,* 31.
178 *One black activist . . .*   Giglio, *Presidency of Kennedy,* 173.
178 *In response, Kennedy . . .*   From the website of the John F. Kennedy Library and Museum (http://www.jfklibrary.org/speeches.htm).
178 *As civil rights . . .*   Strober and Strober, *"Let Us Begin Anew,"* 278.
178 *When, as president, . . .*   Wofford, *Of Kennedys and Kings,* 127.
178 *Asked to attend . . .*   Reeves, *President Kennedy,* 354.

179 *In early 1963, . . .*   Ibid., 463.

179 *He told Wofford, . . .*   Kenney, *Kennedy: Presidential Portfolio,* 100.

179 *"a great change . . .*   Radio and television report to the American people on civil rights, White House, June 11, 1963. From the website of the John F. Kennedy Library and Museum (http://www.jfklibrary.org/speeches.htm).

179 *Kennedy needled McGeorge . . .*   Smith, *Grace and Power,* 245–246.

180 *Kennedy spent much . . .*   Lasky, *J.F.K.: Man and Myth,* 36n.

20. VENERATION FOR KENNEDY

182 *As local politicians . . .*   White, *Making of the President, 1960,* 344.

182 *Theodore White wrote . . .*   White, *In Search of History,* 546.

182 *Charley Bartlett explained, . . .*   Manchester, *Death of a President,* 512.

183 *Joseph Alsop admitted . . .*   Alsop and Platt, *"I've Seen the Best of It,"* 406.

183 *White House aide . . .*   Martin, *Hero for Our Time,* 258.

183 *In 1955, during . . .*   Fay, *Pleasure of His Company,* 172.

183 *Billings had repeated . . .*   Michaelis, *Best of Friends,* 141.

183 *and even pretended . . .*   Smith, *Grace and Power,* 31.

183 *and after the presidential . . .*   Collier and Horowitz, *The Kennedys,* 271.

183 *Billings later said . . .*   Michaelis, *Best of Friends,* 181.

183 *In the first TV . . .*   First televised Nixon-Kennedy presidential debate, September 26, 1960. From the website of the John F. Kennedy Library and Museum (http://www.jfklibrary.org/speeches.htm).

183 *By the campaign's . . .*   White, *Making of the President, 1960,* 303.

183 *Henry Cabot Lodge, . . .*   Parmet, *JFK,* 253.

184 *At the end of . . .*   Reeves, *Question of Character,* 232.

184 *Sinatra even mounted . . .*   Ronald Brownstein, *The Power and the Glitter: The Hollywood-Washington Connection* (New York: Vintage, 1990), 159.

184 *Theodore White slipped . . .*   White, *In Search of History,* 472; White, *Making of the President, 1960,* 145.

184 *At another point, . . .*   Ibid., 171.

184 *William Manchester explains . . .*   Manchester, *Portrait of a President,* 96.

185 *His "reluctance to . . .*   Ibid., 218.

185 *Manchester also fell . . .*   Manchester, *One Brief Shining Moment,* 35–36.

185 *Kennedy "re-established the . . .*   Schlesinger, *A Thousand Days,* 1031.

185 *(Fellow Kennedy aide . . .*   Wofford, *Of Kennedys and Kings,* 176.

185 *When, in front of . . .*   Bradlee, *Conversations with Kennedy,* 135. "C-U-N-T."

185 *Joe Kennedy visited . . .*   Dallas with Ratcliffe, *Kennedy Case,* 209.

186 *Schlesinger observed Kennedy . . .*   Schlesinger, *A Thousand Days,* 689.

186 *Reporter Nancy Dickerson . . .*   Dickerson, *Among Those Present,* 67.

186 *Sorensen recalled that . . .*   Beschloss, *Crisis Years,* 126.

186 *After his marriage . . .*   Smith, *Grace and Power,* 339.

186 *Because of Kennedy's . . .*   Gallagher, *My Life,* 216.

186 *When Jackie called . . .*   White, *In Search of History,* 539.

187 *Joseph Alsop called . . .*   Brown, *JFK: History of an Image,* 10.

187 *Ernest Hemingway wrote, . . .*   Parmet, *JFK,* 7.

187 *Thornton Wilder said . . .*   Manchester, *One Brief Shining Moment,* 160.

187 *Norman Podhoretz, an . . .*   Strober and Strober, *"Let Us Begin Anew,"* 51.

187 *Robert Lowell was . . .*   Paul Mariani, *Lost Puritan: A Life of Robert Lowell* (New York: Norton, 1994), 294.

188 *People struggled to . . .*   Lincoln, *Twelve Years,* 120.

188 *Congressman Roman Puchinski . . .*   Strober and Strober, *"Let Us Begin Anew,"* 52.

188 *Kennedy's barber was . . .*   Manchester, *Portrait of a President,* 114.

188 *The Kennedys had . . .*   Gallagher, *My Life,* 108.

188 *An acquaintance wrote . . .*   Kennedy, *Times to Remember,* 439.

188 *In remote villages . . .*   Bowles, *Promises to Keep,* 453.

188 *Time noted that . . .*   "The Presidency," *Time,* June 7, 1963, 19.

188 *Esquire named Kennedy . . .*   "The Monogram on This Man's Shirt Is J.F.K.," *Esquire,* January 1962, 35.

189 *Dozens of men . . .*   Manchester, *Portrait of a President,* 116.

189 *Ted Kennedy's wife* . . .   Taraborrelli, *Jackie Ethel Joan,* 414.

189 *Long after Kennedy's* . . .   McNamara with VanDeMark, *In Retrospect,* 94.

189 *At auction in 1996,* . . .   Michael Kimmelman, "It's Not Junk If It Was Jackie's," *New York Times,* December 5, 2004, WK3.

190 *They spent the night* . . .   Schlesinger, *A Thousand Days,* 539–540, 561.

190 *But in the morning,* . . .   Ibid., 577.

190 *Jackie asked friend* . . .   Manchester, *Death of a President,* 554.

190 *After hearing of* . . .   Parmet, *Jack,* xiii.

190 *In 1963, he described* . . .   Mailer, *Presidential Papers,* 7.

191 *Frank Sinatra desperately* . . .   Spada, *Peter Lawford,* 326–327.

191 *The first critical* . . .   Beschloss, *Crisis Years,* 636.

21. THE KENNEDY PHOTOGRAPHS

198 *When Dave Powers* . . .   Manchester, *Death of a President,* 643.

198 *Many remarked on* . . .   Martin, *Hero for Our Time,* 519.

22. KENNEDY AS HERO

200 *"Jack had this* . . .   Theodore H. White, "For President Kennedy: An Epilogue," *Life,* December 6, 1963, 158.

200 *In his twenties,* . . .   Hellman, *Obsession,* 27.

201 *He often mentioned* . . .   Ibid., 33.

201 *Certainly, Kennedy resembled* . . .   Buchan, *Pilgrim's Way,* 46.

201 *innumerable gifts, all* . . .   Ibid., 50.

201 *Cecil described Melbourne's* . . .   Cecil, *Young Melbourne,* 9.

201 *In fact, Cecil's* . . .   Ibid., 6.

201 *"If this nation* . . .   Giglio, *Presidency of Kennedy,* 29.

202 *"When I was a* . . .   Baker with King, *Wheeling and Dealing,* 143.

202 *As he said,* . . .   Schlesinger, *A Thousand Days,* 426.

202 *"There's nothing like* . . .   Fairlie, *Kennedy Promise,* 341.

202 *After the Bay* . . .   Goodwin, *Remembering America,* 183.

203 *Kennedy often assigned* . . .   Giglio, *Presidency of Kennedy,* 31.

203 *Without having met* . . .   Halberstam, *Best and Brightest,* 222.

203 *This special forces* . . .   Farber and Bailey, *Columbia Guide to America in the 1960s,* 204.

203 *When the Defense . . .*   Reeves, *President Kennedy,* 117.

204 *When the failure . . .*   Thomas, *Robert Kennedy,* 121.

204 *"If he thinks . . .*   Manchester, *One Brief Shining Moment,* 188.

204 *When Kennedy learned . . .*   Freedman, *Kennedy's Wars,* 169.

23. KENNEDY'S LEGACY

205 *On the very night . . .*   Stein and Plimpton, *American Journey,* 74.

206 *Arthur Schlesinger Jr. . . .*   Smith, *Grace and Power,* 79.

206 *He invited Lincoln . . .*   Reeves, *President Kennedy,* 278.

206 *He asked Donald . . .*   Collier and Horowitz, *The Kennedys,* 289.

206 *Donald later wrote . . .*   Hersh, *Dark Side of Camelot,* 255.

206 *Consider that Kennedy's . . .*   Smith, *Grace and Power,* 401.

206 *Schlesinger acknowledged that . . .*   Schlesinger, *A Thousand Days,* 997.

207 *"Some of us think . . .*   Reeves, *President Kennedy,* 278, citing a Washington, D.C., address, October 3, 1961.

207 *In 1961, Kennedy . . .*   Ibid.

208 *When Sorensen conveyed . . .*   Sorensen, *Kennedy,* 295.

208 *He'd planned to . . .*   Smith, *Grace and Power,* 361.

208 *Although Schlesinger was . . .*   Galbraith, *Journal,* 28.

208 *"I'll write my . . .*   O'Donnell and Powers with McCarthy, *"Johnny, We Hardly Knew Ye,"* 243.

208 *As he knew, . . .*   Bradlee, *Conversations with Kennedy,* 153.

208 *Along the same . . .*   Fay, *Pleasure of His Company,* 5.

209 *Jackie understood, as . . .*   Heymann, *Jackie,* 418.

209 *A week after . . .*   White, *In Search of History,* 539.

209 *She added, "There'll . . .*   Theodore H. White, "For President Kennedy: An Epilogue," *Life,* December 6, 1963, 158.

210 *even in the "Camelot" . . .*   White, *In Search of History,* 545.

210 *After Schlesinger sent . . .*   Beschloss, *Crisis Years,* 24n★.

210 *According to William . . .*   William Manchester, "William Manchester's Own Story," *Look,* April 4, 1967, 62.

210 *She pressed Fay . . .*   Smith, *Grace and Power,* 466.

210 *Jackie was so angry . . .*   "Mrs. Kennedy Bars Gift to Memorial," *New York Times,* December 7, 1966, 92.

210 *When Ben Bradlee . . .*   Smith, *Grace and Power,* 465.

24. KENNEDY—BEGINNINGS AND ENDINGS

212 *"Let us begin anew,"* . . .   Inaugural address, January 20, 1961. From the website of the John F. Kennedy Library and Museum (http://www.jfklibrary.org/speeches.htm).

213 *In his first State* . . .   Sorensen, *Kennedy,* 292.

213 *When, in his speech* . . .   Radio and television report to the American people on the Berlin crisis, White House, July 25, 1961. From the website of the John F. Kennedy Library and Museum (http://www.jfklibrary.org/speeches.htm).

213 *When asked exactly* . . .   Reeves, *President Kennedy,* 317.

214 *With his deep* . . .   Sidey, *Kennedy, President,* 321.

214 *Lem Billings,*   Leaming, *Mrs. Kennedy,* 45; Smith, *Grace and Power,* 32.

214 *Joseph Alsop,*   Heymann, *Georgetown,* 45.

214 *Gore Vidal,*   Smith, *Grace and Power,* 239.

214 *By the end* . . .   Sorensen, *Kennedy,* 478.

215 *Theodore White explained* . . .   White, *In Search of History,* 547.

25. KENNEDY IN VIETNAM

216 *John Kenneth Galbraith* . . .   Galbraith, *Name-Dropping,* 114.

216 *Not long before* . . .   McNamara with VanDeMark, *In Retrospect,* 62.

217 *After Diem's assassination,* . . .   Freedman, *Kennedy's Wars,* 403.

217 *As Schlesinger pointed* . . .   Schlesinger, *Robert Kennedy and His Times,* 780.

217 *Clark Clifford argues* . . .   Clifford with Holbrooke, *Counsel to the President,* 381–382.

217 *In a September 1963* . . .   McNamara with VanDeMark, *In Retrospect,* 62.

218 *"We want the war to be* . . .   Press conference, Washington, D.C., September 12, 1963. From the website of the John F. Kennedy Library and Museum (http://www.jfklibrary.org/speeches.htm).

218 *In the same month,* . . .   McNamara with VanDeMark, *In Retrospect,* 87.

218 *Kennedy expanded the* . . .   Brown, *JFK: History of an Image,* 87.

218 *Secretary of State* . . .   Giglio, *Presidency of Kennedy,* 253–254.

218 *In a 1964* . . .   Collier and Horowitz, *The Kennedys,* 335.

218 *Kennedy, he said,* . . .   Reeves, *Question of Character,* 410.

218 *The text of a speech* . . .   Remarks prepared for delivery at the Trade Mart in Dallas. From the website of the John F. Kennedy Library and Museum (http://www.jfklibrary.org/speeches.htm).

27. KENNEDY IN CRISIS

223 *"Great crises make* . . .   Kennedy, *Profiles in Courage,* 47.

226 *Kennedy charged Eisenhower* . . .   Reeves, *President Kennedy,* 37; Beschloss, *Crisis Years,* 27.

226 *By a 47 to 33* . . .   Kenney, *Kennedy: Presidential Portfolio,* 46.

226 *In his first* . . .   Collier and Horowitz, *The Kennedys,* 263. From the first State of the Union address, Washington, D.C., January 30, 1961.

226 *He treated Castro* . . .   Reeves, *President Kennedy,* 78.

227 *"Everybody wanted to* . . .   Sidey, *Kennedy, President,* 106.

227 *But, as Dean Acheson* . . .   Giglio, *Presidency of Kennedy,* 54.

228 *Indeed, the plan* . . .   Hersh, *Dark Side of Camelot,* 207.

229 *Kennedy described the* . . .   Radio and television report to the American people on the Soviet arms buildup in Cuba, White House, October 22, 1962. From the website of the John F. Kennedy Library and Museum (http://www.jfklibrary.org/speeches.htm).

229 *He agreed with* . . .   Kenney, *Kennedy: Presidential Portfolio,* 169.

229 *When National Security* . . .   Beschloss, *Crisis Years,* 442.

229 *The missiles did* . . .   Giglio, *Presidency of Kennedy,* 192.

229 *McNamara said, "I'll* . . .   Beschloss, *Crisis Years,* 446.

230 *The day after* . . .   Doyle, *Oval Office,* 131.

230 *"It was this* . . .   Schlesinger, *A Thousand Days,* 841.

230 *Had the trade* . . .   Leaming, *Mrs. Kennedy,* 247.

230 *Even Kennedy loyalist* . . .   Giglio, *Presidency of Kennedy,* 215.

230 *It was he who* . . .   Sidey, *Kennedy, President,* 278.

231 *Kennedy denounced the* . . .   Press conference, Washington, D.C., April 11, 1962. From the website of the John F. Kennedy Library and Museum (http://www.jfklibrary.org/speeches.htm).

231 *Bobby sent FBI agents* . . .   Giglio, *Presidency of Kennedy,* 129–130.

231 *Kennedy said, "Do* . . .   Dallek, *Unfinished Life,* 486.

232 *One friend remarked,* . . .   Collier and Horowitz, *The Kennedys,* 253.

28. KENNEDY'S PROMISCUITY

233 *Actor Robert Stack* . . .   Reeves, *Question of Character,* 54.

234 *Marina Sulzberger described* . . .   Smith, *Grace and Power,* 274.

234 *In 1957, when* . . .   Collier and Horowitz, *The Kennedys,* 228.

234 *But as noted by* . . .   Reeves, *Question of Character,* 186.

234 *He wrote notes* . . .   Reeves, *President Kennedy,* 707.

234 *He told a friend,* . . .   Ibid.

234 *The Duke of Devonshire* . . .   Smith, *Grace and Power,* 155.

234 *Clare Boothe Luce* . . .   Beale, *Power at Play,* 76.

234 *George Smathers recalled,* . . .   Reeves, *Question of Character,* 241–242.

234 *Lawyer Clark Clifford,* . . .   Marton, *Hidden Power,* 129–130.

235 *Press Secretary Pierre* . . .   Strober and Strober, *"Let Us Begin Anew,"* 480.

235 *Pat Nixon said* . . .   Matthews, *Kennedy and Nixon,* 177.

235 *A stewardess on* . . .   Heymann, *Jackie,* 230.

235 *Kennedy had a succession* . . .   Sorensen, *Kennedy,* 24.

235 *McGeorge Bundy recalled* . . .   Martin, *Hero for Our Time,* 300.

236 *Harris Wofford argues,* . . .   Wofford, *Of Kennedys and Kings,* 455.

236 *Schlesinger agrees: "Martin* . . .   Arthur M. Schlesinger Jr., "JFK Revisited," *Cigar Aficionado,* November–December 1998.

236 *Elsewhere, Schlesinger made* . . .   Arthur M. Schlesinger Jr., "What the Thousand Days Wrought," *The New Republic,* November 21, 1983, 20.

236 *Ben Bradlee acknowledges* . . .   Bradlee, *A Good Life,* 394.

236 *During the 1960* . . .   Russell Baker, "Kennedy Gives Guidelines for Ethics in Government," *New York Times,* October 18, 1960, 1.

237 *he'd had sex with* . . .   Heymann, *Jackie,* 284–285.

237 *in the Lincoln Bedroom* . . .   "Jack Kennedy's Other Women," *Time,* December 29, 1975, 11.

237 *or had group sex* . . .   Hersh, *Dark Side of Camelot,* 390.

237 *brought an intern* . . .   Smith, *Grace and Power,* 287.

237 *"Jack kept assuring* . . .   Collier and Horowitz, *The Kennedys,* 197.

237 *While giving a journalist* . . .   Heymann, *Jackie,* 292.

238 *Seeing one woman* . . .   Dallek, *Unfinished Life,* 477.

238 *Larry Newman, a* . . .   Hersh, *Dark Side of Camelot,* 230.

238 *One afternoon, Kennedy* . . .   "Kennedy's Other Women," 11.

238 *High-priced New York* . . .   Heymann, *Jackie*, 284–285.

239 *After Bobby Baker* . . .   Baker with King, *Wheeling and Dealing*, 77.

239 *French ambassador Hervé* . . .   Beschloss, *Crisis Years*, 611.

239 *British prime minister* . . .   Smith, *Grace and Power*, 155.

239 *At Palm Beach* . . .   Ibid., 215.

239 *Reporter Maxine Cheshire* . . .   Cheshire with Greenya, *Maxine Cheshire, Reporter*, 55.

240 *Hoover had information* . . .   Thomas, *Robert Kennedy*, 116.

240 *In October 1963,* . . .   Smith, *Grace and Power*, 420.

240 *Hugh Sidey sent* . . .   Talese, *Thy Neighbor's Wife*, 104.

241 *"I didn't make* . . .   Smith, *Grace and Power*, 336.

241 *saying the situation* . . .   Talese, *Thy Neighbor's Wife*, 104.

241 *(For all his* . . .   Tom Wicker, "A Hero's Burial," *New York Times*, November 26, 1963, 2.

241 *Newman recalled a* . . .   Hersh, *Dark Side of Camelot*, 237–238.

241 *"I decided," he explained* . . .   Sorensen, *Kennedy*, 673.

242 *There, he'd had* . . .   Beschloss, *Crisis Years*, 2.

242 *When an attractive* . . .   King with Occhiogrosso, *Tell It to the King*, 94.

242 *Looking back during* . . .   Horne, *Macmillan*, 525.

242 *He criticized the president* . . .   Ibid., 290.

243 *Women smuggled in* . . .   Taraborrelli, *Jackie Ethel Joan*, 673.

243 *Newman recalled, "We* . . .   Hersh, *Dark Side of Camelot*, 228.

243 *"You'd have to say* . . .   Ibid., 230.

243 *The two started* . . .   Ibid., 316.

243 *They spoke dozens* . . .   Beschloss, *Crisis Years*, 141.

243 *(In fact, several* . . .   Bradford, *America's Queen*, 380.

244 *Hoover learned about* . . .   Thomas, *Robert Kennedy*, 169.

244 *Kennedy spent that* . . .   Spada, *Peter Lawford*, 330.

244 *On June 29, 1963,* . . .   James D. Horan and Dom Frasca, "High U.S. Aide Implicated in V-Girl Scandal," *New York Journal-American*, June 29, 1963, A1.

244 *Two days later,* . . .   Giglio, *Presidency of Kennedy*, 268.

244 *they told him that* . . .   Ibid.

244 *Bobby threatened to* . . .   Ibid.

244 *The FBI had no* . . .   Beschloss, *Crisis Years,* 610.

244 *And where was Kennedy* . . .   Marton, *Hidden Power,* 128.

245 *Only a few* . . .   Hersh, *Dark Side of Camelot,* 399.

245 *Rometsch was a* . . .   Heymann, *Jackie,* 371–372. Baker later went to prison for income tax evasion, theft, and conspiracy to defraud the government.

245 *Kennedy had asked* . . .   Baker with King, *Wheeling and Dealing,* 80.

245 *she made at least* . . .   Hersh, *Dark Side of Camelot,* 390.

245 *"She was very* . . .   Ibid., 389.

245 *In August,* . . .   Thomas, *Robert Kennedy,* 256.

245 *The FBI and* . . .   Smith, *Grace and Power,* 419.

245 *In September and* . . .   Clark Mollenhoff, "U.S. Expels Girl Linked to Officials," *Des Moines Register,* October 26, 1963, 1; Cabell Phillips, "Baker Inquiry Is Asked If German Woman's Ouster by U.S. Involved Security," *New York Times,* October 29, 1963, 17.

245 *While the Baker* . . .   Smith, *Grace and Power,* 419.

245 *On November 15, 1963,* . . .   Leaming, *Mrs. Kennedy,* 327.

246 *That week, the* . . .   Bradlee, *A Good Life,* 258.

29. KENNEDY'S EXPLOITS

236 *Inga Arvad told* . . .   Blair and Blair, *The Search for JFK,* 142.

236 *Marilyn Monroe told* . . .   Anthony Summers, *Goddess: The Secret Lives of Marilyn Monroe* (New York: Macmillan, 1985), 224.

236 *Secret Service logs* . . .   Leaming, *Mrs. Kennedy,* 263–264.

236 *One JFK girlfriend* . . .   Heymann, *Jackie,* 149.

236 *Judith Exner came* . . .   Exner with Demaris, *My Story,* 245.

237 *Joan Lundberg Hitchcock,* . . .   Reeves, *Question of Character,* 173.

237 *Kennedy and Torbert* . . .   Parmet, *JFK,* 305.

237 *Smathers recalled, "Jack* . . .   Collier and Horowitz, *The Kennedys,* 197.

237 *Ellen Rometsch reported* . . .   Hersh, *Dark Side of Camelot,* 390.

238 *Kennedy placed another* . . .   Smith, *Grace and Power,* 147.

238 *Twenty-year-old* . . .   Hersh, *Dark Side of Camelot,* 237.

238 *When Fiddle told* . . .   Martin, *Hero for Our Time,* 316.

239 *Marion "Mimi" Beardsley* . . .   Smith, *Grace and Power,* 287.

239 *Kennedy was sexually* . . .   Hamilton, *JFK: Reckless Youth,* 358.

239 *Kenneth Tynan's diary* . . .   John Lahr, ed., *The Diaries of Kenneth Tynan* (New York: Bloomsbury, 2001), 38–39.

240 *"Jack was always* . . .   Smith, *Grace and Power*, 145.

240 *During the 1963 cruise* . . .   Ibid., 364–365.

240 *Bobby Baker recalled,* . . .   Baker with King, *Wheeling and Dealing*, 78.

240 *One of his lovers* . . .   Collier and Horowitz, *The Kennedys*, 175.

241 *he told Clare* . . .   Martin, *Hero for Our Time*, 54.

241 *told Harold Macmillan,* . . .   Horne, *Macmillan*, 290.

241 *There is no* . . .   Heymann, *Jackie*, 284; Bradford, *America's Queen*, 145; Marton, *Hidden Power*, 128; Giglio, *Presidency of Kennedy*, 267; Goodwin, *Fitzgeralds and Kennedys*, 723.

241 *"We're a bunch* . . .   Reeves, *President Kennedy*, 291.

242 *When an aide* . . .   Leamer, *Kennedy Men*, 404.

242 *Dutton, Jim Reed,* . . .   Smith, *Grace and Power*, 154, 337–339.

30. KENNEDY'S COOL

247 *He didn't like* . . .   Strober and Strober, *"Let Us Begin Anew,"* 29.

248 *He literally signed* . . .   Lowe, *Portrait*, 82.

248 *"Sometimes," Clark Clifford* . . .   Clifford with Holbrooke, *Counsel to the President*, 304.

248 *While serving in the* . . .   Hamilton, *JFK: Reckless Youth*, 549. Letter of June 24, 1943.

248 *During the agonizing* . . .   Beschloss, *Crisis Years*, 285.

248 *While his newborn* . . .   Leamer, *Kennedy Men*, 697.

248 *Reporter Laura Bergquist* . . .   Martin, *Hero for Our Time*, 476.

248 *Walking into a party,* . . .   Blair and Blair, *The Search for JFK*, 142.

248 *Kennedy evaluated his* . . .   Leamer, *Kennedy Men*, 452.

248 *When guests at* . . .   Martin, *Hero for Our Time*, 493.

249 *For example, in* . . .   Matthews, *Kennedy and Nixon*, 32.

249 *In a nod to* . . .   Sidey, *Kennedy, President*, 325.

249 *During the presidential* . . .   Bradlee, *Conversations with Kennedy*, 20.

249 *When asked in* . . .   Hersh, *Dark Side of Camelot*, 24.

250 *Not long after* . . .   Sidey, *Kennedy, President*, 54.

250 *At the birthday* . . .   Leaming, *Mrs. Kennedy*, 199.

250 *"Well, I guess* . . .   Goodwin, *Remembering America*, 146.

250 *When Arthur Schlesinger* . . .   Schlesinger, *A Thousand Days,* 162.

250 *When a reporter* . . .   Press conference, Washington, D.C., May 9, 1962. From the website of the John F. Kennedy Library and Museum (http://www.jfklibrary.org/speeches.htm).

250 *In his comments* . . .   Hamilton, *JFK: Reckless Youth,* 645.

250 *When Jackie gave* . . .   Bradford, *America's Queen,* 131.

251 *When Alfred Kazin* . . .   Schlesinger, *A Thousand Days,* 744.

251 *"He observes the* . . .   Manchester, *Portrait of a President,* 116.

251 *When he was introduced* . . .   Goodwin, *Remembering America,* 117.

251 *Of his phone* . . .   Galbraith, *Journal,* 6.

251 *Of his American* . . .   Schlesinger, *A Thousand Days,* 910.

251 *Two weeks after* . . .   Reeves, *President Kennedy,* 106.

251 *When a friend* . . .   Bradlee, *Conversations with Kennedy,* 234.

252 *During the Kennedys'* . . .   Beschloss, *Crisis Years,* 186.

252 *He said during* . . .   Thomas, *Robert Kennedy,* 61.

252 *When Twentieth Century* . . .   Taraborrelli, *Jackie Ethel Joan,* 173.

252 *Undersecretary of State* . . .   Lasky, *J.F.K.: Man and Myth,* 525.

252 *Although Schlesinger repeatedly* . . .   Arthur M. Schlesinger, foreword to *Of Poetry and Power,* edited by Glikes and Schwaber, vi.

253 *Clark Clifford observed,* . . .   Clifford with Holbrooke, *Counsel to the President,* 304.

253 *In 1956, when* . . .   Leuchtenburg, *Shadow of FDR,* 76.

253 *In his public* . . .   Wofford, *Of Kennedys and Kings,* 382.

253 *He didn't like* . . .   Collier and Horowitz, *The Kennedys,* 289.

253 *in fact, when* . . .   Hamilton, *JFK: Reckless Youth,* 50.

254 *whom Joe described* . . .   Cassini, *In My Own Fashion,* 302.

31. KENNEDY'S HEALTH

256 *According to Robert* . . .   Dallek, *Unfinished Life,* 76, 77, 104.

257 *If Kennedy did* . . .   Ibid., 105.

258 *In addition to* . . .   Reeves, *President Kennedy,* 668, note accompanying p. 42 ("Addison's disease").

259 *Addisonians taking cortisone* . . .   Smith, *Grace and Power,* 33.

259 *In December 1962,* . . .   Ibid., 331.

259 *Kennedy biographer Robert* . . .   Dallek, *Unfinished Life,* 705.

260 *Kennedy radiated health . . .*   Travell, *Office Hours,* 320; James Reston Jr., "That 'Damned Girdle': The Hidden Factor That Might Have Killed Kennedy," *Los Angeles Times,* November 22, 2004, B9.

260 *In 1953, at a time . . .*   Paul F. Healy, "The Senate's Gay Young Bachelor," *Saturday Evening Post,* June 13, 1953, 26.

260 *To keep himself . . .*   Sorensen, *Kennedy,* 38.

260 *He once told . . .*   Beschloss, *Crisis Years,* 189.

262 *In 1940, he contracted . . .*   Robert Dallek, "The Medical Ordeals of JFK," *Atlantic Monthly,* December 2002, 54.

264 *His chronic back . . .*   Leamer, *Kennedy Men,* 299.

264 *In October 1954, . . .*   Beschloss, *Crisis Years,* 189.

264 *It was at this . . .*   Ibid.

265 *Between mid-May and . . .*   Leamer, *Kennedy Men,* 543.

32. KENNEDY'S LIES

267 *For example, after . . .*   Anthony Lewis, "President's Back Strain at Tree Planting Is Disclosed," *New York Times,* June 9, 1961, 1.

267 *After he collapsed . . .*   Collier and Horowitz, *The Kennedys,* 167.

267 *After seven months . . .*   "Senator Kennedy Recovers and Returns to the Job," *New York Times,* May 24, 1955, 1.

267 *in fact, Kennedy . . .*   Parmet, *Jack,* 317.

267 *Dr. Janet Travell . . .*   Travell, *Office Hours,* 319.

268 *In 1957, after . . .*   Ibid., 320.

268 *In 1959, he claimed, . . .*   Blair and Blair, *The Search for JFK,* 573.

268 *Around the same . . .*   Burns, *John Kennedy,* 156.

268 *Sometimes Kennedy told . . .*   Ibid.

268 *In a dig at . . .*   Parmet, *JFK,* 17.

268 *Striking back during . . .*   W. H. Lawrence, "Johnson Backers Urge Health Test," *New York Times,* July 5, 1960, 19.

268 *Asked about his . . .*   Reeves, *President Kennedy,* 24.

268 *He told Schlesinger, . . .*   Blair and Blair, *The Search for JFK,* 574.

268 *When his press . . .*   Reeves, *President Kennedy,* 44.

269 *Secret Service agent . . .*   Leamer, *Kennedy Men,* 543.

269 *Kennedy didn't know, . . .*   Dallek, *Unfinished Life,* 399.

269 *He also installed . . .*   Travell, *Office Hours,* 312.

269 *he had a special mattress* . . .   Leamer, *Kennedy Men,* 523.

269 *Even as president,* . . .   Schlesinger, *A Thousand Days,* 776.

270 *Kennedy later suggested* . . .   Hamilton, *JFK: Reckless Youth,* 380. A November 30, 1959, letter from William Boulet, president, Wilfred Funk, Inc., to Senator John F. Kennedy read, "In answer to your letter dated November 24, 1959, the records available indicate that the total sales of your publication 'Why England Slept' were approximately 12,000 copies." Hamilton, *JFK: Reckless Youth,* 842, note accompanying p. 380 ("actual sales").

270 *For example, a major* . . .   Cabell Phillips, "How to Be a Presidential Candidate," *New York Times,* July 13, 1958, SM11.

270 *"a back injury* . . .   Ibid.

270 *(who at least* . . .   Smith, *Grace and Power,* 56.

270 *"I worked as hard* . . .   Reeves, *Question of Character,* 142. See also Dallek, *Unfinished Life,* 210.

270 *Rose Kennedy acknowledged* . . .   Leamer, *Kennedy Women,* 467.

271 *according to biographer* . . .   Parmet, *Jack,* 323–332.

271 *James MacGregor Burns* . . .   Collier and Horowitz, *The Kennedys,* 207n★.

271 *Sorensen later explained,* . . .   Beschloss, *Crisis Years,* 127.

33. KENNEDY AS MUSE

273 *In his 1940* . . .   John F. Kennedy, *Why England Slept* (New York: Wilfred Funk, 1940), xxii.

274 *Among musicians, Kennedy's* . . .   Spada, *Peter Lawford,* 253.

275 *After Kennedy's victory,* . . .   Taraborrelli, *Jackie Ethel Joan,* 33.

276 *Norman Mailer, with* . . .   Norman Mailer, *An American Dream* (New York: Vintage International, 1963), 1.

276 *Kennedy invited renowned* . . .   Glikes and Schwaber, *Of Poetry and Power,* 9.

276 *Of Poetry and Power,* . . .   Ibid.

277 *Mailer's adulatory Esquire* . . .   Mailer, "Superman Comes to the Supermarket," in *Presidential Papers,* 59.

277 *Kennedy observed, "It* . . .   Schlesinger, *A Thousand Days,* 116.

277 *When the movie* . . .   Gallagher, *My Life,* 270.

277 *Novelist Ward Just* . . . Just, *Jack Gance*, 184.

278 *When a friend* . . . O'Donnell and Powers with McCarthy, *"Johnny, We Hardly Knew Ye,"* 451.

34. KENNEDY—QUESTIONS HE RAISED

279 *His brother Bobby* . . . Parmet, *Jack*, 15.

280 *Off the air,* . . . King with Occhiogrosso, *Tell It to the King*, 93.

280 *The Kennedys offered* . . . Reeves, *President Kennedy*, 324.

281 *That in November* . . . Burns, *John Kennedy*, 83.

281 *which prompted one* . . . Ibid.

281 *That, as Manchester* . . . Manchester, *One Brief Shining Moment*, 60.

281 *That Jack and Jackie* . . . Gore Vidal, "President Kennedy," in *United States: Essays, 1952–1992* (New York: Random House, 1993), 799.

281 *That for almost* . . . Donovan, *PT 109*, 88.

281 *"The singers were* . . . Manchester, *Portrait of a President*, 150.

282 *That just two* . . . O'Donnell and Powers with McCarthy, *"Johnny, We Hardly Knew Ye,"* 25.

282 *Secretary of State* . . . Alsop, *The Center*, 186.

282 *Until Jackie ordered* . . . Gallagher, *My Life*, 224.

35. KENNEDY ALCHEMY

284 *Journalist Tom Wicker* . . . Wicker, *Kennedy without Tears*, 16.

285 *Dean Rusk reflected,* . . . Strober and Strober, *"Let Us Begin Anew,"* 485.

285 *Ted Sorensen argued,* . . . Sorensen, *Kennedy*, 758.

285 *Journalist Hugh Sidey* . . . Sidey, *Kennedy, President*, x.

285 *Joe Kennedy couldn't* . . . Hersh, *Dark Side of Camelot*, 89.

286 *Theodore White maintained* . . . White, *In Search of History*, 474.

286 *Arthur Schlesinger Jr. listed* . . . Schlesinger, *A Thousand Days*, 1031.

286 *Sorensen, for example,* . . . Sorensen, *Kennedy*, 7.

286 *Pierre Salinger wrote,* . . . Salinger, *With Kennedy*, 364.

286 *Ben Bradlee acknowledged,* . . . Bradlee, *Conversations with Kennedy*, 12.

286 *Chester Bowles: "No* . . . Bowles, *Promises to Keep*, 443.

287 *Helen Thomas: "If* . . . Thomas, *Dateline: White House*, 37.

287 *John Kenneth Galbraith:* . . .   Strober and Strober, "*Let Us Begin Anew,*" 492.

287 *Harold Macmillan: "Perhaps* . . .   Horne, *Macmillan,* 526.

288 *As Norman Mailer* . . .   Mailer, "Superman Comes to the Supermarket," in *Presidential Papers,* 47.

288 *Joe Kennedy understood* . . .   Parmet, *Jack,* 329.

288 *Then, after only* . . .   Parmet, *JFK,* 98.

288 *Schlesinger recalled Kennedy's* . . .   Schlesinger, *A Thousand Days,* 207.

289 *As ambassador to France* . . .   Beschloss, *Crisis Years,* 674.

289 *Sorensen wrote, "I think* . . .   Sorensen, *Kennedy,* 758.

289 *One politician scoffed* . . .   Schlesinger, *A Thousand Days,* 726.

289 *Nixon groused to* . . .   H. R. Haldeman, *The Haldeman Diaries* (New York: Putnam, 1994), 125.

290 *Dave Powers recalled* . . .   O'Donnell and Powers with McCarthy, "*Johnny, We Hardly Knew Ye,*" 55.

290 *When lawyer Newton* . . .   Parmet, *Jack,* 339.

290 *Norman Mailer suggested* . . .   Mailer, *Presidential Papers,* 38, 41–42.

290 *When Kennedy visited* . . .   Beschloss, *Crisis Years,* 604.

290 *Secretary of State* . . .   Smith, *Grace and Power,* 382.

290 *Here was a young* . . .   Goodwin, *Fitzgeralds and Kennedys,* 780.

291 *I used to* . . .   Ibid., 780–781.

291 *One friend observed,* . . .   Strober and Strober, "*Let Us Begin Anew,*" 57.

291 *Of the 1960 campaign,* . . .   White, *Making of the President, 1960,* 319–320.

291 *Larry Newman, Kennedy's* . . .   Hersh, *Dark Side of Camelot,* 21.

291 *Ben Bradlee recalled* . . .   Bradlee, *Conversations with Kennedy,* 10.

291 *Dean Rusk: "He* . . .   Strober and Strober, "*Let Us Begin Anew,*" 156.

291 *State Department official* . . .   Doyle, *Oval Office,* 101.

291 *Charley Bartlett reflected,* . . .   Leamer, *Kennedy Women,* 538.

291 *After Kennedy died,* . . .   James Reston, "What Was Killed Was Not Only the President but the Promise," *New York Times,* November 15, 1964, 24.

292 *Ted Sorensen wrote,* . . .   Sorensen, *Kennedy,* 751.

292 *Red Fay recalled, . . .*   Fay, *Pleasure of His Company,* 261–262.

292 *Cambodia's Prince Sihanouk . . .*   Schlesinger, *A Thousand Days,* 1029.

292 *When it fell to . . .*   Manchester, *Death of a President,* 409.

292 *Her composed TV . . .*   For an audio clip of Jacqueline Kennedy's address, go to http://www2.uol.com.br/speakup/collection.

292 *Concluding her remarks . . .*   Shulman, *"Jackie"!,* 134.

292 *And while the . . .*   Beschloss, *Crisis Years,* 304, citing a Gallup poll of August 19, 1962.

293 *Early in his term, . . .*   Reeves, *President Kennedy,* 73.

293 *Gallup polls showed . . .*   Reeves, *Question of Character,* 2.

293 *After the Cuban . . .*   Smith, *Grace and Power,* 327.

293 *(Furthermore, in the . . .*   Manchester, *Portrait of a President,* 89.

293 *In the 1962 . . .*   Beschloss, *Crisis Years,* 557.

293 *Joseph Alsop asked . . .*   Manchester, *Death of a President,* 534.

293 *Reporter Laura Bergquist . . .*   Martin, *Hero for Our Time,* 568.

293 *Poet Kathleen Raine . . .*   Glikes and Schwaber, *Of Poetry and Power,* 2.

293 *About 175 million . . .*   Hamilton, *JFK: Reckless Youth,* 812.

293 *The funeral was even . . .*   Parmet, *Jack,* xii.

293 *In France, Charles . . .*   Beschloss, *Crisis Years,* 676.

293 *The American ambassador . . .*   Mulvaney, *Diana & Jackie,* 146.

294 *When an American . . .*   Goodwin, *Remembering America,* 232.

37. WHO KILLED JOHN F. KENNEDY?

297 *Fellow marine Kerry . . .*   Posner, *Case Closed,* 33–34.

298 *On September 25, Oswald . . .*   Ibid., 164.

298 *He had expected . . .*   Ibid., 195.

298 *On October 14, . . .*   Mallon, *Mrs. Paine's Garage,* 42.

298 *On November 19–20, . . .*   Parmet, *JFK,* 344.

299 *He had told . . .*   Posner, *Case Closed,* 33.

299 *The conspiracy theorists . . .*   Ibid., 470.

299 *First, marksmanship specialists . . .*   Ibid., 20–21n★.

300 *The bullet has also . . .*   Ibid., 341–342.

301 *He told a police . . .*   Manchester, *Death of a President,* 276.

301 *The commission's rushed . . .*   Tim Weiner, "A Blast at Secrecy in Kennedy Killing," *New York Times,* September 29, 1998, A17.

303 *The credibility of . . .*   Mallon, *Mrs. Paine's Garage,* 193.

303 *Although many blame . . .*   Posner, *Case Closed,* 464.

304 *Witnesses, instead of . . .*   Ibid., 483–499.

304 *When Oswald's grave . . .*   Parmet, *JFK,* 348.

304 *For instance, those . . .*   Goldberg, *Enemies Within,* 134.

305 *Ruby had always . . .*   Posner, *Case Closed,* 356.

305 *Reporter Tony Zoppi . . .*   Ibid., 374.

38. FORTUNE'S FAVORITE

308 *As he campaigned . . .*   Sorensen, *Kennedy,* 173.

308 *During the 1962 . . .*   Salinger, *With Kennedy,* 271.

309 *Worse, one of Baker's . . .*   Bradford, *America's Queen,* 260.

310 *At his November . . .*   Harold Chase and Allen Lerman, eds., *Kennedy and the Press: The News Conferences* (New York: Thomas Y. Crowell Company, 1965), 520.

311 *In the summer . . .*   Thomas, *Robert Kennedy,* 275.

311 *Corbin continued to . . .*   Hersh, *Dark Side of Camelot,* 445.

311 *Hoover, too, might . . .*   Leamer, *Kennedy Women,* 584.

311 *Mark Raskin, a . . .*   Leamer, *Kennedy Men,* 691–692.

312 *In his 1963 . . .*   Smith, *Grace and Power,* 356–357.

312 *the very next day, . . .*   Radio and television report to the American people on civil rights, White House, June 11, 1963. From the website of the John F. Kennedy Library and Museum (http://www.jfklibrary.org/speeches.htm).

312 *As he left . . .*   Dallek, *Unfinished Life,* 625.

312 *After Berlin, he . . .*   Smith, *Grace and Power,* 382.

312 *Polls taken abroad . . .*   William Manchester, "Then: 1963," *New York Times,* November 4, 1973, 321.

312 *In mid-November, Kennedy . . .*   Ibid.

312 *His physical condition . . .*   Parmet, *JFK,* 337.

312 *Kennedy had even . . .*   O'Donnell and Powers with McCarthy, *"Johnny, We Hardly Knew Ye,"* 39.

313 *"We can say . . .*   Sorensen, *Kennedy,* 750.

313 *Jackie hadn't traveled . . .*   Smith, *Grace and Power,* 423.

313 *"To think that . . .*   West with Kotz, *Upstairs at the White House,* 276.

313 *Kennedy's eagerness to* . . .   Gallagher, *My Life,* 341.

314 *Efforts to shield* . . .   O'Donnell and Powers with McCarthy, *"Johnny, We Hardly Knew Ye,"* 19.

314 *During his June* . . .   Smith, *Grace and Power,* 382.

314 *Kennedy rode in* . . .   Lowe, *Portrait,* 172.

314 *(The bubble top* . . .   Posner, *Case Closed,* 263n.

314 *And because Kennedy* . . .   King with Occhiogrosso, *Tell It to the King,* 96.

314 *"Would Lincoln have* . . .   Schlesinger, *A Thousand Days,* 675.

314 *He observed, "I* . . .   Strober and Strober, *"Let Us Begin Anew,"* 502.

314 *"Sometimes . . . the promise* . . .   Buchan, *Pilgrim's Way,* 50.

315 *Jackie, too, could* . . .   Anthony, *As We Remember Her,* 189.

316 *In a notebook* . . .   Buchan, *Pilgrim's Way,* 60.

39. MY KENNEDY

319 *"This country is* . . .   Remarks intended for delivery to the Texas Democratic State Committee, Austin, Texas, November 22, 1963. From the website of the John F. Kennedy Library and Museum (http://www.jfklibrary.org/speeches.htm).

Select Bibliography

Forty Ways to Look at JFK rests on the work of more comprehensive biographers. Kennedy's life, character, and presidency have inspired a huge, fascinating literature, and I hope my own brief account will inspire readers to read further. Listed below are the principal works consulted.

Adler, Bill, ed. *The Kennedy Wit*. New York: Citadel Press, 1964.

Alsop, Joseph, and Adam Platt. *"I've Seen the Best of It": Memoirs*. New York: Norton, 1992.

Alsop, Stewart. *The Center: People and Power in Political Washington*. New York: Harper and Row, 1968.

Anthony, Carl Sferrazza. *As We Remember Her: Jacqueline Kennedy Onassis in the Words of Her Family and Friends*. New York: HarperCollins, 1997.

Baker, Bobby, with Larry L. King. *Wheeling and Dealing: Confessions of a Capitol Hill Operator*. New York: Norton, 1978.

Baldridge, Letitia. *In the Kennedy Style*. New York: Doubleday, 1998.

Barnouw, Erik. *Tube of Plenty: The Evolution of American Television*. 2nd ed. New York: Oxford University Press, 1990.

Barthes, Roland. *Camera Lucida: Reflections on Photography*. Translated by Richard Howard. New York: Hill and Wang, 1981.

Beale, Betty. *Power at Play: A Memoir of Parties, Politicians, and the Presidents in My Bedroom*. Washington, D.C.: Regnery Gateway, 1993.

Berlin, Isaiah. *The Hedgehog and the Fox*. Chicago: Ivan R. Dee, 1953.

Beschloss, Michael R. *The Crisis Years: Kennedy and Khrushchev, 1960–1963.* New York: Edward Burlingame Books, 1991.

Blair, Joan, and Clay Blair Jr. *The Search for JFK.* New York: Berkley Publishing Corp., 1976.

Boorstin, Daniel J. *The Image.* New York: Vintage Books, 1961.

Bowles, Chester. *Promises to Keep: My Years in Public Life, 1941–1969.* New York: Harper and Row, 1971.

Bradford, Sarah. *America's Queen: The Life of Jacqueline Kennedy Onassis.* New York: Penguin Books, 2000.

Bradlee, Benjamin C. *Conversations with Kennedy.* New York: Norton, 1975.

———. *A Good Life: Newspapering and Other Adventures.* New York: Simon and Schuster, 1995.

———. *That Special Grace.* New York: Lippincott, 1963.

Brown, Thomas. *JFK: History of an Image.* Bloomington: Indiana University Press, 1988.

Bruno, Jerry, and Jeff Greenfield. *The Advance Man.* New York: Morrow, 1971.

Bryant, Traphes, with Frances Spatz Leighton. *Dog Days at the White House.* New York: Macmillan, 1975.

Buchan, John. *Pilgrim's Way.* Cambridge, U.K.: Riverside Press, 1940.

Burns, James MacGregor. *John Kennedy: A Political Profile.* New York: Avon, 1959.

Cassini, Oleg. *In My Own Fashion.* New York: Simon and Schuster, 1987.

Cecil, David. *Melbourne: The Young Melbourne and Lord M* in one volume. London: Reprint Society, 1939.

Clifford, Clark, with Richard Holbrooke. *Counsel to the President.* New York: Random House, 1991.

Collier, Peter, and David Horowitz. *The Kennedys: An American Drama.* New York: Summit Books, 1984.

Corry, John. *The Manchester Affair.* New York: Putnam, 1967.

Dallas, Rita, with Jeanira Ratcliffe. *The Kennedy Case.* New York: Putnam, 1973.

Dallek, Robert. *An Unfinished Life.* New York: Little, Brown, 2003.

Dickerson, Nancy. *Among Those Present: A Reporter's View of Twenty-five Years in Washington.* New York: Random House, 1976.

Donaldson, Sam. *Hold On, Mr. President!* New York: Random House, 1987.

Donovan, Robert J. *PT 109: John F. Kennedy in World War II.* New York: McGraw-Hill, 1961.

Doyle, William. *Inside the Oval Office: The White House Tapes from FDR to Clinton.* New York: Kodansha International, 1999.

Exner, Judith, with Ovid Demaris. *My Story.* New York: Grove Press, 1977.

Fairlie, Henry. *The Kennedy Promise: The Politics of Expectation.* Garden City, N.Y.: Doubleday, 1973.

Farber, David, and Beth Bailey. *The Columbia Guide to America in the 1960s.* New York: Columbia University Press, 2001.

Fay, Paul B., Jr. *The Pleasure of His Company.* New York: Harper and Row, 1966.

Felsenthal, Carol. *Power, Privilege, and the "Post": The Katharine Graham Story.* New York: Putnam, 1993.

Freedman, Lawrence. *Kennedy's Wars: Berlin, Cuba, Laos, and Vietnam.* New York: Oxford University Press, 2000.

Galbraith, John Kenneth. *Ambassador's Journal.* Boston: Houghton Mifflin, 1969.

———. *Name-Dropping: From FDR On.* New York: Houghton Mifflin, 1999.

Gallagher, Mary Barelli. *My Life with Jacqueline Kennedy.* New York: Paperback Library, 1969.

Giglio, James N. *The Presidency of John F. Kennedy.* Lawrence: University Press of Kansas, 1991.

Glikes, Erwin A., and Paul Schwaber, eds. *Of Poetry and Power: Poems Occasioned by the Presidency and by the Death of John F. Kennedy.* New York: Basic Books, 1964.

Goldberg, Robert Alan. *Enemies Within: The Culture of Conspiracy in Modern America.* New Haven, Conn.: Yale University Press, 2001.

Goodwin, Doris Kearns. *The Fitzgeralds and the Kennedys.* New York: Simon and Schuster, 1987.

Goodwin, Richard N. *Remembering America: A Voice from the Sixties.* Boston: Little, Brown, 1988.

Graham, Katharine. *Personal History.* New York: Knopf, 1997.

Halberstam, David. *The Best and the Brightest.* New York: Ballantine, 1969.

Hamilton, Nigel. *JFK: Reckless Youth.* New York: Random House, 1992.

Hellman, John. *The Kennedy Obsession: The American Myth of JFK.* New York: Columbia University Press, 1997.

Hersh, Seymour M. *The Dark Side of Camelot.* New York: Back Bay Books, 1997.

Heymann, C. David. *The Georgetown Ladies' Social Club.* New York: Atria Books, 2003.

———. *A Woman Named Jackie.* New York: Lyle Stuart Books, 1989.

Horne, Alistair. *Harold Macmillan.* Vol. 2, *1957–1986.* New York: Viking, 1989.

Just, Ward. *Jack Gance.* New York: Houghton Mifflin, 1989.

Kennedy, John F. *Profiles in Courage.* New York: Pocket Books, 1955.

Kennedy, Rose. *Times to Remember.* Garden City, N.Y.: Doubleday, 1974.

Kenney, Charles. *John F. Kennedy: The Presidential Portfolio.* New York: Public Affairs, 2000.

King, Larry, with Peter Occhiogrosso. *Tell It to the King.* New York: Putnam, 1988.

Klapp, Orrin E. *Symbolic Leaders: Public Dramas and Public Men.* Chicago: Aldine, 1964.

Klein, Edward. *All Too Human: The Love Story of Jack and Jackie Kennedy.* New York: Pocket Books, 1996.

Koestenbaum, Wayne. *Jackie under My Skin.* New York: Plume Books/Penguin, 1995.

Krock, Arthur. *Memoirs: Sixty Years on the Firing Line.* New York: Funk and Wagnalls, 1968.

Kutler, Stanley I. *The Wars of Watergate: The Last Crisis of Richard Nixon.* New York: Knopf, 1990.

Lasky, Victor. *J.F.K.: The Man and the Myth.* New Rochelle, N.Y.: Arlington House, 1963.

Latham, Caroline, and Jeannie Sakol. *The Kennedy Encyclopedia.* New York: New American Library, 1989.

Leamer, Laurence. *The Kennedy Men, 1901–1963: The Laws of the Father.* New York: Perennial, 2001.

———. *The Kennedy Women: The Saga of an American Family.* New York: Villard Books, 1994.

Leaming, Barbara. *Mrs. Kennedy: The Missing History of the Kennedy Years.* New York: Free Press, 2001.

Leuchtenburg, William E. *In the Shadow of FDR.* Ithaca, N.Y.: Cornell University Press, 1983.

Lieberson, Goddard, ed. *John Fitzgerald Kennedy . . . As We Remember Him.* New York: Atheneum, 1965.

Lincoln, Evelyn. *My Twelve Years with John F. Kennedy.* New York: Bantam Books, 1965.

Lindholm, Charles. *Charisma.* Cambridge, U.K.: Basil Blackwell, 1990.

Lippmann, Walter. *Public Opinion.* New York: Free Press, 1922.

Lowe, Jacques. *Portrait: The Emergence of John F. Kennedy.* New York: Bramhall House, 1961.

———. *Remembering Jack: Intimate and Unseen Photographs of the Kennedys.* New York: Bulfinch Press, 2003.

Lubin, David M. *Shooting Kennedy: JFK and the Culture of Images.* Berkeley: University of California Press, 2003.

Mailer, Norman. *The Presidential Papers.* New York: Putnam, 1963.

Malcolm, Janet. *Diana & Nikon: Essays on Photography.* New York: Aperture, 1997.

Mallon, Thomas. *Mrs. Paine's Garage: And the Murder of John F. Kennedy.* New York: Pantheon Books, 2002.

Manchester, William. *The Death of a President.* New York: Harper and Row, 1967.

———. *One Brief Shining Moment.* Boston: Little, Brown, 1983.

———. *Portrait of a President.* Boston: Little, Brown, 1962.

Manso, Peter, ed. *Mailer: His Life and Times.* New York: Simon and Schuster, 1985.

Martin, Ralph G. *A Hero for Our Time.* New York: Macmillan, 1983.

Marton, Kati. *Hidden Power: Presidential Marriages That Shaped Our Recent History.* New York: Pantheon, 2001.

Matthews, Christopher. *Kennedy and Nixon: The Rivalry That Shaped Postwar America.* New York: Touchstone, 1996.

McNamara, Robert S., with Brian VanDeMark. *In Retrospect: The Tragedy and Lessons of Vietnam.* New York: Times Books, 1995.

Michaelis, David. *The Best of Friends: Profiles of Extraordinary Friendships.* New York: Morrow, 1983.

Mulvaney, Jay. *Diana & Jackie: Maidens, Mothers, Myths.* New York: St. Martin's Griffin, 2002.

O'Donnell, Kenneth P., and David F. Powers with Joe McCarthy. *"Johnny, We Hardly Knew Ye."* Boston: Little, Brown, 1970.

O'Neill, Tip, with William Novak. *Man of the House: The Life and Political Memoirs of Speaker Tip O'Neill.* New York: Random House, 1987.

Parmet, Herbert S. *Jack: The Struggles of John F. Kennedy.* New York: Dial Press, 1980.

———. *JFK: The Presidency of John F. Kennedy.* New York: Dial Press, 1983.

Posner, Gerald. *Case Closed: Lee Harvey Oswald and the Assassination of JFK.* New York: Random House, 1993.

Quirk, Lawrence J. *The Kennedys in Hollywood.* New York: Cooper Square Press, 2004.

Reeves, Richard. *President Kennedy.* New York: Simon and Schuster, 1993.

Reeves, Thomas C. *A Question of Character: A Life of John F. Kennedy.* New York: Free Press, 1991.

Rhea, Mini, with Frances Spatz Leighton. *I Was Jacqueline Kennedy's Dressmaker.* New York: Fleet Publishing, 1962.

Salinger, Pierre. *With Kennedy.* New York: Doubleday, 1966.

Sante, Luc. *Evidence.* New York: Farrar, Straus and Giroux, 1992.

Sassoon, Donald. *Becoming Mona Lisa.* New York: Harvest Book, 2002.

Saunders, Frank, with James Southwood. *Torn Lace Curtain: Life with the Kennedys.* New York: Pinnacle Books, 1982.

Schlesinger, Arthur M., Jr. *Robert Kennedy and His Times.* Boston: Houghton Mifflin, 1978.

———. *A Thousand Days.* Boston: Houghton Mifflin, 1965.

Selkirk, Errol. *JFK for Beginners.* New York: Perigee Books, 1988.

Shaw, Mark. *The John F. Kennedys: A Family Album*. New York: Farrar, Straus and Giroux, 1964; rev. ed., New York: Rizzoli, 2000.

Shaw, Maud. *White House Nannie*. New York: New American Library, 1965.

Shulman, Irving. *"Jackie"! The Exploitation of a First Lady*. New York: Pocket Books, 1970.

Sidey, Hugh. *John F. Kennedy, President*. New York: Atheneum, 1963.

Smith, Sally Bedell. *Grace and Power: The Private World of the Kennedy White House*. New York: Random House, 2004.

Sobieszek, Robert A. *The Art of Persuasion: A History of Advertising Photography*. New York: Harry N. Abrams, 1988.

Sontag, Susan. *On Photography*. New York: Anchor Books, 1977.

Sorensen, Theodore C. *Kennedy*. New York: Harper and Row, 1965.

———. *The Kennedy Legacy*. New York: Macmillan, 1969.

Spada, James. *Peter Lawford: The Man Who Kept the Secrets*. New York: Bantam Books, 1991.

Stein, Jean, interviewer and George Plimpton, ed. *American Journey: The Times of Robert Kennedy*. New York: Harcourt Brace Jovanovich, 1970.

Strober, Gerald S., and Deborah H. Strober. *"Let Us Begin Anew": An Oral History of the Kennedy Presidency*. New York: HarperPerennial, 1993.

Suares, J. C., and J. Spencer Beck. *Uncommon Grace: Reminiscences and Photographs of Jacqueline Bouvier Kennedy Onassis*. Charlottesville, Va.: Thomasson-Grant, 1994.

Summers, Anthony, and Stephen Dorril. *Honeytrap*. London: Coronet Books, 1988.

Szarkowski, John. *Mirrors and Windows: American Photography since 1960*. New York: Museum of Modern Art, 1978.

Talese, Gay. *Thy Neighbor's Wife*. Garden City, N.Y.: Doubleday, 1980.

Taraborrelli, J. Randy. *Jackie Ethel Joan*. New York: Warner Books, 2000.

Thomas, Evan. *Robert Kennedy: His Life*. New York: Simon and Schuster, 2000.

Thomas, Helen. *Dateline: White House*. New York: Macmillan, 1975.

Thompson, Jerry L. *Truth and Photography*. Chicago: Ivan R. Dee, 2003.

Travell, Janet. *Office Hours: Day and Night.* New York: World Publishing, 1968.

West, J. B., with Mary Lynn Kotz. *Upstairs at the White House.* New York: Coward, McCann and Geoghegan, 1973.

White, Theodore H. *America in Search of Itself: The Making of the President, 1956–1980.* New York: Warner Books, 1982.

———. *In Search of History.* New York: Harper and Row, 1978.

———. *The Making of the President, 1960.* New York: Atheneum, 1988.

Wicker, Tom. *JFK and LBJ: The Influence of Personality upon Politics.* New York: Morrow, 1968.

———. *Kennedy without Tears: The Man beneath the Myth.* New York: Morrow, 1964.

Wills, Garry. *The Kennedy Imprisonment.* New York: Little, Brown, 1981.

Wofford, Harris. *Of Kennedys and Kings.* New York: Farrar, Straus and Giroux, 1980.

Acknowledgments

My deep thanks go to the three people who made *Forty Ways to Look at JFK* possible: my agent, Christy Fletcher; my editor, Nancy Miller; and my husband, Jamie Rubin.

Special thanks also to: Nicolas Checa, Susan Cohan, Jacob Collins, Elizabeth Craft, Elizabeth Factor, Dana Hoey, Deirdre Lanning, Freda Richardson, Bob Rubin, Judy Rubin, Drew Schiff, Diana Walker, and especially Reed Hundt.

And thanks to my parents, Jack and Karen Craft, who gave me not only enthusiastic support but also exceedingly useful editorial suggestions.

Index

378   INDEX

Permission Acknowledgments

TEXT

Grateful acknowledgment is made to the following for permission to reprint previously published materials:

Berkley Publishing, a division of Penguin Group (USA) Inc.: Excerpts from *The Search for JFK* by Joan Blair and Clay Blair, Jr., copyright © 1976 by Joan Blair and Clay Blair, Jr. Reprinted by permission of Berkley Publishing, a division of Penguin Group (USA) Inc.

Farrar, Straus, and Giroux, LLC: Excerpts from *Of Kennedys and Kings: Making Sense of the Sixties* by Harris Wofford, copyright © 1980 by Harris Wofford. Reprinted by permission of Farrar, Straus, and Giroux, LLC.

Georges Borchardt, Inc.: Excerpt from *The Kennedys* by Peter Collier and David Horowitz, copyright © 1984 by Peter Collier and David Horowitz. Reprinted by permission of Georges Borchardt, Inc.

HarperCollins Publishers Inc.: Excerpts from *Kennedy* by Theodore C. Sorensen, copyright © 1965, renewed 1993 by Theodore C. Sorensen. Reprinted by permission of HarperCollins Publishers Inc.

Houghton Mifflin Company: Excerpts from *A Thousand Days: John F. Kennedy in the White House* by Arthur M. Schlesinger, Jr., copyright © 1965, renewed 1993 by Arthur M. Schlesinger, Jr. All rights reserved. Reprinted by permission of Houghton Mifflin Company.

International Creative Management, Inc.: Excerpts from *The Crisis Years* by Michael Beschloss, copyright © 1991 by Michael R. Beschloss. Reprinted by permission of International Creative Management, Inc.

Little, Brown and Co., Inc., and International Creative Management, Inc.: Excerpts from *The Dark Side of Camelot* by Seymour Hersh, copyright © 1997 by

Seymour M. Hersh. Reprinted by permission of Little, Brown and Co., Inc., and International Creative Management, Inc.

Little, Brown and Co., Inc.: Excerpts from *"Johnny We Hardly Knew Ye"* by Kenneth P. O'Donnell, copyright © 1970, 1972 by Kenneth P. O'Donnell, David F. Powers and Joe McCarthy. Reprinted by permission of Little, Brown and Co., Inc.

Random House, Inc.: Excerpts from *JFK: Reckless Youth* by Nigel Hamilton, copyright © 1992 by Nigel Hamilton; excerpts from *Grace and Power* by Sally Bedell Smith, copyright © 2004 by Sally Bedell Smith. Reprinted by permission of Random House, Inc.

Scribner, an imprint of Simon & Schuster Adult Publishing Group and Sll/ Sterling Lord Literistic, Inc.: Excerpts from *A Hero for Our Time* by Ralph G. Martin, copyright © 1983 by Bandwagon, Inc. Reprinted by permission of Scribner, an imprint of Simon & Schuster Adult Publishing Group, and Sll/ Sterling Lord Literistic, Inc.

Simon & Schuster Adult Publishing Group: Excerpts from *President Kennedy—Profile of Power* by Richard Reeves, copyright © 1993 by Reeves-O'Neil, Inc. Reprinted by permission of Simon & Schuster Adult Publishing Group.

Gerald S. Strober and Deborah Hart Strober: Excerpts from *"Let Us Begin Anew": An Oral History of the Kennedy Presidency* by Gerald S. Strober and Deborah H. Strober, copyright © 1993 by Gerald S. Strober and Deborah H. Strober (Harper-Collins Publishers Inc., 1993). Reprinted by permission of Gerald S. Strober and Deborah Hart Strober.

David F. White: Excerpts from *The Making of the President* by Theodore H. White, copyright © 1961 by Theodore H. White, copyright renewed 1989 by Beatrice K. H. White, David F. White and Heyden White. Reprinted by permission of David F. White on behalf of David F. White and Heyden Rostow.

W. W. Norton & Company, Inc.: Excerpts from *Conversations with Kennedy* by Ben Bradlee, copyright © 1975 by Benjamin C. Bradlee. Reprinted by permission of W. W. Norton & Company, Inc.

The Wylie Agency Inc.: excerpts from *The Presidential Papers* by Norman Mailer, copyright © 1963 by Norman Mailer. Reprinted by permission of The Wylie Agency Inc.

PHOTOGRAPHS

Page 10: *During an August 1963 press conference* . . . Photo courtesy of Getty Images; **Page 14:** *Naval lieutenant Jack Kennedy sits aboard* . . . Photo courtesy of Getty

Images; **Page 30:** *March 1963. Photographers crowd to snap* . . . Photo courtesy of Getty Images; **Page 35:** *1946. A young, gaunt, and tan Jack Kennedy* . . . Photo courtesy of AP/Wide World Photos; **Page 48:** *John F. Kennedy waves to the crowd.* Photo courtesy of Vytas Valaitis/Getty Images; **Page 54:** *March 1963. President Kennedy is a blur* . . . Photo courtesy of STF/AFP/Getty Images; **Page 70:** *John Kennedy walking in the dunes.* Photo courtesy of Mark Shaw/Photo Researchers; **Page 136:** *July 15, 1960. Senator John Kennedy faces photographers* . . . Photo © Bettmann/CORBIS; **Page 141:** *1962. President Kennedy claps while watching* . . . Photo © Bettmann/CORBIS; **Page 142:** *March 28, 1958. At home in Georgetown* . . . Photo courtesy of Ed Clark/Getty Images; **Page 143:** *The cover of Life shows Senator John Kennedy* . . . Photo courtesy of Hy Peskin/Getty Images; **Page 144:** *July 1963. Jack Kennedy skips stones across the water* . . . Photo courtesy of Hy Peskin/Getty Images; **Page 146:** *May 1962. Actress Marilyn Monroe stands between* . . . Photo courtesy of Cecil Stoughton/Getty Images; **Page 147:** *A thoughtful President Kennedy takes a quiet moment* . . . Photo © CORBIS; **Page 161:** *November 1963. Members of the Kennedy family gather* . . . Photo courtesy of Getty Images; **Page 193:** *Density: January 1961. At the inaugural ball* . . . Photo courtesy of Paul Schutzer/Getty Images; **Page 194:** *Meditation: January 20, 1961. President Kennedy delivers* . . . Photo courtesy of Joseph Scherschel/Getty Images; **Page 195:** *Familiarity: 1960. Jack, Jackie, and Caroline relax* . . . Photo courtesy of Mark Shaw/ Photo Researchers; **Page 196:** *Knowledge in the Viewer: 1948. The Kennedys gather* . . . Photo © CORBIS; **Page 198:** *Dramatic Irony: 1960. President-elect John Kennedy stands* . . . Photo courtesy of AP/Wide World Photos; **Page 199:** *August 1963. President Kennedy walks with his son* . . . Photo © CORBIS; **Page 221:** *July 1953. Jack and Jackie Kennedy relax* . . . Photo courtesy of Hy Peskin/Getty Images; **Page 221:** *1960. Supporters surround John Kennedy* . . . Photo courtesy of Paul Schutzer/Getty Images; **Page 222:** *1960. John Kennedy has a moment of reflection* . . . Photo courtesy of Paul Schutzer/Getty Images; **Page 223:** *November 1960. President-elect Kennedy holds his daughter* . . . Photo courtesy of Paul Schutzer/Getty Images; **Page 223:** *1961. President Kennedy and Mrs. Kennedy return to the White House.* Photo © Bettmann/CORBIS; **Page 224:** *1961. President Kennedy talks on the telephone* . . . Photo courtesy of Paul Schutzer/Getty Images; **Page 310:** *1963. John Kennedy Jr. plays while his father works* . . . Photo © CORBIS; **Page 321:** *September 1960. During the presidential campaign* . . . Photo courtesy of Paul Schutzer/ Getty Images; **Page 323:** *John Fitzgerald Kennedy 1917–1963.* Photo courtesy of Mark Shaw/Photo Researchers